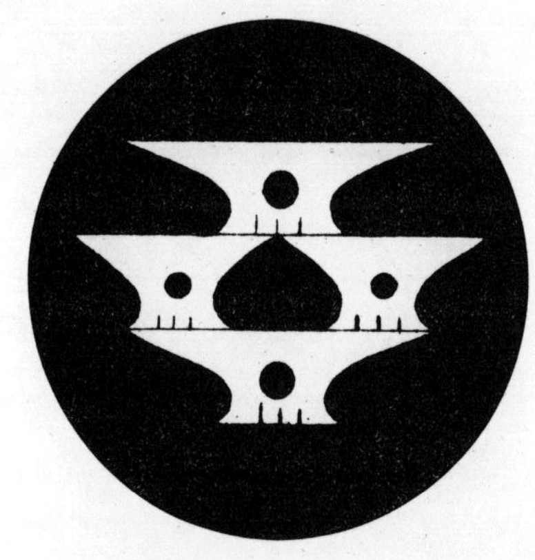

Also by Karen Green

How to Cook His Goose (And Other Wild Games), with Betty Black

The Great International Noodle Experience

Winners!

Japanese Cooking for the American Table

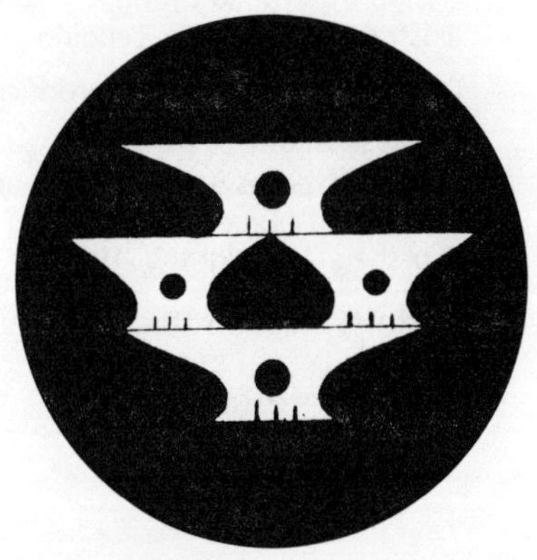

by Karen Green

J. P. TARCHER, Inc., Los Angeles · Distributed by Houghton Mifflin Company, Boston

Library of Congress Cataloging in Publication Data

Green, Karen.
Japanese cooking for the American table.

Bibliography: p. 155
Includes index.
1. Cookery, Japanese. I. Title
TX724.5.J3G68 1982 641.5952 82-10397
ISBN 0-87477-215-X

J. P. Tarcher, Inc.
9110 Sunset Blvd.
Los Angeles, CA 90069

Design by Cynthia Eyring
Illustrated by Jeanette Lendino

MANUFACTURED IN THE UNITED STATES OF AMERICA

P 10 9 8 7 6 5 4 3 2 1

First Edition

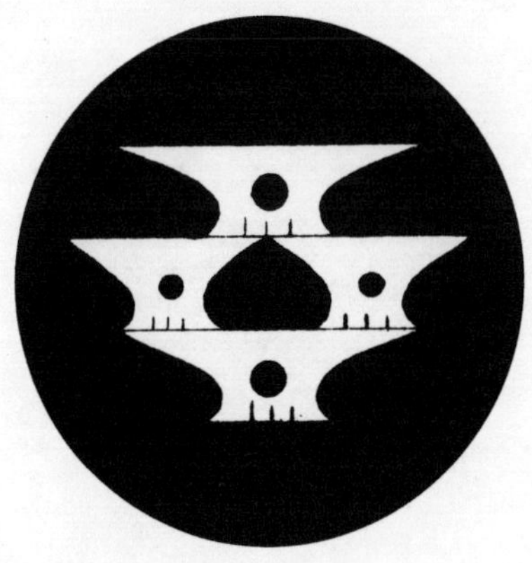

With love to my mother and best friend, Betty Schwartz

CONTENTS

ACKNOWLEDGMENTS

As I write these final words, I want to include the numerous people who assisted me with this book. But the list would take several pages, and I know there are space limitations. Though your name may not be printed here, it is secure in my heart.

Special thanks to my dear husband, Bill, for his patience, artistic talents, and support in satisfying both my intellectual and hunger cravings; to my wonderful young sons, Jonathon and Jeffrey, for never complaining about eating Japanese foods instead of hot dogs and pizza; to my loving mother and fellow author, Betty Schwartz, for carefully reading every handwritten word of my first draft and helping me polish the grammar; to my friend and fellow food writer-Oriental cooking instructor, Susan Slack, for also reading my original notes and offering many excellent suggestions; to my friend and Japanese cooking instructor, Matao Uwate, for guiding me in my search to understand traditional Japanese cooking; and to my tea ceremony instructor, Soyu Koizumi, for sharing her inner peace and home.

I would also like to thank Matsuo Someka, Hidemi Ayukawa, and Masami, of the Ikeda Bakery in Los Angeles, for generously spending many hours with me and sharing the secrets of baking Japanese sweets and snacks; Mickie Kuono and Itamae Kengi, of Koto Restaurant in Newport Beach, for sharing their sashimi and sushi expertise; Hitoshi Komiyama, of Mifune Restaurant in Los Angeles, for sharing his noodle expertise; Suki Han, of Han's Market in Irvine, Jim Hikida, of Jim's Market in Costa Mesa, and Nori Takatani, of Anzen Hardware in Los Angeles, for answering countless questions about Japanese ingredients and utensils; and Diane Plocher, of JFC International, Inc., Japanese food wholesaler-distributors, and George Eisenberg and Gail Conners, of International Vintage Wine Company, sake importers, for their kind replies to questions necessary to my research.

I am also most grateful to my agent, Jane Jordan Browne, for believing in this book when it was only a title; and to my publisher, Jeremy Tarcher; my editor, Janice Gallagher; my production manager, Derek Gallagher; and to copy editor Diana Rico, production coordinator Georgia Griggs, and the entire staff of J. P. Tarcher, Inc., for their encouragement, interest, and trust. And, finally, my thanks to all my family, friends, and readers for tasting my recipes. I love you all.

KAREN GREEN
June 1982

AN INVITATION TO JAPANESE COOKING

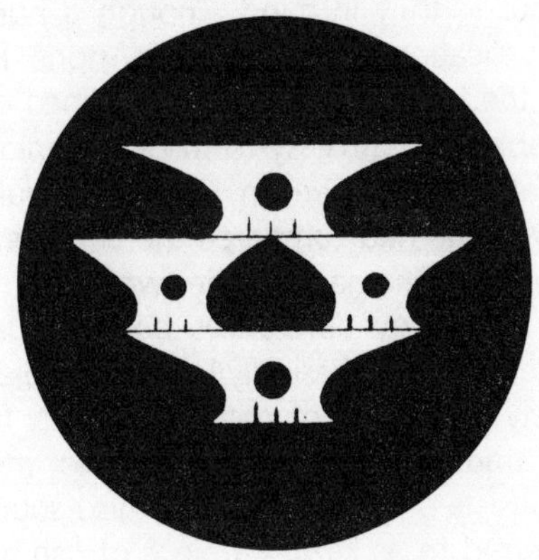

I have been asked many times how I came to write a Japanese cookbook. The inference seems to be that to dedicate oneself to an in-depth study of Japanese cookery, one has to be Japanese, have a Japanese spouse, or have lived several years in Japan. Not so.

My penchant for the cuisine of Japan is based upon a keen interest in that country's fine, artistic hand with simple, healthy, seasonal foodstuff. All over the United States, Japanese restaurants—splashy, large, corporation-owned and simple, small, family-run ones—are popping up. As I frequented these establishments, my love for Japanese fare grew, and I found I wanted to re-create many of these dishes in my own home for family and friends to enjoy.

I spent many days wandering through the marketplaces of Los Angeles's and San Francisco's Japanese communities, talking with the proprietors about their goods, and comparing these products with those available at our major markets. At the Zen Buddhist Temple in Los Angeles's Little Tokyo, I observed and cooked alongside one of the city's renowned food specialists. I visited a great number of Japanese restaurants and bakeries, looking over the shoulders of their chefs, testing recipes with their staffs. I cooked with Japanese friends in their homes to better my understanding of family-style cookery. I corresponded with Japanese food and wine importers, and I read a great number of traditional Japanese cookbooks, written in both English and Japanese.

During this period of intensive research, I found that no Japanese cookbook had been written with the American public truly in mind. Though a number of beautiful publications were available, none fully encompassed the knowledge that I had gained or had a highly readable text with easy-to-follow techniques and recipes that the American public would find tasteworthy. None had compared the cuisines and offered a rewarding marriage of the two.

There are many differences between Japanese and American cookery, basically in the ingredients and in the variety and types of recipes selected for each meal. The traditional Japanese morning meal, for example, consists of a small bowl of miso soup; some protein, referred to as kazu—a piece of fish, chicken, tofu, or egg, often left over from the previous day; some seaweed (nori, wakame, and hijiki are most popular); a tiny salty-sour plum (umeboshi); rice; pickles; and tea—all served at the same time. A typical Japanese bento lunch includes a cup of soup (usually a clear broth with garnishes), a few slices of raw fish (sashimi) with condiments, a piece of fried shrimp (tempura), some slices of fish sausage (kamaboko), several small portions of cooked vegetables, pickles, rice, and tea. All Japanese meals end with boiled rice, pickles, and tea. For a sweet touch, you might find fresh fruit or sweetened beans. Pastries and other baked goods are rarely, if ever, served with a Japanese meal. Instead, you might enjoy these as an informal snack or as part of the very formal tea ceremony.

Should you wish to serve a traditional Japanese meal to your family, you can select a number of dishes to prepare. I find, however, that Americans prefer larger portions and fewer courses, so the servings indicated are designed for the American appetite.

Traditional Japanese recipes call for a substantial amount of sugar, which seems to balance the saltiness of the soy sauce and miso. Following American health trends to reduce salt and sugar intake, I have cut back on these items and have increased the use of lemon juice, sake, and mirin. I find the resulting taste and appearance similar and far more healthy. In addition, I have eliminated the use of MSG (monosodium glutamate) and other artificial flavor enhancers. Also, few traditional recipes call for marinades, and if marinades are used, they involve only a short time or a mere brushing on of sauce at the last minute. For American tastes, I have increased the time for marinating, allowing a better opportunity for seasonings to penetrate.

Another distinct difference in this cookbook as compared to other Japanese cookbooks is in organization. Before you can follow a recipe, you must be familiar with the necessary ingredients and utensils. I have featured these chapters in the beginning sections of this book. Whenever possible, I have suggested a substitute that is readily available to the American kitchen. In classifying the recipe chapters, I have given attention to the needs of the American table. I have started with the basic stock of Japanese cookery, dashi, and have followed this with soups and stews. Aware of American interest in sashimi and sushi, I have placed this chapter next. Then I discuss salads and vegetables and next move to a special section on tofu and miso, spotlighting these recipes for the health-aware and vegetarian American tables. The recipe chapters continue with the main and side courses, grouped according to cooking techniques, in the same manner that we approach our American meals, and then end with the sweet course and beverages.

You will find the instructions simple. To ease anyone's intimidation with regard to cooking something new, each recipe offers tips, advice, and necessary fundamentals.

My recipes are invitations to creativity. If you cannot locate an authentic Japanese ingredient or utensil, substitute something available. If you do not like the seasoning called for, feel free to substitute another. If you like a certain recipe but would prefer it sweeter or spicier, adjust it to your taste.

I have tried to impart my enthusiasm for Japanese cookery. Through studying this cuisine, we can learn the art of enhancement, rather than of masquerade, by offering foods that are not complicated with heavy sauces, not laden with overpowering seasonings. We can learn to be versatile, using what is readily available at the height of its season and at the low end of its cost. We can learn how the preparation and serving of foods can be respected for their aesthetic value as well as their nutritional value. By studying Japanese cuisine, we can discover an ancient appreciation of nature's bounty.

Tabete kudasai. Please eat.
Kampai. Toast: to your health.

INGREDIENTS

I wish I could escort you on a shopping tour of Japanese markets, with their shelves of brightly packaged dry goods, refrigerators and freezers of exotic ready-to-cook items, and coolers filled with unusual greens and starches. But since that is impossible, I think it necessary at this point in the book to introduce you to the ingredients you will be using. Watch carefully for special handling tips and precooking advice; the time-consuming part of Japanese cookery is the advance work, but once this is completed, the recipes are a cinch.

As Japanese cookery becomes more popular throughout the United States and as the Asian population increases, more and more neighborhood markets are opening up. Most major supermarkets are also greatly expanding their oriental foods sections. If you can't obtain certain ingredients, feel free to make substitutions. Also, refer to the Where to Go for More Information section for the addresses of mail-order suppliers and other sources.

ABURA: Cooking oil. Vegetable oils are used almost exclusively; rarely will you need butter, animal fat, or olive oil. Oil from deep frying is often reused. Some people feel the added flavors from different ingredients improve the cooking oil. To save, filter this oil through a fine-meshed strainer and store in a dark, cool spot. There are several special oils, such as goma abura, a dark sesame oil used in small quantities to flavor cooking oil and simple broth soups and salads, and tempura abura, a combination of processed vegetable oils bottled specifically for cooking tempura.

AGAR-AGAR (KANTEN): Japanese gelatin. A dried sea vegetation processed from a red seaweed (tengusa), used as a jelling agent, particularly for sweets. It congeals quickly without refrigeration and all fruits, including pineapple, will set in it. Sold dried in translucent, colored and clear brittle sticks and in shredded and powdered forms. Stored in airtight containers, its shelf life is several years. Available at oriental markets and many health-food stores. Can substitute gelatin.

AJINOMOTO: MSG (monosodium glutamate). Although many traditional Japanese recipes include this chemical seasoning, because of American tastes and dietary awareness I have eliminated it, substituting herbs and dried seasonings. Besides, an artificial enhancer isn't necessary if ingredients are fresh.

AONORIKO: Powdered green laver, a member of the seaweed family. Used as seasoning and as garnish. Available bottled.

AZUKI BEANS (ADZUKI): Dried small red beans. Require soaking several hours or overnight before use. Most often prepared with sugar and/or honey to be eaten as a sweet. Available at most major markets and oriental and health-food stores. Can substitute other small red beans.

BUTA: Pork. Next in popularity after fish and fowl as a source of protein. Also called ton.

CHA (OCHA): Tea. This revered beverage is the main refreshment of the Japanese people and practically forms a culture in itself. Some teas are (1) matcha (hiki-cha), a bright green powdered tea used primarily for ceremonial purposes, expensive; (2) gyokuro, an excellent green tea leaf, difficult to acquire; (3) sencha, green tea made from very tender leaves, the quality used for company, a sipping tea; (4) bancha, the lowest quality and most commonly drunk as a thirst quencher; (5) hojicha, bancha leaves roasted to produce a smoky-tasting tea; and (6) genmaicha, a blend of tea leaves and roasted brown rice kernels. The word *agari,* referring to Japanese tea, is used only at the sushi bar. The following beverages are brewed like tea: (1) mugicha, a wheat tea made from roasted, unpolished barley, served chilled in the summer; available loose and in tea bags; (2) kobu-cha, a liquid beverage, almost a broth, made of powdered kombu and hot water; (3) habucha, stinkweed-seed tea; and (4) sakura-yu, a cherry tea used for celebrations, made from salted cherry blossoms. American black tea is referred to as kocha. Chinese and Indian teas are also black. See Beverages chapter for further discussion of tea brewing and the tea ceremony.

CHIKUWA: Fish cake. This variety is cylindrical with a central hole. Available in most major markets. See *kamaboko.*

DAIKON: Japanese white radish, available all year. Generally about 3 feet long and weighing 1 to 2 pounds. Many Japanese markets sell cut chunks. I've also seen medium-size daikon grouped in bunches. Select firm daikon. The entire vegetable is edible. A versatile vegetable, it is served raw and grated (squeeze out excess liquid) as an accompaniment to many sushi bar recipes, sunomono, tempura sauce, and others. It can be pickled or cooked in numerous fashions. In your refrigerator vegetable bin, it stays fresh for several weeks. A form of daikon, kiri-boshi daikon or sengiri

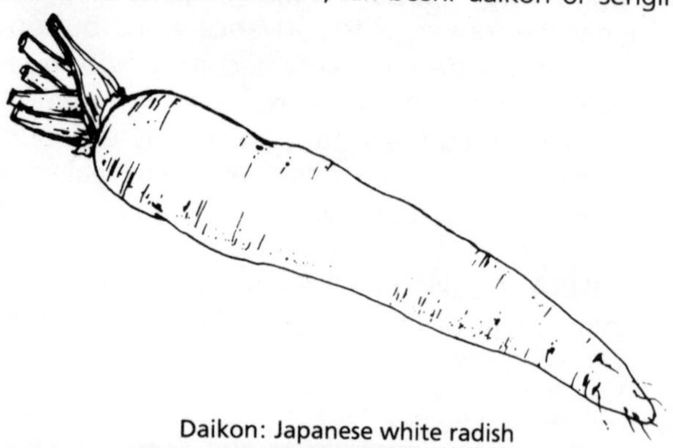

Daikon: Japanese white radish

daikon, is shredded, pickled, and dried, and packaged in cellophane bags; it keeps for several weeks in your refrigerator. Softened and braised, it becomes a vegetable dish. Yellow, pickled daikon, or takuan, available refrigerated in oriental markets, is a popular sushi ingredient. You can substitute turnips or bottled white horseradish.

DAIZU: Dried soybeans. Require soaking before simmering; readily available at oriental markets and health-food stores.

DASHI: Basic stock, essential to Japanese cookery. Made primarily from katsuo bushi, dried bonito flakes resembling sawdust, and kombu, a dark, dried kelp or sea tangle. See instructions in The Basic Stock: Dashi chapter. When in a pinch, try instant dried dashi, dashi-no-moto, which is similar to bouillon cubes or crystals and is available in both small cubes and oversized "tea" bags. (Even Japanese chefs recommend dashi-no-moto.) If you do not like the fishy taste or aroma of dashi, you can substitute another stock, such as chicken, beef, or vegetable stock or clam juice, although the resulting dish will greatly differ.

DENBU: Cooked, ground fish or seafood. Usually a bright pink or brown with a sweet taste. A popular ingredient for sushi combinations.

EDA MAME: Fresh soybeans. The pods are long and bright green. They are available fresh in the late spring through summer months and can be found all year frozen in their pods in oriental markets. Boil them in their pods and offer as a healthy snack. Shell and salt the beans as you eat, discarding the pods. Can substitute lima beans or other legumes for many recipes.

ENDO: Peas. Fresh or frozen green peas are often used in Japanese recipes.

ENOKITAKE (ENOK, ENOKE): Slender white mushrooms, packaged in cellophane. Major markets are now carrying them. Look for fresh heads and stems. Cut off and discard the very bottom of the stems. Popular raw (add some to your next salad) and cooked in soups and one-pot dishes.

FU: Dried wheat gluten. High in protein and low in starch, fu is a unique ingredient. A variety of decorative shapes are available, most popular of which are arare, little balls or hail, used in soups; hana, little flowers, used in soups; kuruma, small wheels or round rolls, used in soups and simmered dishes; shona, long, flat, crackerlike, used in miso soup. Soften in tepid water for 5 to 10 minutes (it expands greatly), then squeeze dry. Can substitute parboiled, decoratively shaped pasta or croutons.

FUKI: Coltsfoot. Rhubarblike green. The long green hollow stalk is edible. Preparation includes salting, parboiling to draw out the bitter taste, then removing of any stringy veins. Store in refrigerator. Can substitute celery.

FURIKAKE: A popular seasoning mixture of dried bonito, seaweeds, sesame seeds, sugar, salt, and MSG.

GARI: Ginger seasoned in vinegar. Paper-thin slices of gari are eaten, particularly with sushi, to refresh the palate. Often tinted bright pink.

GINKGO NUTS (GINNAN): Seeds of the mature female ginkgo or maidenhair tree. To prepare the fresh nuts for cooking, three outer layers must be removed: (1) a yellow pulpy outer covering is first removed (this is usually done by the farmers before the nuts are sent to the markets); (2) a thin, but hard, white nut case must be cracked; and (3) a thin, brownish skin needs to be rubbed off. (Place nuts in hot water to aid in this last step.) After these layers are removed, the raw white nuts are ready for further cooking. They are popular in steamed, deep-fried, skewered, grilled, and one-pot dishes. Store in refrigerator. Also available precooked and canned.

GOBO: Burdock root. These skinny, firm, woody-looking roots are a little thicker than your fingers and about 1½ feet long. Keeps in refrigerator vegetable bin for several weeks. Advance preparation: Scrub well; do not peel. Immediately soak in a vinegar-water (su water) solution to remove the alkaline flavor and retain the crunchy texture and white color. If cut and exposed to the air without soaking, it will turn a dark reddish

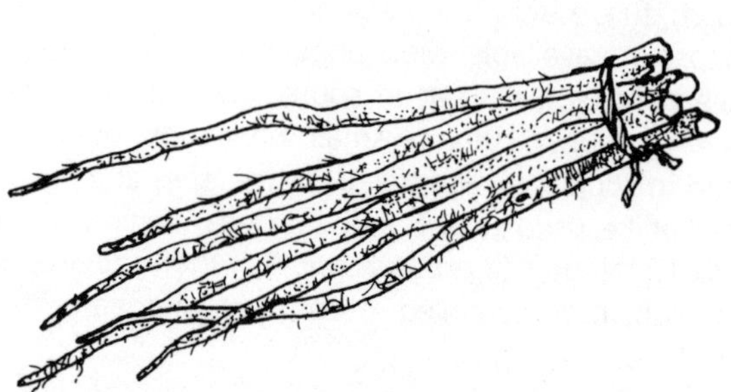

Gobo: Burdock root

brown. Burdock may irritate your hands when you scrub it, so wear gloves. To further tenderize boiled gobo, pound it lightly with a wooden mallet or surikogi.

GOHAN: Cooked polished white rice. Preparation includes 30 to 60 minutes of washing, rinsing, draining, and soaking repeatedly with fresh water until no more milky liquid appears. This process shortens cooking time as well as prevents gumminess. Refer to *kome.*

GOMA: Sesame seeds. Used extensively. Unless otherwise stated, recipes call for the white variety. Black ones are most often used as a garnish. Categories are unhulled white (shiro goma), hulled white (muki goma), black (kuro goma) and a mixture of black and coarse salt (goma shio). Dry roasting in a sesame toaster or skillet brings out the full aroma and flavor (see Dry Roasting section of Advance Preparation chapter for instructions). Seeds stored in an airtight container will keep for several years. Available in the oriental and spices sections of major markets and at health-food stores.

HAKUSAI: Chinese cabbage. Also called celery cabbage and nappa cabbage. Compact heads up to 16 inches long. The outer leaves often have dark spots, but do not toss them. Keeps refrigerated for about a week. Used raw for salads and salted pickles; very popular in one-pot dishes and soups. Can substitute the most available variety of cabbage.

HARUSAME: Bean "gelatin" noodles. Commonly called Japanese vermicelli or cellophane noodles. Easily

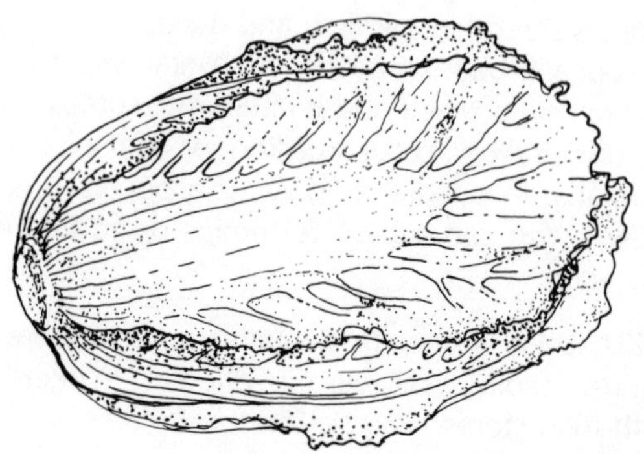

Hakusai: Chinese cabbage

available dried and packaged in many markets' oriental sections.

HASU: Lotus root. See *renkon.*

HIJIKI: Dried sea vegetation. Black, resembles licorice. Soak in warm water for at least 30 minutes; then drain hijiki and squeeze dry. Used primarily in soups and salads.

HIYAMUGI: Fine, varicolored, thin wheat-flour noodle. Used primarily in cold dishes; popular during the summer months. Resembles somen.

KAKI: Persimmon, available fresh September through early December; eaten fresh as a dessert. The Japanese variety is not as tart as American persimmons. Dried persimmons are eaten as a snack.

KAMABOKO: Fish-paste cakes. This is the generic name for a variety of pureed, mixed (often bound with a starch), then steamed, sometimes grilled, fish products. Some are brightly colored—you will often see white rolls with a hot pink covering. Fish most commonly used are cod, shark, and croaker. Sliced into

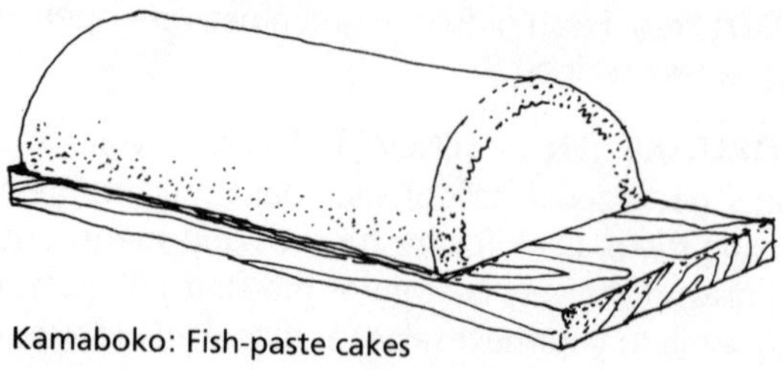

Kamaboko: Fish-paste cakes

decorative shapes and eaten as a snack, lunch dish, or added to many soups, one-pot, noodle, or simmered dishes. Available refrigerated in oriental markets and in most major supermarkets.

KANPYO (KAMPYO): Dried gourd (squash) shavings. Skin of a Japanese fruit. Long, ribbonlike, and edible, kanpyo is dried and packaged in cellophane. Before use, reconstitute by rinsing in water, rubbing with salt, then soaking in water for several hours to overnight (the salt rub will hasten softening); or parboil. Terrific for tying vegetable bundles and tofu bundles. Also used in sushi and vegetable dishes. For tying, you can substitute thread or kitchen string.

KANTEN: Sea vegetation product for jelling. See *agar-agar.*

KASHI: Confection or sweets.

KATAKURIKO: Potato starch. Used as a sauce thickener (first dissolve in water) and to coat foods before frying. You can substitute cornstarch or arrowroot.

KATSUO BUSHI (KATSUOBUSHI): Dried bonito flakes. Most often katsuo bushi resembles sawdust, though it is also sold in larger shavings and strips. It looks woody and smells fishy. Used primarily for making dashi, occasionally as a garnish for cooked vegetables and sunomono. Packaged in paper or cellophane bags or boxes. Check the date for freshness and use within 6 to 12 months. Store at room temperature in an airtight container. Available in the oriental section of most major markets.

KIKURAGE: Thin, dark mushrooms, sold dried. Nicknamed wood or tree ears; also called jelly mushrooms. They are very black and brittle. When reconstituted, they will greatly expand and soften, though still be chewy, so don't use too much at once. Stored dried in an airtight container, their shelf life is several years. Easily available at oriental markets.

KINAKO: Soy flour. A very nutritious variety of flour also available in health-food stores. Often used for Japanese confections. Refrigerate after opening, as soy flour is highly perishable.

KINOME: Pepper tree leaves. In spring, the Japanese pepper tree yields new leaves. These are used as a garnish for soups, simmered foods, tofu recipes, and grilled foods. They are added to recipes both for their minty taste, and to symbolize spring. If not available, substitute watercress, parsley, cilantro, or celery leaves. The pods of the same tree yield Japanese pepper, or sansho.

KISHIMEN: Broad, flat noodles. Made of flour, salt, and water. Similar to udon, though larger and wider.

KOMBU (KONBU): Dried, cultivated kelp or sea tangle. This dark sea vegetation is primarily used for making dashi, though often used for vegetables, sunomono, and sushi recipes. Store sheets at room temperature in an airtight container. Shredded kombu is also available and is used primarily in deep-fried and sauteed dishes. Shiro kombu is white kombu. Reconstituted, it is a favorite sushi ingredient.

KOME (OKOME): Raw hulled rice, the mainstay of the Japanese diet. Japanese people prefer short-grained rice—for example, California Rose and Blue Rose. Store in an airtight container at room temperature. Refer to *gohan.*

KONNYAKU: Gelatinous yam cake made from a tuber. There are two forms: (1) shiro konnyaku, a pearly white cake that is refined, and (2) kuro konnyaku, a dark-speckled, unrefined cake. Konnyaku has no calories and is bland, so it easily absorbs other flavors. Popular for its jellylike texture. Available refrigerated in oriental markets. It is sometimes packaged as alimentary paste in water. At home, continue to refrigerate, and once package is opened, store any leftover cake in fresh water changed daily. Unopened packages keep for several weeks. Preparation requires parboiling or dry roasting to firm up the texture. Slices of konnyaku, served with condiments and dipping sauce (konnyaku sashimi), are a vegetarian delicacy. Related to shirataki.

KURI (KURII): Chestnuts. If you are a newcomer to fresh chestnut preparation, do not be turned away by the hard outer shell. As for the gingko nut, several steps are required to reach the flavorsome inner nut. There are different schools of thought on cracking the nut. The long technique involves working with a sharp paring knife and completely shelling before cooking; this method is tedious. Instead, I take a few short cuts. With the point of a sharp knife, carefully cut an X into the flat side. Do not pierce or cut into the nutmeat. Then place the nuts in boiling water for about 10 minutes. Drain and rinse. As soon as they are cool enough, peel off the outer shell and rub off the bitter brown skin. You may find it easier to do this with the aid of your knife. The whitish chestnut is now ready for further cooking according to the recipe. Fresh chestnuts are easy to locate during the autumn and early winter months. Canned or dried chestnuts can be substituted, but fresh are much better. Refer to page 142 for further discussion of handling tips.

KUROMAME: Black beans. This legume should be stored in a dark dry place, and like most legumes it must be soaked before use. You can substitute turtle beans.

KURUMI: Walnuts. Occasionally, Japanese recipes suggest your grinding walnuts, in a similar manner as sesame seeds, as the base for a sauce.

KUZU (KUDZU): Japanese arrowroot. Used to coat foods before deep frying, resulting in a crystallike coating; as a thickener for sauces and soups (first dissolve in water), resulting in a glossy sauce; as a jellying agent, particularly for sweets; as a noodle ingredient; and as a broth ingredient. Sold in small boxes, the powder is lumpy and should be sifted or strained before use. Can substitute arrowroot, cornstarch, or flour. The general formula for substitution is 1 tablespoon flour for 1 teaspoon kuzu; 1 tablespoon arrowroot for 1½ teaspoons kuzu; and 1 tablespoon cornstarch for 4½ teaspoons kuzu.

KYURI: Cucumber. Japanese cucumbers are very crisp and smaller, more narrow, and less watery than American and European cucumbers. When substituting, I prefer the unwaxed European cucumber with its edible skin. To remove excess bitterness from cucumbers, cut off the bottom inch of the stem end and rub the flesh sides together. The liquid that rises is the bitter-tasting part.

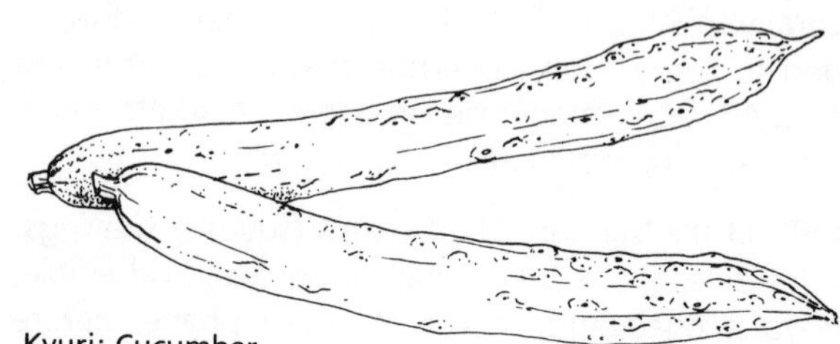

Kyuri: Cucumber

MATSUTAKE: Very large and very expensive Japanese mushrooms. Considered by many mushroom aficionados to be the king of mushrooms. Sold fresh in the autumn months, they are also called pine mushrooms because they grow under the red pine trees in the mountains. Preparation requires careful inspection, wiping, and trimming. Keep whole or in large pieces and do not overcook. They are popular broiled with a basting sauce or simmered and cooked with rice. Best cooked within one or two days of purchase. Available canned. Can substitute giant fresh mushrooms.

MEMMI: Japanese seasoned soup starter. This concentrated liquid base used for soups and noodle dishes includes soy sauce, sugar, seasonings, and bonito extract. Must be diluted. Available bottled.

MENRUI: Noodles. This is the generic name for the entire family of noodles. The three major classifications are soba, somen, and udon, plus hiyamugi, kishimen, ramen, and often harusame and shirataki. See individual types for explanation of classes and associated products.

MIKAN: Mandarin orange or tangerine. Mikan juice, which is high in vitamin C, has long been popular for curing colds. Fresh mikans are available early winter through early spring. Can substitute fresh tangerines or canned mandarin oranges.

MIRIN: Sweet, syrupy rice wine, related to sake. Alcoholic content is approximately 13 to 14 percent. Used for cooking, not drinking. The shelf life of opened mirin is far better than that of sake because it has a high sugar content. If not available, substitute 2 parts sake to 1 part sugar (or more sugar to taste), heat to dissolve sugar, and reduce liquid by half. Light sherry or sweet sherry can be substituted.

MISO: Fermented soybean paste. Miso, along with tofu, is the backbone of the Japanese health-food repertoire. Miso is made from sieved soybeans mixed with a grain (rice malt or barley), salt, water, and *Aspergillus oryzae,* a mold starter that encourages fermentation. There are numerous flavors, colors, and textures. The three classifications are (1) aka, red to dark brown, pungent; (2) chu, medium to golden color, mild; and (3) shiro, white to pale tan, mellow and slightly sweet. To introduce your family to miso, it is best to start with the sweeter varieties. Purchase small containers, tasting the different types until you find those you most enjoy. Generally, the lighter the color, the sweeter the miso. The darker misos tend to be saltier.

Considered an excellent product for a low-fat diet, miso is composed primarily of unsaturated and cholesterol-free oils. Miso can be used as a condiment or a relish, a seasoning agent, a pickling agent, a tenderizer, a soup or sauce base (like a bouillon cube), a soup or sauce thickener, a dressing or topping, a spread, or a marinade. (Miso should be added to a soup at the last minute; overcooked miso can spoil a recipe.) Many varieties can be stored at room temperature; however, the sweeter ones should be refrigerated. Should any mold appear, simply scrape off as you would from cheese. Easy to obtain at most major markets, health-food stores, and oriental markets.

MITSUBA: Trefoil. An herb, distantly related to flat-leafed parsley, but tasting quite similar to celery leaves. Used raw as a garnish and in cooked dishes, such as simmered and tempura recipes. Keeps well refrigerated if you place the stems in a glass of cold water and gently encase the leafy top with a plastic produce bag. (This trick to extend the life of mitsuba works for all herbs, even parsley.) If not available, substitute celery leaves, sorrel, parsley, watercress, or cilantro.

MOCHI (OMOCHI, MOCHIGOME): Sweet, glutinous rice. Used for special occasions and special recipes, such as for pounded and steamed rice cakes and with azuki beans for sekihan. Premade mochi cakes are available fresh, frozen, and dried, ready to be eaten, grilled, toasted, or added to other recipes. Check the label to see if they're filled with sweet beans. You'll find them at oriental specialty shops and Japanese confection shops in white and shades of pink and pale green.

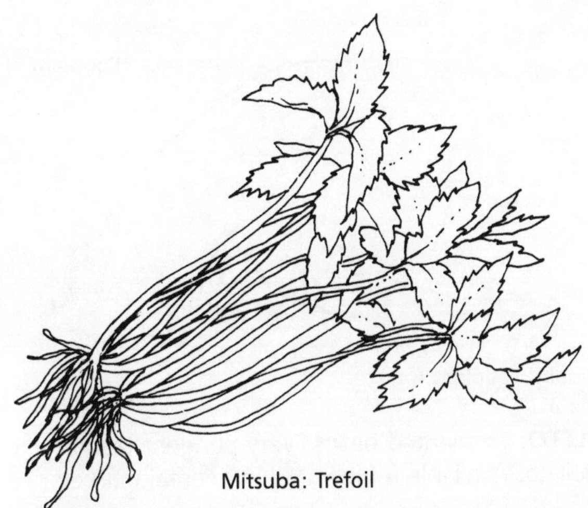

Mitsuba: Trefoil

MOCHIKO: Sweet rice flour, used to make dumplings and sweets. These confections are served during the tea ceremony and for snacks. To use as a sauce thickener, first dissolve in cold water.

MOYASHI: Bean sprouts. Not as popular in Japanese cookery as in Chinese, but they're gaining in use, particularly in Americanized Japanese recipes. Fresh bean sprouts are easy to obtain.

NAMEKO: Slippery orange or gold mushrooms. These mushrooms have a slimy texture and a rich, earthy flavor. Often used in soups, one-pot dishes, and salads. Available fresh, bottled, and canned.

NASHI: Pears. A popular dessert.

NASUBI: Eggplant. Same handsome, deep purple color as the American eggplant, but considerably smaller and more cylindrical. The skin is tender and should not be peeled. Preparation requires salting or parboiling slices or fingers. Easy to obtain. If you are substituting American eggplant, use 1 small American for every 5 Japanese eggplants. (Pictured overleaf.)

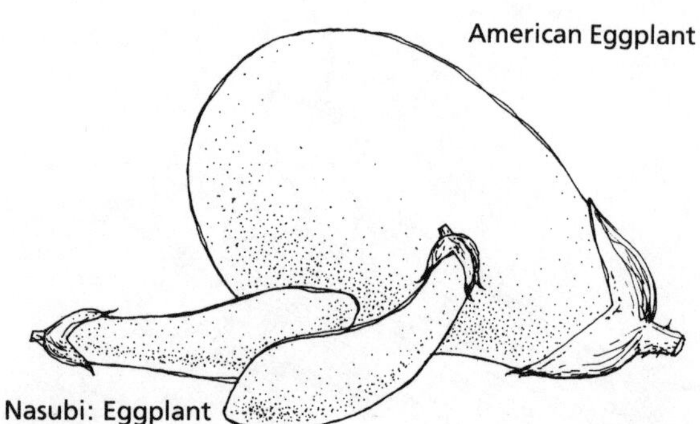

NATTO: Fermented beans. Very pungent tasting and smelling. Available refrigerated in oriental markets.

NEGI (NAGANEGI): Long onions. These are longer and thicker than scallions, but not as big as leeks. They have a surprisingly delicate flavor, so try to locate. Used sliced and chopped for any recipe requiring onions. A must for sukiyaki. Can substitute scallions (green onions).

NIBOSHI: Dried small sardines. Sold in cellophane packages. Eaten as a snack and used in several recipes, particularly niboshi dashi, a sardine-based stock. Store in airtight containers at room temperature. Obtainable in the oriental section of most major markets.

NIMIKU: Garlic.

NINJIN: Carrots.

NORI: Referred to as seaweed, but actually laver, a type of sea vegetation. Nori is the king of the sea vegetation family, which also includes kombu, wakame, hijiki (the four most popular), plus several others. Dried and available in thin, crisp, dark greenish-black sheets, usually 6-inch to 10-inch squares. Different qualities and types available. Easy to locate in the oriental section of major markets. (See information on dry roasting—page 46—for directions on crisping nori.)

A must for sushi roll making (norimaki)—nori is used to completely encase the rice and other ingredients. It is also used in strips to circle or attach other sushi recipes (see pages 68–74). Cut into very thin strips, crumbled or flaked, nori is used as a garnish for many dishes. Preflaked nori is also available. Store in an airtight container at room temperature or freeze for long periods of time.

NUKA: Bran of rice. This is the fine brown skin that is removed from brown rice during the rice-polishing process. It is reserved for other purposes, most often for pickling. Adds crispness to vegetables.

OKARA (KARA): Soy pulp. A by-product of the soybean into soy milk into tofu-making process, consisting of the solids remaining after the liquid has been filtered. Grainy, like cornmeal, and a good source of protein. Obtainable at oriental markets and health-food stores.

PANKO: Japanese-style bread crumbs. They are white and untoasted and considerably coarser than American or Italian. Sold in cellophane bags, panko gives your fried foods an excellent outer crust. Substitute homemade bread crumbs.

RAMEN: Chinese-style noodles, often prepackaged with dehydrated soup mix.

RENKON: Lotus root. Also called hasu. One of nature's surprises, this is my favorite Japanese vegetable because of the contrast between its outer and inner appearances. Carefully peel this ugly brown root, and you will find canallike holes. Slice into circles of desired thickness, and you will have flowerlike vegetables. Immediately upon peeling and slicing, soak in a su water solution to hold the color. Stored unpeeled in the refrigerator, lotus root will keep about a week. Popular vegetable for deep frying and simmered or pickled dishes; also eaten raw with a sweet vinegar dressing.

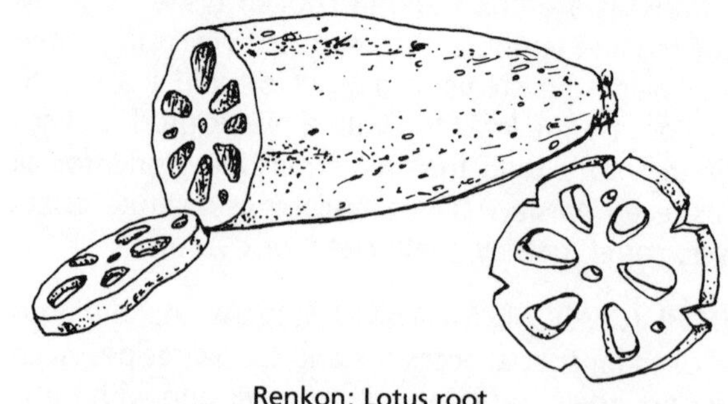

Renkon: Lotus root

Try tossing some raw slices with a salad for an unusual crunchy addition.

SAKANA: Fish, seafood, and shellfish. When purchasing fish, select firm flesh with no fishy odor or slimy appearance. Fillets are best with the skin still on one side. For whole fish, it is important to leave the head intact; a headless fish is thought to bring misfortune. Choose only fish with shiny, clear eyes—grayish, dull eyes signal old fish.

Oriental markets offer a handsome variety of fish species. You will find many unique-looking whole fish and sections of fish. Fish collars (the fleshy area around the neck bones), cheeks, heads, and backbones (with spines) are prized eating.

In the recipe chapters, I will list fish suggestions. If a particular species is not fresh or available, substitute another fish that is. In fish cookery, freshness is of primary importance.

Here's a list of the most popular of fish in Japanese cookery. Each is savored for its own reasons, some raw, some cooked, and some both raw and cooked.

Albacore: Shiro maguro. Peachy to rose in color, the flesh is soft. Available fresh July through October. Popular for sashimi and sushi. Also refer to *tuna*.

Barracuda: Kamasu. The Japanese prefer to eat the younger, smaller fish, about 8 inches long.

Carp: Koi. Symbolizes love and strength. Very important fish for Boys' Day or Children's Day.

Clams: There are many varieties. The most favored include (1) akagai (ark shell or pepitona clam), peachy to reddish—the stringlike part around the body, himo, is also edible—generally imported frozen; (2) aoyagi (red clam), orange, parboiled before served, imported frozen, similar to American quahog; (3) awabi (abalone), peachy to grayish, very chewy; (4) hamaguri (Pismo clam); (5) kaibashira (large scallop), also called tairagai, adductor muscles of great clam; (6) kobashira (small scallop), light gold, actually the generic name for the succulent muscles that perform the opening and closing motion of all clams; (7) mirugai (geoduck), also called horseneck clam, light peach, the long neck is most often eaten raw; and (8) torigai (cockle), black with white, very chewy, imported frozen.

Cod: Tara. Includes several fish, most prominently Atlantic cod and codfish. Haddock is related. Served many ways. Often used for fish cakes (kamaboko and chikuwa).

Crab: Kani (gani). Reportedly, there are eight hundred varieties of edible crabs in Japan. Generally eaten cooked. Popular for sushi.

Eel: There are basically two types of eel—freshwater (unagi) and saltwater (anago). Unagi is the most popular. Both types are cooked and brushed with a thick sweet sauce (tare) for a sushi dish. You can buy eel already cooked and glazed to use in sushi or other recipes. Some people like to recook and season them.

Globefish: Fugu. There is much talk about fugu, a fish that is related to the blowfish and is highly poisonous unless properly handled. It is difficult to find in the United States. In Japan it is a specialty at fugu restaurants. The toxin is located in the liver and ovaries, so for a Japanese chef to be permitted to prepare fugu, he must first pass several government tests and be licensed.

Halibut: Hirame. A whitefish, the flesh is a delicate white to pink. Thinly sliced, it is very popular as sashimi. It is often rolled into a flower shape, the center then filled with roe. Also refer to whitefish.

Herring: Nishin. Though a tasty fish, herring is most prized for its roe (fish eggs) rather than its flesh. (See *Roe*—next page.)

Mackerel: Saba. A family of several varieties, including Spanish mackerel, North American mackerel, and North American Pacific mackerel. Considered especially delicious in the fall months, when the fish have no eggs. (Legend has it that if a wife eats mackerel during these months, she will be barren.) Oily, full-flavored fish. It is generally marinated with a salt-vinegar solution and served for sushi. Horse mackerel (ma-aji) is also popular.

Octopus: Tako. Always preboiled (though many sushi bar devotees think it is raw), it is popular for sushi and sashimi and in salads. The tentacles, which are naturally gray, turn a burgundy color when boiled. Also available canned and dried.

Oysters: Kaki. Eaten raw and cooked.

Pompano: Koban aji. Most preferred are the very small pompano, about 3 inches long. Cleaned and whole, they are especially enjoyed deep fried.

Prawn (shrimp): Ebi. Shrimp, jumbo shrimp, prawns, and sometimes lobster are grouped together in this category. A popular sushi item, it is precooked and pinkish. Ama ebi is raw shrimp, still grayish and a sushi delicacy. The heads, also a delicacy, are cut off and fried. *Odori* refers to shrimp eaten live. Shrimp is a popular ingredient for many cooked recipes, most notably tempura, teppan, and teriyaki.

Red sea bream: Tai. This category also includes red snapper, perch, red porgy, yellow porgy, black porgy, sea bream. A sweet, lean, pinkish whitefish, it is most often served whole at ceremonial and holiday meals, symbolizing wealth and good fortune. Also popular for sushi.

Roe: Fish eggs. Very popular item, particularly for sushi (often with a raw egg yolk), in salads and appetizers, and as a garnish. There are many varieties enjoyed, most commonly cod roe (tarako), herring roe (kazunoko), flying-fish roe (tobiko), smelt or capelin roe (masago or shishamo), sea urchin roe (uni), and salmon roe (ikura). Kazunoko, nicknamed yellow diamonds because of their price, are yellow and firm (the color often enhanced by a marinade of mirin, soy sauce, and stock). Tobiko are small, bright orange eggs that seem to pop when you eat them. A common sushi item is tobiko with raw quail-egg yolks on top of rice, wrapped with nori. Masago resembles tobiko in appearance and taste, though they are even smaller. Both orangy eggs are salty. Uni, the sexual gland of the sea urchin, consists of a small bundle rather than individual pieces. A golden yellow, uni is not salty but a little nutty or sweet. The most popular and commonly available of these varieties is ikura. Salmon roe are the largest of the egg shapes and are a shiny, reddish orange. If you've eaten red caviar, you've tasted ikura.

Salmon: Sake. Cooked, smoked, cured, or salt marinated. Whole salmon is a popular New Year's Day dish. Salmon is never served raw, even for sushi, though cured salmon is a popular sushi ingredient. Grilled salmon collars and heads are delicious.

Sardine: Iwashi. This family also includes herring, kippers, and bloaters. Available fresh (whole and fillets) and dried. Niboshi (boiled and dried) is an important ingredient for a type of dashi. Kohada, Japanese shad, is a small, sardinelike fish, often marinated in vinegar and served as sushi.

Sea bass: Suzuki. Includes black sea bass. Its firm, mild, white flesh is extremely popular as sashimi, especially when thinly sliced like hirame. The striped sea bass is related, but since it travels through fresh water to spawn, it is not advisable to eat it raw.

Skipjack tuna: Katsuo. Tuna family, also includes bonito. Best in the spring as sashimi (tataki). Catching and eating this tuna symbolizes spring's coming. Its full-flavored flesh is a deep rose. Dried bonito flakes are necessary in making dashi.

Squid: Ika. Squid can vary from as small as a single inch up to a giant size of many feet. Cuttlefish is often grouped with squid, though it differs, containing a large internal cuttlebone. Squid skin must be peeled off (see pages 43–44), revealing a flesh that is a chalky white; it is eaten both raw and cooked. The tentacles, simmered in seasoned broth, make delicious hors d'oeuvres.

Trout: Masu. Includes rainbow, steelhead, and salmon trout. A much-favored cooked fish, introduced to Japan from the Pacific coast.

Tuna: Maguro. Related to the mackerel family, includes albacore. With its rich red flesh, it is probably the most popular of all fish for sushi and sashimi. See also *yellowtail.*

Whitefish: Shiromi. A large classification of fish, also called flatfish. Includes sea bass, halibut, rock cod, red snapper, flounder, turbot, sole, dabs (sand dabs), and sea bream. Used in many cooked recipes and especially popular sliced paper thin for sashimi. See also *red sea bream.*

Yellowtail: Tuna family. Includes the prized bluefin tuna. The Japanese name changes according to the size of the fish and the section of its flesh. Buri is a full-grown fish over 35 inches. Hamachi is a year-old fish, about 30 to 35 inches. The head and spine are especially delicious when grilled. The smaller fish are warasa, inada, and wakashi. The favored part of the tuna is the fatty or oily belly (toro). Also enjoyed are the fillet of red meat (akami) and the pinkish meat between the toro and akami (chutoro). These terms will help you when you select sushi or sashimi.

SAKE (NIHON SHU): Rice wine, the most popular of all Japanese alcoholic beverages. Clear, colorless, and containing 12 to 18 percent alcohol, it is generally served slightly heated (to about 100° F.). As a result of Western influence, it is now served chilled over ice as well. Often compared to beer because of the ingredients and fermentation process, sake is as good as the quality of its water and of its rice. Since long aging is not necessary, there are no vintage years. Sake is also used as a cooking wine for balancing salty ingredients and for flavoring and tenderizing, as is mirin, a sweet, syrupy rice wine. Store in a cool, dark place; once it is opened, drink or use sake for cooking as soon as possible. You may substitute dry sherry.

SAKE KAZU (KASUZUKE): The mash left over after the liquid has been drained off during the sake-making process. Used to marinate foods as well as to top hot rice, farmer style. Available at oriental markets.

SANSHO: Japanese pepper, the aromatic berries of the prickly ash tree, dried and crushed to a fine powder. Most fragrant, sansho is available in the oriental section of many markets. Can substitute powdered black pepper. The leaves of the same tree are also used in cooking (see *kinome*).

SATO: Sugar. Traditional Japanese recipes call for great amounts of sugar, particularly in glazes or sauces to brush on grilled foods, in vinegar-based dressings and sauces for rice and salads, and in simmered dishes. The sugar balances the tartness of vinegar and the saltiness of soy sauce. In most recipes, an equal amount of honey can be substituted for the sugar.

SATO IMO: Field or country potatoes. Available at many produce stands under the name "taro potatoes." A member of the yam family, it has a dark brown, fuzzy outside and is smooth and grayish inside. To prepare, peel with a sharp knife, removing all brown spots, and soak in water 30 minutes. Boil in rice water (water reserved from the rice-rinsing process) or add some raw rice to the boiling water—this helps reduce the potato's gooey texture. Then rinse and use in your recipe. Select small, well-rounded potatoes and store in the refrigerator. You can substitute small new potatoes.

SATSUMA IMO: Sweet potato. Reddish outer skin with a golden yellow interior. The flesh is not as sweet as that of American yams or sweet potatoes. Used in fairly thick slices for tempura, and when sweet simmered, serves as a confection. You may substitute yams or sweet potatoes.

SAYA ENDO: Snow peas. Crisp, young pea pods. Some cooks snap off the flowery stem ends to string them but unless you're careful, the pods will open. (Therefore I skip that step.) Most recipes have you blanch them to add at the last minute. Easily available fresh, also frozen.

SHARI (SUSHI MESHI): Sushi rice. Steamed rice tossed with a dressing made of vinegar, sugar, and salt. You will find a powdered mix for this easy-to-make dressing at most oriental markets and oriental sections of major markets.

SHICHIMI TOGARASHI: Seven-spice hot pepper. A popular powdered combination of pungent and aromatic seasonings, including dried hot pepper, rape seeds, poppy seeds, sesame seeds, mustard seeds, hemp seeds, pepper leaf, and dried tangerine, orange, or lemon peel. Sold in tins and bottles.

SHIITAKE: Dried mushrooms. These are the most commonly used oriental mushrooms. In Japan, they are available fresh during the autumn through spring. To reconstitute, soak in warm water for several hours (minimum 3 to 5 hours, better yet, 24 hours). When studying Chinese cooking, I found these mushrooms could be used after 30 minutes of soaking, and then the tough center core could be cut out and discarded. The Japanese technique of longer soaking results in a more tender texture, and you can use the entire mushroom with the core, making for less waste of a costly item. These mushrooms are high in vitamins and minerals, as is the soaking liquid, which should be reserved to add to other recipes (or to water your household plants). Popular in salads and in grilled, braised, simmered, and one-pot dishes. You can substitute American mushrooms, but shiitake are easy to obtain and especially tasty.

SHINMA: New rice. This special, highly esteemed rice is harvested in the late summer and early autumn. Requires less water and a shorter cooking time than the usual rice. Available at oriental markets.

SHIO: Salt. Coarse salt is most often used. Aji shio is MSG-coated salt—90 percent salt and 10 percent MSG. Though it is frequently used in Japanese cookery, for health reasons I prefer to use plain salt.

SHIRATAKI: Thin, transparent, gelatinous noodles made from a tuberous root starch (devil's tongue root). Also called snake, palm, and shining waterfall. Contains no calories or nutrients and is used primarily in sukiyaki and mizutaki. Related to konnyaku. Sold dried in plastic bags and soft in cans and water packed in the refrigerator section of oriental markets and many major markets.

SHISO: Aromatic, somewhat minty green leaf of the beefsteak plant. A popular garnish and sushi ingredient. Available fresh in the summer and fall, and sometimes in winter, too. You may substitute fresh mint leaves or basil leaves. There's also a reddish-purple shiso. A different species, it is used primarily in making pickled plums, umeboshi, and confections.

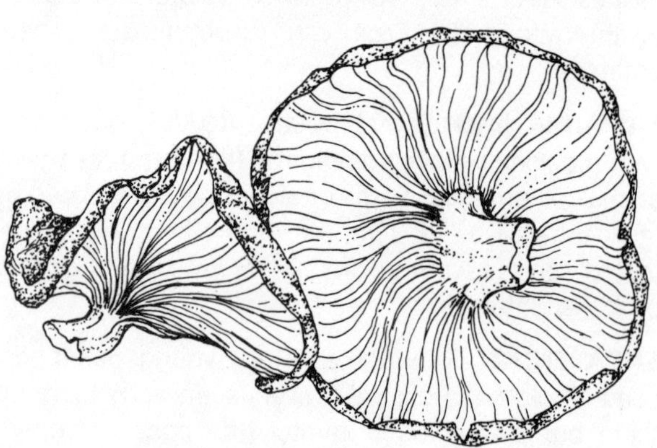

Shiitake: Dried mushrooms

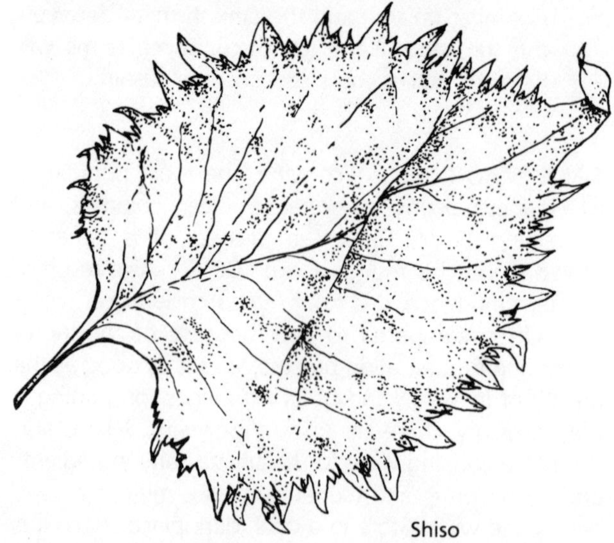

Shiso

SHOGA: Fresh ginger (gingerroot). Since fresh ginger is generally available in the produce section of most markets, please, please do not substitute the powdered variety. Peel off the brown outer skin of only as much as you need, then wrap the remaining root in plastic and store in the refrigerator or the freezer. Although the ginger will become spongy from freezing, the taste remains the same, and it is excellent for ginger juice. Grate ginger while it's still nearly frozen. When you have the time, grate extra ginger, wrap small bundles (about a teaspoonful) in wax paper squares, and keep in your freezer for future use. Ginger can also be stored refrigerated in alcohol (vodka, sake, sherry). If mold appears, simply cut off and discard that part. Gari, vinegared ginger slices, are a popular condiment, particularly for sushi. Beni shoga is red pickled ginger.

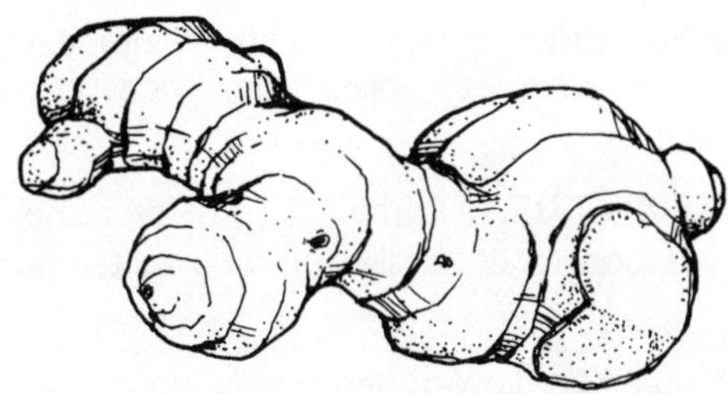

Shoga: Gingerroot

SHÓYU (SÓYA): Japanese soy sauce, made from soybeans, grain (cracked, roasted wheat, or barley), salt, water, and rice enzymes. This mixture is naturally fermented for 1 to 2 years, then filtered and bottled. Soy sauce should be a rich reddish brown and translucent. There are several kinds to choose from.

Dark soy sauce is slightly salty (about 18 percent salt); it is used to enhance flavor in broiled and boiled foods (with sugar, salt, and/or water), in seasoned sauces, with pickling ingredients, as a soup base (with miso and stock), and as a dipping sauce for noodles, sashimi, sushi, and other cooked recipes. Thin soy sauce, lighter in color, is used for light-colored sauces and stocks. Low-sodium soy sauce is also available.

American and Chinese soy sauces, in comparison, are considered synthetic or chemical products. They are not brewed or fermented but are generally made with hydrolyzed vegetable protein, flavorings, colorings (such as caramel and corn syrup) and preservatives. This process involves only a few days, and the resulting soy sauce is thicker than the Japanese.

All soy sauces should be stored at room temperature. The shelf life is several years; however, if some water evaporates, the sauce may taste even saltier than usual. Always shake soy sauce before you pour. No substitute for soy sauce is possible.

SHUNGIKU: Garland chrysanthemum. (Resembles ornamental chrysanthemum leaves.) Nicknamed chop suey leaves. May be eaten raw, though some prefer them blanched. Very popular ingredient for sukiyaki and one-pot dishes or cooked by itself with soy sauce and seasonings. I've also enjoyed them wrapped in nori like a sushi roll. To keep fresh, wrap stems in damp paper towels and refrigerate. You may substitute dandelion leaves (tampopo), spinach, chard, or mustard leaves (karashina). Or grow your own from seeds.

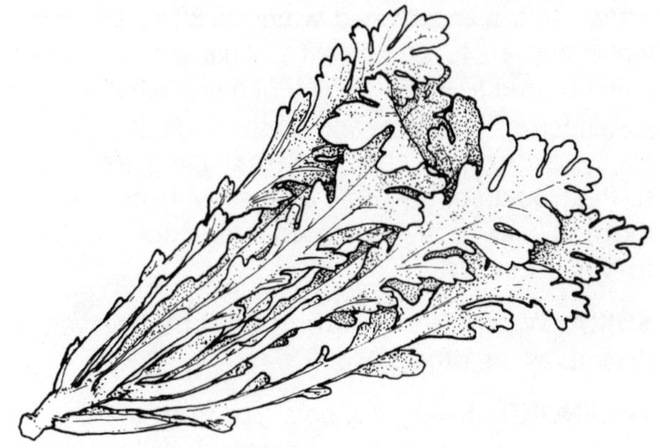

Shungiku: Chrysanthemum

SOBA: Buckwheat noodles. These thin grain noodles come in several colors and flavors, primarily buckwheat (grayish-beige), as well as cha soba (green tea flavored and colored), yaki soba (yellow noodles for stir frying) and chuka soba (yellow noodles for soups and salads). Available dried and fresh, in the refrigerator or freezer

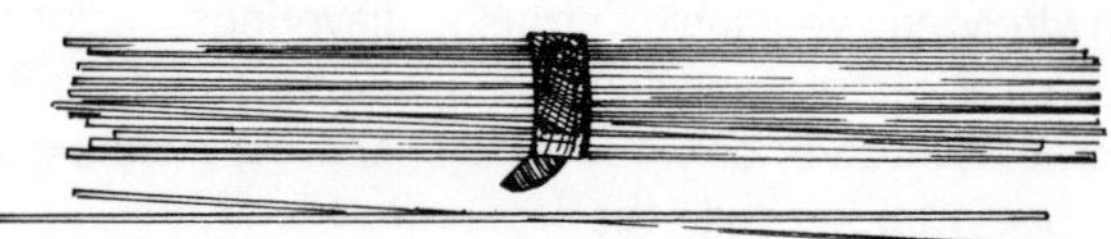

Soba: Buckwheat noodles

section of major markets and oriental food stores. You can substitute thin whole wheat or other noodles.

SOMEN: Thin white noodle, similar to vermicelli. Somen is most often eaten at room temperature or chilled. Excellent for salads and the like. Tamago zomen (somen) is a light yellow enriched egg noodle. You can substitute thin spaghetti or vermicelli.

SU: Rice vinegar. Japanese vinegar, naturally sweet and very mild, is most important for seasoning, dressing, tenderizing, and washing foods. It is available at most major markets. You can substitute cider vinegar or fresh lemon juice.

Throughout this book, you'll find reference to *su water.* This is an acidated water of 80 to 90 percent water and 10 to 20 percent vinegar (or to taste). Su water is used to hold the color of many vegetables and to tenderize, marinate, and wash foods. It's also necessary to use on your hands when shaping rice for sushi so that you do not become covered with sticky rice. To make su water: Use about 2 to 3 teaspoons of vinegar to 1 quart of water.

SUIKA: Watermelon. A favorite fresh fruit. Served as a dessert, as are other melons.

TAKENOKO: Bamboo shoots, cut from the bamboo plant as it throws out new seasonal stalks. You can purchase them fresh at Japanese produce stands, particularly during the spring. If the husks are still intact, you will need to peel them and then boil the shoots for about an hour to rid them of bitterness. However, I have found fresh bamboo shoots already husked and parboiled at the local Japanese markets. If you have never eaten fresh bamboo shoots, with their nutty flavor, you are in for a visually rewarding as well as tasteworthy experience. If using canned bamboo

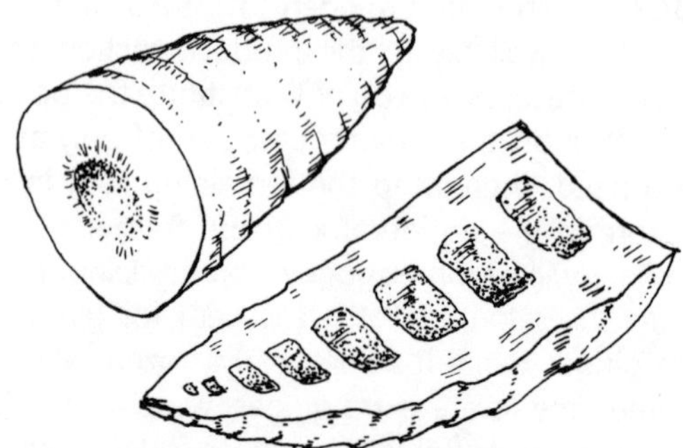

Takenoko: Bamboo shoots

shoots, try to find whole shoots so that you can shape the cylinders yourself. To refresh canned shoots, parboil in fresh water for a few seconds, rinse, and drain. Leftover bamboo shoots can be kept for several days (even weeks) in the refrigerator; simply store in fresh water, changing it daily.

TAMAGO: Eggs. Popular in Japanese cuisine, eggs are found raw, steamed, boiled, fried, poached, and/or sweetened.

TEMPURA ABURA: Combination of processed vegetable oils bottled especially for cooking tempura. See *abura.*

TEMPURA KO: Low-gluten wheat flour, used especially for tempura batter. All-purpose flour can be substituted.

TENTSUYU: Dipping sauce for tempura. Available bottled and canned; usually condensed requiring dilution with water. Easy to make at home. (See page 123.)

TOFU: Soybean cake; bean curd. Often referred to as *o-tofu,* "honorable tofu," it is a source of inexpensive, high-quality protein, rich in minerals and vitamins, free from chemical toxins and cholesterol, low in saturated fats and calories, and easy to digest. The custardlike cakes of fresh tofu are generally packaged in plastic containers with water. To store for several days, it is best (though not necessary) to change this water daily and to keep the container covered in the refrigerator. You can also freeze tofu.

Tofu is easily available at most major markets,

oriental markets, and health-food stores in many different forms—the most common being: (1) regular tofu (momen tofu), (2) silken tofu (kinugoshi tofu), and (3) firm tofu (Chinese-style toufu). Other forms are: (4) deep-fried tofu pouches and puffs (aburage, age), (5) deep-fried tofu cutlets, cakes, or cubes (atsu-age or nama-age), (6) deep-fried tofu burgers (ganmo), (7) pressed and savory pressed tofu (toufu-kan), (8) grilled (yaki-dofu), and (9) freeze-dried tofu (koya-dofu).

You can simply drain the fresh cakes, cut them into small squares, and add to simple recipes, such as soups, salads, and omelets. However, as you become more familiar with the qualities and varieties of tofu, you will want to put forth the effort on the preparation required. The basic fresh cakes must be properly drained of their excess liquid. There are several simple techniques: (1) slicing and draining—cut cakes about ½ inch thick and place on paper towels, cover with additional paper towels and let drain at least 30 minutes, changing the towels at least once; (2) colander draining—place whole cakes on a small, flat colander, cover, and refrigerate several hours or overnight; (3) pressing—wrap cakes in kitchen towels and refrigerate several hours or overnight; (4) slanting—wrap cakes in kitchen towels and for at least 30 minutes allow to drain on cutting board placed in kitchen sink at an angle; (5) parboiling—cut tofu into small rectangles or squares and parboil about 5 minutes, drain (an excellent way to refresh old tofu); (6) squeezing and crumbling—wrap tofu in cheesecloth, kitchen towels, or tofu sack, twist and squeeze to extract remaining liquid, empty squeezed and crumbled tofu into working bowl (for this method, it is best to have drained the tofu by one of the other techniques); and (7) scrambling—crumble tofu into skillet, heat while stirring, about 4 minutes, using a wooden spoon or chopsticks, until tofu is crumbled and dry; strain to drain.

The deep-fried tofu products need advance preparation to rid them of excess oil. Tofu pouches, cutlets, cubes, and triangles should be placed in boiling water for a few minutes; use chopsticks to push the tofu down into the water, or you can place them in a colander and douse with boiling water. Completely drain, then cut these tofu open into desired shapes. In many recipes, tofu pouches should first be cut in half, then parboiled, and next cut into desired shapes. This step is to rid the insides of excess oil. Some recipes require that deep-fried tofu be broiled, toasted, or grilled. Soak freeze-dried tofu about 5 minutes, then firmly press between the palms of your hands to squeeze dry. Instant tofu is also available; follow package instructions.

TOGARASHI: Dried hot red peppers. Used as a spicy seasoning with daikon, cabbage, and other ingredients. Available whole and powdered. Store in your pantry spice shelves. You can substitute other dried small red chili peppers or cayenne pepper.

TONKATSU SOSU: Dark sauce traditionally served with fried pork cutlets (tonkatsu). Available in bottles. You can substitute Worcestershire sauce.

TORI: Chicken. The part of the breast enjoyed sashimi style, called sasami, is the tender inner fillet. Recipes including *tori* in the name signal that the main ingredient is chicken; for example, yakitori is broiled chicken.

TSUKEMONO: Japanese-style pickles. Served with every Japanese meal as an accompaniment, particularly at the end of the meal with rice. There are six basic types of pickles, depending upon the pickling agent: salt, miso, nuka, vinegar, sake lees (or sake kazu), and koji (cooked rice, barley, or soybeans that have been mixed with the *Aspergillus oryzae* mold, then incubated, as in the making of soy sauce).

UDO: A Japanese vegetable similar to fennel or spikenard. Raised without sunlight, it is white and delicate. Generally eaten raw with a vinegar dressing; occasionally added to soups as a garnish. Available spring to autumn. You can substitute fennel, celery (first remove all strings), or asparagus.

UDON: Soft, thick, large white noodles (round or flat), made from flour, salt, and water. Available fresh in the refrigerator or freezer sections of oriental markets and many major markets. Also available dried. You can substitute other thick, flat pastas.

UMEBOSHI: Pickled Japanese plum. A popular ingredient for rice balls and many sushi recipes. Available in cans and bottles and in the refrigerator section of oriental markets. Recently I have found small boxes of chewable tablets of freeze-dried plum extract candy, umeboshi-jun, composed of plum and beefsteak plant leaves.

UME-SHU: Plum wine. Sweet wine made of the green fruit of the plum tree. It is served chilled in summer, at room temperature in winter.

WAKAME: Dried sea vegetation. It is used reconstituted, primarily in salads and soups. Soaking time varies, depending upon quality. Generally, 15 minutes to 1 hour is sufficient, then drain and squeeze dry. Cut off tough parts. The nutritious soaking liquid can be reserved for other use.

WAKEGI: Scallions. Commonly chopped, diced, and minced as a garnish for soups, salads, sauces, and noodle recipes.

WARABI: Bracken fern, fiddlehead, or fiddler's fern. A mountain vegetable, it must be soaked in su water before being added to recipes.

WASABI (SABI): A member of the horseradish family resembling celery root. The edible part is the root, which must be peeled and then grated. However, fresh wasabi is rarely sold in the United States. Powdered wasabi is the "mustard" of Japanese cookery. It is a must for sushi and sashimi. To reconstitute, place a small amount of powder in a small mixing bowl, add a few drops of water, and mix thoroughly with a chopstick until you have a thick pungent paste. Cover and let rest for 15 minutes to allow the flavors to mellow. Add to taste to soy sauce for a dipping sauce for sashimi, or dab a little on the raw fish slices for sushi before placing on the vinegared rice. Leftover paste can be stored covered in the refrigerator. Tins of powder are easy to obtain at most major markets, oriental food stores—even fresh fish markets. Plastic tubes of wasabi paste are making an appearance at many oriental markets. Once they are opened, refrigerate. You can substitute bottled white horseradish or spicy dried mustard for a similar taste.

YAMA IMO: Mountain yam. Bumpy on the outside and somewhat gooey on the inside. Peeled and grated, it is eaten raw with fresh tuna or with boiled rice and egg. It is also boiled or fried for a number of Japanese recipes. You will find these potatoes at oriental markets, generally stored in sawdust-filled crates. Peel only the amount you need and store the remaining tuber (keeps for several weeks) in the refrigerator vegetable bin. You can substitute yam.

YUBA: Soy-milk film. When soy milk is heated, the film that forms on the surface of the milk is called yuba. Yuba can be homemade or reconstituted from dried form (sheets, rolls, or strips). Soy milk and dried yuba are available at health-food stores as well as at oriental markets.

YUZU: Aromatic citron. About the size of a tangerine, yuzu is used primarily for its aromatic rind, as a garnish for soups, simmered dishes, pickles and relishes, and sweet dishes. Available November through January. Substitute lime or lemon peel.

EQUIPMENT

To set up your kitchen for Japanese cooking, it is not necessary to run out to an Oriental market or hardware store to purchase every piece of equipment. There are many items in your pantry that will easily substitute.

But let's say you were given the opportunity to completely outfit your kitchen in the Japanese style. You would certainly be purchasing the following pieces of equipment, for which I also indicate substitutions.

APRON (KAPPOGI): A special apron for cooking. For everyday cooking, I prefer my machine-washable, no-iron butcher's apron, but I don my kappogi for entertaining.

BAMBOO MAT (MAKI-SU or SUDARE): Matchsticklike bamboo, woven with string into an 8-inch to 10-inch square mat. Slightly dampened, it is used for forming certain sushi dishes, such as norimaki, into rolls. A maki-su is fairly inexpensive, so, if you plan to make sushi rolls, do invest in this item.

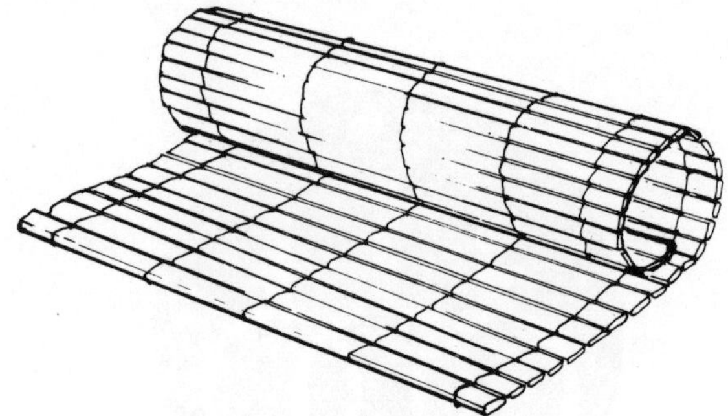

Bamboo Mat: Maki-su or Sudare

CERAMIC SERVING AND EATING BOWL (DONBURI): Deep-footed, large bowl with a lid, used primarily for recipes featuring a bed of rice or noodles with a protein topping. *Donburi* refers to the particular recipe as well as to the serving piece. Deep soup bowls can be substituted.

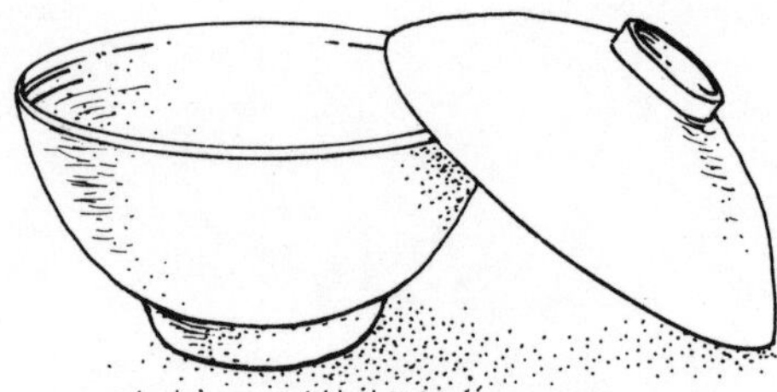

Ceramic Serving and Eating Bowl: Donburi

CHARCOAL BRAZIER (KONRO or SHICHIRIN): Made of baked earthenware and used for grilling, broiling, and one-pot dishes. You can substitute your broiler or a portable electric burner as necessary.

CHARCOAL GRILL (HIBACHI): Small, cast-iron grill, used tableside to broil or barbecue. You can substitute a patio barbecue or kitchen broiler.

CHOPSTICKS (HASHI): There are several different varieties of chopsticks. Those for eating are generally plain or lacquered wood. Disposable ones, called wari-basi, are generally used in restaurants. To introduce novices to handling chopsticks, jam a small, thick piece of paper at the top between the two ends to separate them and tightly secure with a rubber band; you now have a springlike chopstick apparatus. Chopstick etiquette dictates that one eat from the narrow end and use the broad end for serving oneself from a communal bowl. Longer and thicker chopsticks are used for cooking. When a table is properly set, hashi are placed on holders, called hashi oki, generally made of pottery or ceramic.

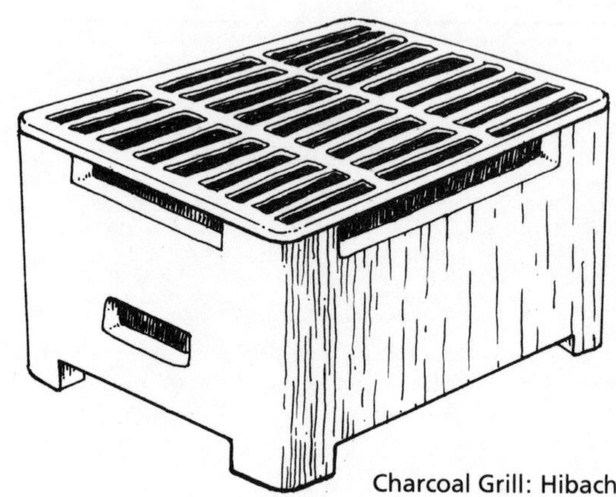

Charcoal Grill: Hibachi

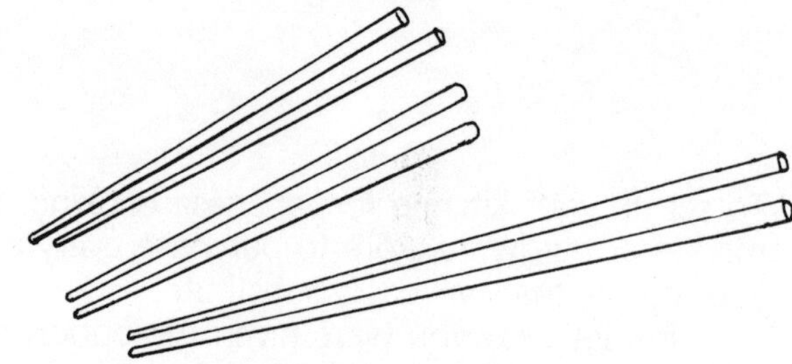

Chopsticks: Hashi

COLANDER (ZARU): Used for draining washed and cooked foods, for salting, tossing, arranging foods attractively, for tableside cooking (as in sukiyaki), and for serving (as in tempura and cold noodles). The large, slightly concave round or square colanders drain food faster and better than American-style colanders with-

Colander: Zaru

out crowding or crushing the ingredients. Modern models are made of brightly colored plastic. Some also have a draining bottom tray (to catch the water) and a top cover.

CUTTING BOARD (MANAITA): The size is generally about 19 inches square. You can substitute any cutting board.

DEEP-FRYING EQUIPMENT: Deep frying (agemono) requires several pieces of equipment. (1) Pot (agemono-nabe or tempura-nabe): heavy and deep, retains heat well. Usually thick cast iron or brass. If substituting, use a heavy deep fryer; I like to use my wok. (2) Net ladle (ami-shakushi or agedame): A fine wire mesh ladle used for skimming the oil (also excellent for skimming fat from soups and stocks). You can substitute a slotted metal spoon. (3) Oil drainer (abura-kiri): A shallow pan with a rack for draining. You can substitute a colander, strainer, sieve, or cookie rack. (4) Handy long narrow chopsticks with wood ends for handling and sharp-pointed metal ends for turning frying foods.

Deep frying pot: Agemono-nabe or Tempura-nabe

DROPPED LID (OTOSHI-BUTA): A unique but simple piece of equipment that hastens simmering without permitting the liquid to boil. The lid, usually made of cypress or cedar, is about an inch smaller in diameter than the cooking pot and has a handle for easy placement and removal. You drop the lid directly on top of the simmering foods so that the heat penetrates while some vapor slowly evaporates. Since the liquid will not boil rapidly, the ingredients will not bounce around and break up. Wood dropped lids are available in several diameters. Metal lids that are smaller in diameter don't work as well because they are too heavy and the food may pick up some metallic aftertastes. Circles cut from cooking parchment can be substituted. You can weight these slightly with chopsticks or wooden cooking spoons.

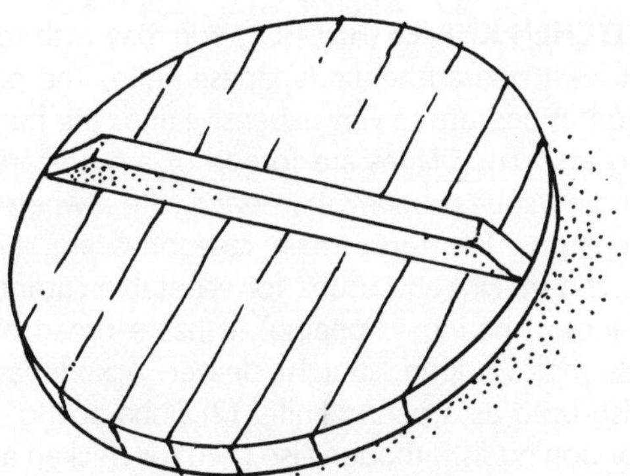

Dropped lid: Otoshi-Buta

FISHBONE TWEEZERS (HONE-NUKI): These metal boning tweezers are excellent for removing small bones from fish fillets without ripping the flesh. You can substitute eyebrow tweezers.

GRATER (OROSHI-GAME): Flat, prickly metal (usually aluminum) graters; I find the 9-inch size the most helpful. The fine sharp teeth are used primarily for grating ginger and horseradish. The cupped well at the bottom collects gratings juices. You can use your standard American grater on the fine side. Or try crushing ginger in your garlic press.

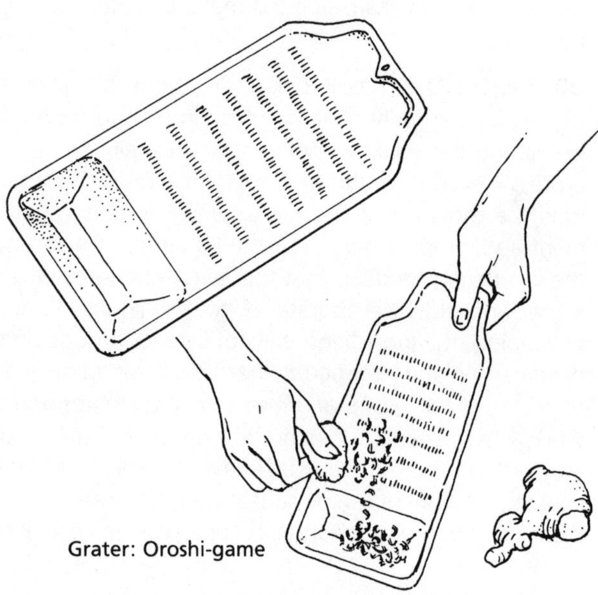
Grater: Oroshi-game

KITCHEN KNIVES (HOCHO): You may wish to invest in at least one authentic Japanese knife. The prices vary from moderate to very expensive (into the hundreds of dollars). The blades are forged of a high-carbon steel and must be properly sharpened with a whetstone and kept dry. The three main categories are: (1) Nagiri-bocho (nakiri) and usuba for vegetable cutting (slicing, mincing, paring, chopping). It has a broad blade and resembles a long, straight cleaver. A kodeba-bocho is also used as a paring knife. (2) Deba-bocho, primarily for boning fish, though also used for chicken and meat. It has a heavy, sharp tip and is somewhat tapered. (3)

Knives: Hocho

Takobiki-bocho, yanagiba, and ryuba are sashimi slicers. The takobiki has a blunt, pointless end, and the yanagiba and ryuba have pointed, willow-blade cutting edges. All are long with very thin blades. Refer to *whetstones* for care of knives.

LACQUERED SOUP BOWLS (OWAN): Individual soup bowls with lids. Plastic coating rather than lacquer is often substituted for economy. To clean, rinse and dry—do not soap or scour lacquered utensils.

Lacquered Soup Bowls: Owan

LINEN CLOTH (SARASHI): Used for straining stocks, wrapping vegetables and tofu to squeeze out excess liquid, wrapping fish to be marinated in miso, and many other similar jobs. You can substitute several layers of cheesecloth or kitchen towels.

LUNCH BOX (BENTO): These individual lunch boxes are made of a thin metal, such as tin. They're divided into two compartments, one for rice and the other for kazu (a protein of some kind, often left over from another meal). There are also more luxurious, larger lunch boxes with more compartments, called maku no uchi.

METAL MOLD (NAGASHI-BAKO/NAGASHIKAN): Generally made of seamless aluminum, this two-part metal

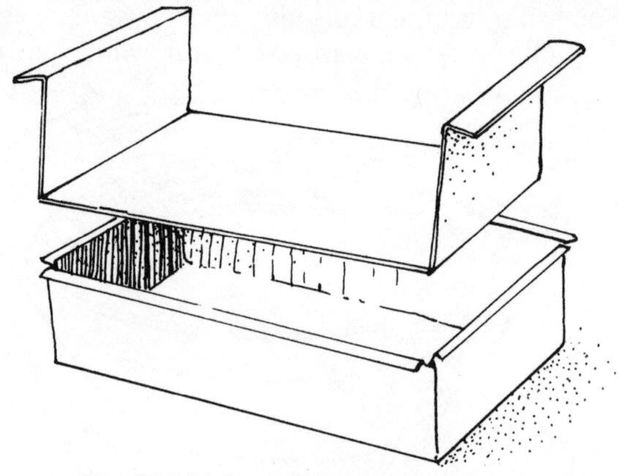
Metal Mold: Nagashi-bako/Nagashikan

mold has a removable inner tray. It is used for several Japanese recipes, such as chilled gelatin and steamed sweetened eggs. To unmold, you simply remove the inner tray by the sides. You can substitute a heat-proof mold or casserole for the cooked recipes and a plastic mold for the chilled.

MORTAR AND PESTLE (SURIBACHI AND SURIKOGI): The suribachi is usually made of ceramic or other earthenware, sometimes of plastic. The outside is generally glazed brown; the inside is tan with circular and straight grids that act as a grinder. Often the bottom has plastic or rubber grips to prevent sliding. Use this to grind small portions of toasted sesame seeds and to mix, crush, and blend many ingredients for a thick sauce, such as a sesame miso or tofu sauce. To clean, wash with water only and wipe dry. The large, cedar-wood surikogi is the pestle. You can also use it for beating foods as you would use a metal meat tenderizer. You can substitute a mortar and pestle, a food processor, or a blender.

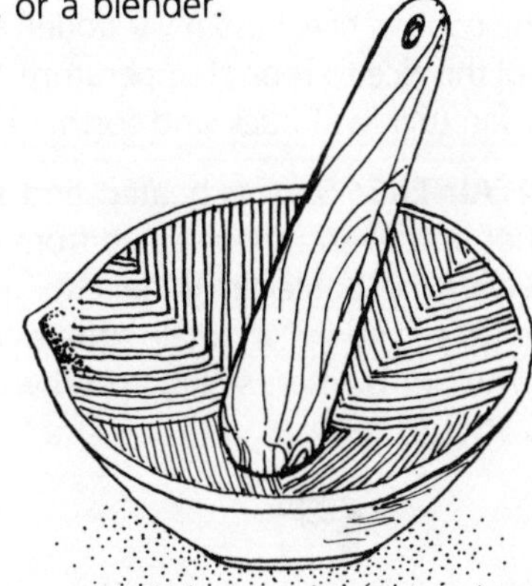

Mortar and Pestle: Suribachi and Surikogi

NEW YEAR'S DAY BOX (JUBAKO): Compartmental, tiered box for serving New Year's Day foods, handy at home or on a picnic. You can substitute serving platters, particularly a lazy Susan–style divided tray.

PICKLING TUB (TARU): Traditionally, vegetables to be salt pickled were placed in wooden or ceramic tubs like crocks, then covered with a weighted wooden lid. A plastic container is now available with a built-in lid-and-weight gadget (shokutaku-tsuke). You can substitute a wood, ceramic, porcelain, plastic, or glass dish. Add vegetables and salt (or pickling sauce), place plastic wrap or wax paper on top of the vegetables, and weight down.

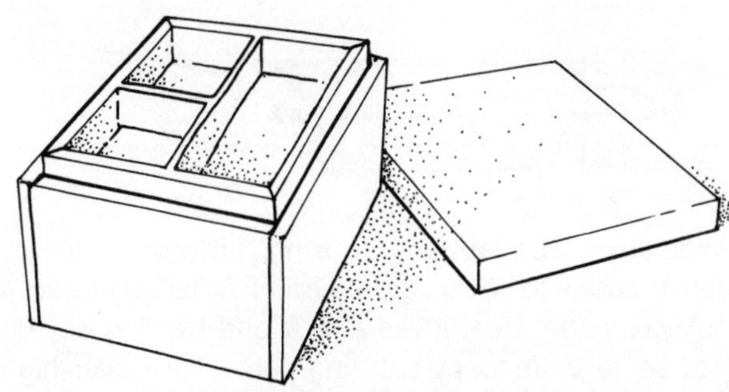

New Year's Day Box: Jubako

POTS AND PANS (NABE): You can purhase traditional Japanese pieces or, in most cases, use what you have on hand. Foods are also served directly from a nabe. (1) Donabe: An earthenware, clay casserole pot with a lid, glazed only on the inside. This can be used on the stove top or in the oven. (2) Oyako nabe: Small skillet with one long, upright handle on the side that facilitates combining ingredients—you simply shake the pan. Used primarily in oyako donburi recipe. You can substitute another small skillet and stir the ingredients with chopsticks. (3) Sukiyaki nabe: A shallow, round, heavy cast-iron skillet used for making sukiyaki. This is a handsome piece of equipment for stove-top braising or stewing or grilling of meat, fish, poultry, and

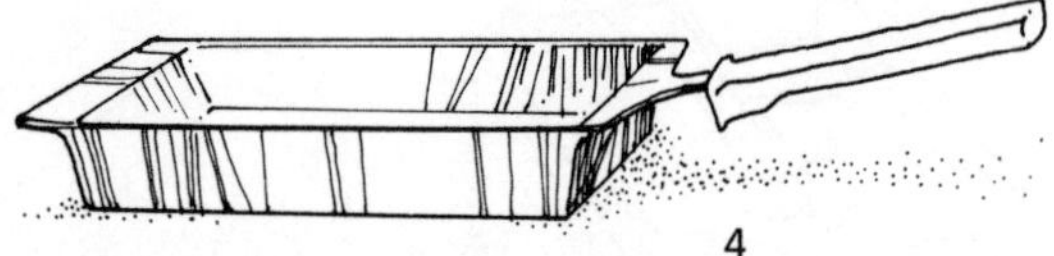

vegetables. For tableside cooking, however, I find it much easier to use a large electric skillet. To clean a sukiyaki nabe, treat it like a wok and hand-wash; do not scrub with soapy scouring pads. Place over high heat and dry, then rub with a paper towel dampened with a little cooking oil and heat slightly to seal. (4) Tamago nabe (tampago yaki nabe/maki yaki nabe): A rectangular skillet for making cylindrical Japanese omelets. If you are interested in preparing Japanese rolled omelets to be served warm or chilled or thin rectangular egg sheets that you slice into shreds, you must have a tamago nabe. Some are made of cast iron, others, aluminum. The best are made of copper with a tin coating. Do not scrub to clean—you may destroy the surface coating. Instead, clean with a cloth and wipe with cooking oil. (5) Tempura nabe: A heavy, cast-iron pot used for deep frying. The top has a rim that turns inward and thus prevents hot oil from splattering. (6) Teppan: A heavy, flat, cast-iron skillet for cooking teppan-yaki. You can substitute a griddle or a large electric skillet.

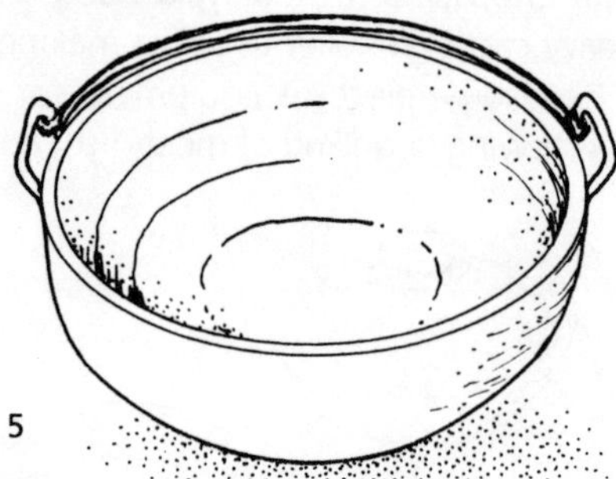

RICE-MAKING SUPPLIES: For proper cooking of rice, several pieces of equipment are necessary. Nowadays, many homes have electric rice cookers. These are very simple to operate. All you need do is assemble and plug in. Making Japanese-style rice the traditional method is also very simple. You need a heavy pot with a tight lid.

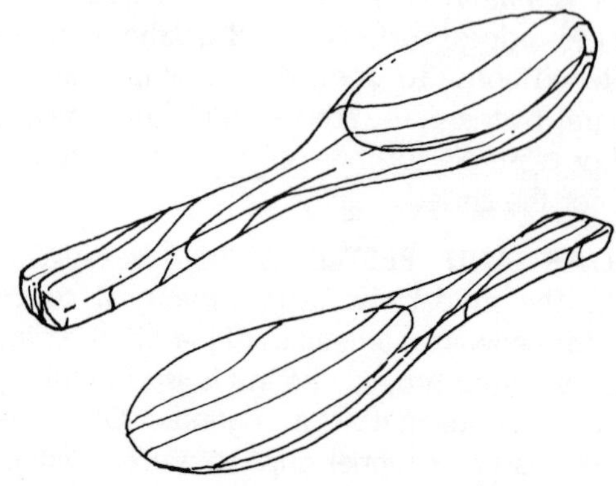

Rice Paddles: Samogi/shamoji

To secure the lid on my pot so that no steam escapes, I weight it down with a stone pestle. For stirring, fluffing up, and serving, use a wooden rice paddle (samogi/shamoji). For sushi rice, you will need a rice tub (handai or sushi oke), made of fragrant cedar, in which you place the cooked rice. I use my wooden salad bowl. Then, to cool this rice to room temperature, you should wave a flat fan (uchiwa) back and forth.

SAKE CONTAINERS: Sake is heated and served in a tokkuri, liquor bottle, and then sipped from a sakezuki, small stoneware or porcelain wine cup. Sometimes, chilled sake is served in a small square cedar box, masuzake. The rim is often salted and the alcohol enjoyed like a shot of tequila.

Sake set

SCRUB BRUSH (TAWASHI): These strange-looking, even ugly, scrubbers are made of natural palm fiber and are ideal for scrubbing root vegetables and pots. You can substitute a synthetic vegetable scrubber.

SESAME SEED TOASTER (GOMAIRI): This is a small, tinny skillet with a wire mesh attached lid that secures tightly. Use this on the stove top to toast or dry roast your sesame seeds a few seconds over high heat, which brings out the full flavor of the seeds. You can use an ordinary dry skillet, but the toasting sesame seeds will pop all over your stove.

Sesame Seed Toaster: Gomairi

SKEWERS (KUSHI): Bamboo skewers are used for chicken, kaboblike hibachi foods, when adding small ingredients, such as hard-cooked quail eggs to a one-pot dish, to prevent shrimp from curling, and to pierce food to check for doneness. The flat skewers are best so food will not turn. It is best to presoak these for recipes requiring high heat, so that the bamboo doesn't burn. Long stainless-steel skewers are used for small whole fish. Generally, several skewers are placed in these fish so they can hold the desired shape and can be turned easily during cooking.

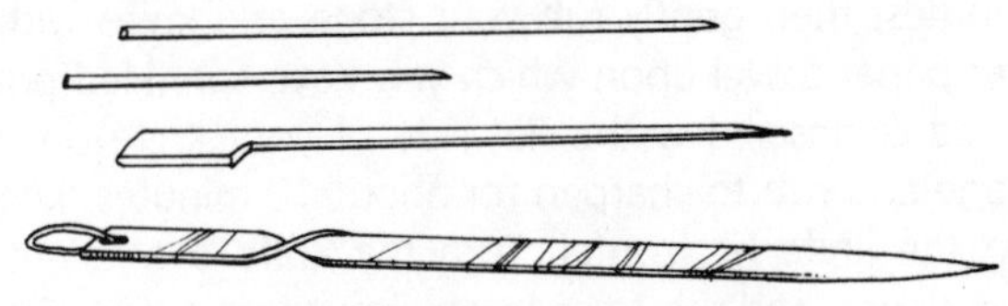

Skewers: Kushi

SLICER (BENRINA): To slice vegetables, such as cucumbers, thinly, you may wish to purchase this small, rectangular, boxlike gadget. Some come with extra blades for shredding. You can achieve similar results with a mandoline, a food processor, or a sharp knife.

STEAMERS (MUSHIKI): There are two types of steamers: (1) metal (generally aluminum), most often square with several tiers and round holes, and (2) bamboo, the more familiar and traditional Chinese steamers, with bamboo and wood slats or trays. Several round steamers can be placed on top of one another. If you do not own a steamer, you can use a fish poacher or can easily construct your own device by placing a footed wire rack or several metal rings (empty small metal cans, such as pineapple or tuna, with tops and bottoms removed) in steaming liquid in a Dutch oven, topping this with a heat-proof cooking dish filled with the food, then covering with the Dutch oven lid. To prevent condensation from dripping down on the steaming food, wrap a tea towel under and around the lid.

STOVE-TOP BROILER (YAKIAMI/SAKANAYAKI): These inexpensive two-part gadgets include a dripping tray with slits to allow the heat to rise and a stand-up wire grill with handles. Assemble and place on top of your burner, and you will turn your stove into a grill. This simulates a charcoal brazier, hibachi, or toaster. The only difficulty is in controlling the splattering of the basting sauces.

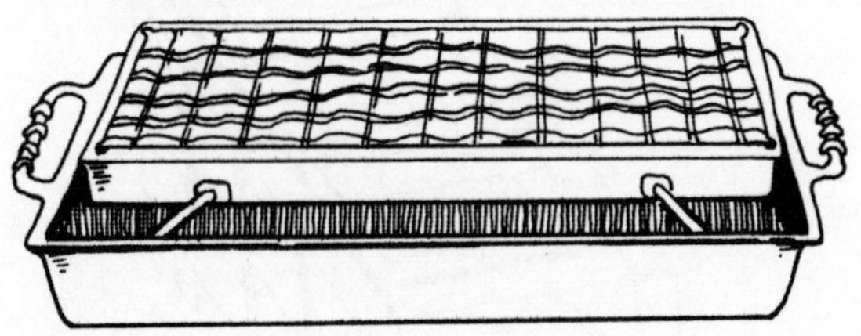

Stove-Top Broiler: Yakiami/Sakanayaki

STRAINERS (URAGOSHI): Several recipes require strainers or sieves for straining or mashing. The traditional Japanese equipment consists of a fine-mesh net that is very tightly stretched over a circular form. Foods to be strained are poured over the mesh into a bowl. Foods to be mashed to a puree are forced into a bowl through the strainer with a rice paddle. You will find many other uses for this, including sifting powdered sugar and straining stocks. You can substitute

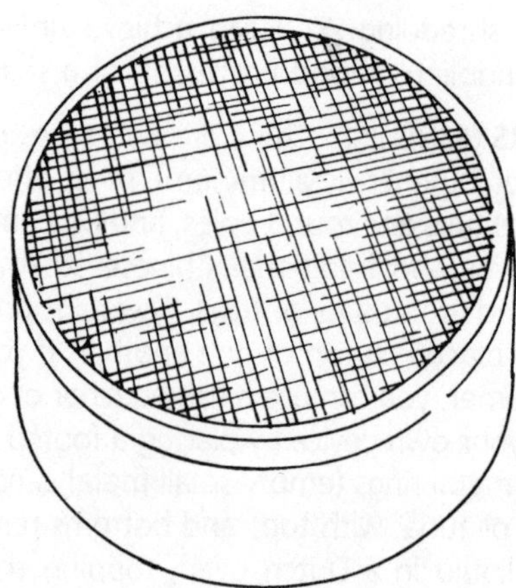
Strainer: Uragoshi

small-holed colanders, sieves, and strainers, and, for the mixing, a food processor or blender.

SUSHI PRESS (OSHIWAKU): Wooden box or mold with an inner lid for pressing sushi. Some molds have decorative inner patterns that will help you to press small, geometric sushi loaves—you will need this type if you plan to make sushi loaves. Inexpensive plastic molds are easily available.

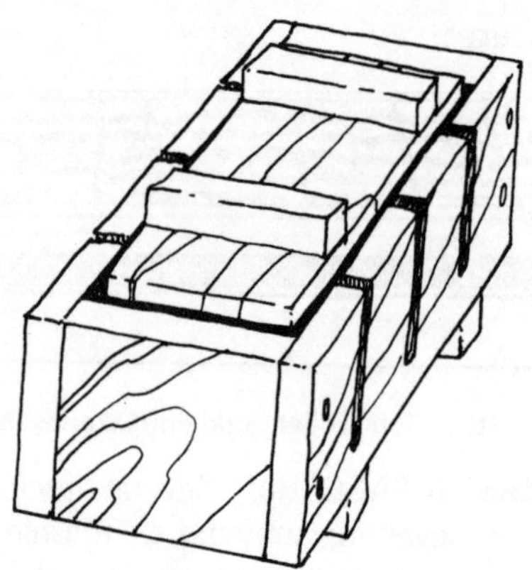
Sushi Press: Oshiwaku

TEA CEREMONY UTENSILS: The best serving bowls, plates, and cups are used. Necessary items for the host or hostess include portable brazier and sunken hearth (furo, ro), glazed tile on which the brazier rests (shikiita), teakettle (okama), container for the rinse water (kensui), bamboo water ladle (hishaku), cold-water container (mizusashi), lid rest to hold the hot kettle's lid (futa-oki), container for tea (cha-ire, usuchaki, depending upon the type of tea), tea scoop (chashaku), bamboo tea whisk (chasen), tea bowl (chawan), small white cloth, dampened, for wiping the bowl (chakin), silk wiping cloth (fukusa), a fabric case with another small silk napkin inside (fukusa bassami, kobukusa), and a folding fan (sensu). Foods are presented on platters, in bowls, and on lacquerware. Sometimes a fuchidaka, a five-tiered layered box, or a kashi-bachi, a special bowl, is used for confections.

WET TOWELS (OSHIBORI): If you frequent a Japanese restaurant, particularly the sushi bar, you are familiar with these hot, damp, fragrant towels for cleansing the hands. To make: use linen or terry cloth, the size of a hand towel. Dampen with hot water to which you might add a few drops of jasmine or another fragrance. Wring out excess water and roll up like a tube. Wrap individually in foil and keep warm in a low oven, or wrap in plastic and reheat later in a microwave oven.

WHETSTONES (TOISHI): There are three different kinds of whetstones for traditional hocho attention. For the first step in caring for your knives, you need an arato, which is a very rough stone. The second step requires a medium-textured stone, aoto. Finally, a fine-textured stone, a shirato, is used for smoothing and finishing. If using only one whetstone, follow these steps: wet the stone with water and let sit for about 10 minutes, then gently rub your stone and knife with a wet paper towel upon which you have sprinkled powdered cleanser. Lay the flat side of your knife on the stone and rub to sharpen for about 10 minutes, keeping the knife horizontal. Turn the knife over, slanted side down, and rub to sharpen about four times. Wash your knife and dry with a dish towel; wrap blade in paper towels and put away. Wash and dry whetstone.

ADVANCE PREPARATION

CUTTING AND SLICING

The following list will illustrate the attention given to proper cutting and slicing of foods in Japanese cooking. In the recipe pages, I will refer to the English translations.

KUSHIGATA-GIRI: Quarter, as you would a lemon or tomato.

MEN-TORI: Peel the skin or outer surface, such as with potatoes. Often the edges are beveled.

KAKUMUKI: Peel the surface and remove both ends. Often the vegetable is further shaped into a hexagon, a popular shape for carrots. Thought to evoke a turtle, a hexagon symbolizes old age because a turtle lives a long life.

WA-GIRI: Round slices. Cylindrical vegetables, such as carrots, are often thinly sliced (also referred to as koguchi-giri).

HANGETSU-GIRI: Half-moons or crescents are cut from the round slices.

ICHO-GIRI: Quartered. Round slices are cut into fourths, evoking a fan.

SHIKISHI-GIRI: Squares. Rectangles and cubes are often cut into small squares.

TANZAKU-GIRI: Rectangles. Cylindrical vegetables are often cut into thick slices and then into rectangles.

RAN-GIRI: Cut on diagonal. Cylindrical vegetables are often cut at an angle into about 1-inch pieces. If you roll the vegetable a half-turn after each cut, this is called naname-giri. These steps are similar to the Chinese roll-cutting technique.

SEN-GIRI: Cut into matchstick-size juliennes.

SAINOME-GIRI: Chop coarsely.

MIJIN-GIRI: Mince.

SASAGAKI: Cut into slivers, as you would sharpen a pencil. Resembles shavings. Most often used for carrots and gobo.

KATSURA-MUKI: Cut into a thin, continuous sheet. Daikon and cucumbers are most often cut in this manner. You would slice around the outside surface, continuing until you have one long sheet. This is very difficult and takes a steady hand, a sharp knife, and lots of practice. Sometimes these sheets are tightly rolled and then sliced into curls, kaminari. Soak these curls in ice water to set the shape.

KIKUKA-GIRA (KIKKA-KABU): Cut to resemble chrysanthemums. Take a thick circle of vegetable, such as daikon, and hold it on the chopping block with a pair of chopsticks (apart and parallel). Slice the top in one direction at ⅛-inch to ¼-inch intervals, then slice in the other direction. The chopsticks bordering the daikon will act as buffers and prevent you from slicing through the bottom of the vegetable.

Vegetables are often cut into decorative shapes or edible garnishes. This is done to enhance a particular dish as well as to symbolize a special season or holiday.

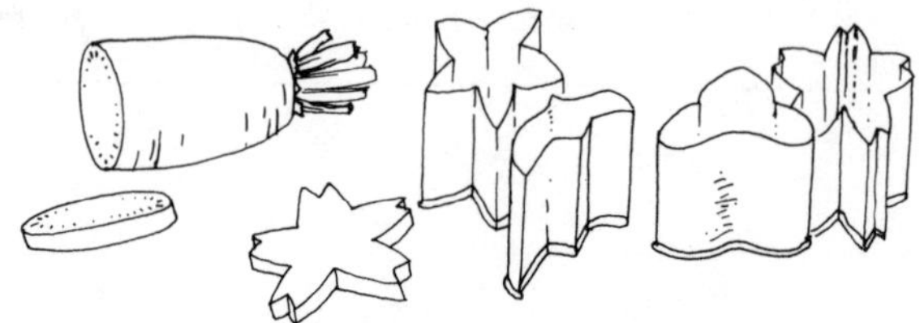

Cutters and their results

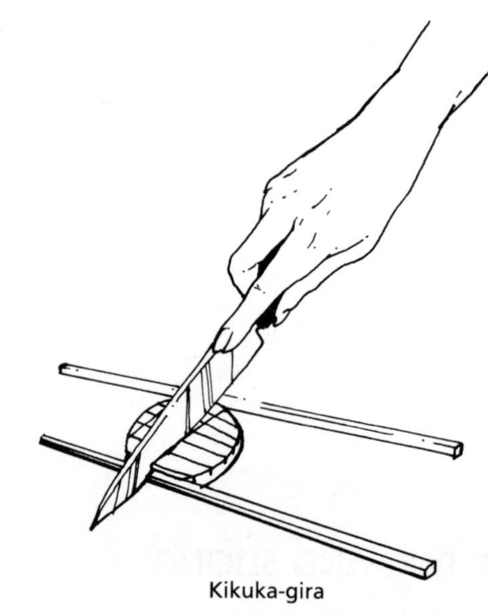

Kikuka-gira

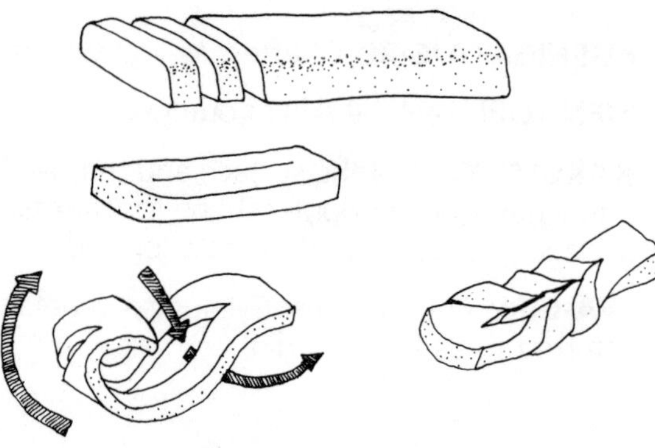

Konnyaku: Yam cakes

Basic traditional shapes include flowers and plum blossoms (hanagata). You can do this artistic cutting by hand or opt for a set of inexpensive, charming cutters. There are also a few trick cuts that need to be done by hand: Lemon rind (yuzu) is usually cut into thin strips; then these strips are sliced and threaded or split to resemble pine needles or leaves. Yam cakes (konnyaku) are often sliced into thin rectangles, then a center slit is cut, and one is threaded or twisted through this slit. The konnyaku slices now resemble braids (tazuna). Soaked mushroom caps (shiitake) are often kept whole, an X is sliced into the outer surface, and the mushroom is bent to expose the inner flesh. Lotus root (renkon) slices are occasionally trimmed so that each thin slice approximates a flower. Chilled Japanese-style omelet (tamago) and cucumbers are often sliced at angles to resemble bamboo shoots or mountains (yamagata).

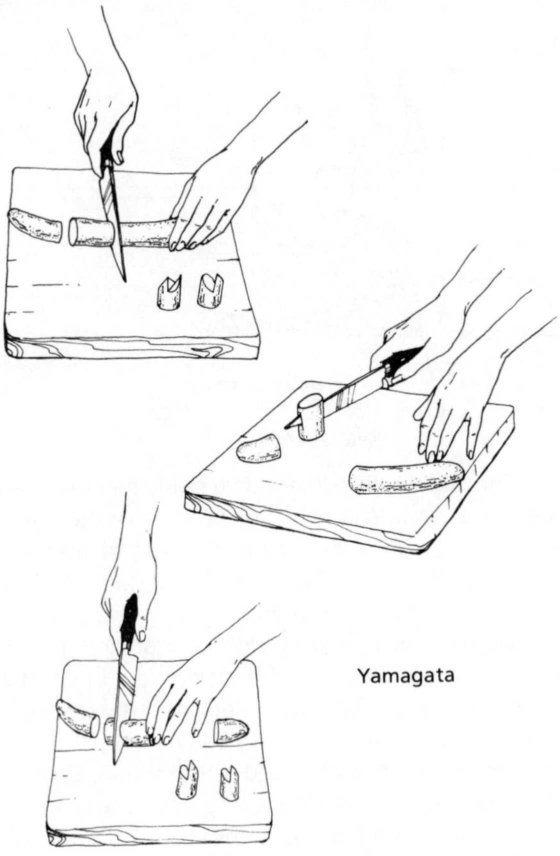

Yamagata

CLEANING, FILLETING, AND BONING FISH

Freshness of ingredients is of utmost importance in Japanese cookery. To ensure the freshness of your fish and seafood, you should understand the basic Japanese techniques of cleaning, filleting, and boning.

Since knives are not brought to the Japanese table, fish and seafood (as well as fowl and meat) are almost always cut into bite-size pieces that can be handled easily with chopsticks. Although fish is also cooked whole, its soft flesh can easily be separated with chopsticks.

Whole Fish

Lay out fish horizontally on a cutting board or newspaper with the head on the right. Lift up the small fin on the top near the head. Place the blade of a sharp knife behind this fin. The knife should be almost perpendicular to the fish (about one o'clock). Chop off the head. With a small fish, you can cut off the head in one motion; larger fish may require several motions. With some large fish, you may have to place the blade in the proper position and then hit the knife with a kitchen mallet. Discard the head or keep and clean for another recipe.

Find the "belly button" of the fish—a small depression or dot on the belly. Place the tip of your knife in this depression and slit open the stomach, cutting in the direction of the neck. Place the wide part of the knife blade into the belly and scrape out and discard entrails.

To fillet cleaned fish, hold your knife with your right hand and hold the fish down firmly with your left. Take the knife and place it horizontally right above the backbone and the neck area. Cut through the skin and flesh, working in a back-and-forth motion, proceeding from the neck to the tail. Remove the top fillet. Place

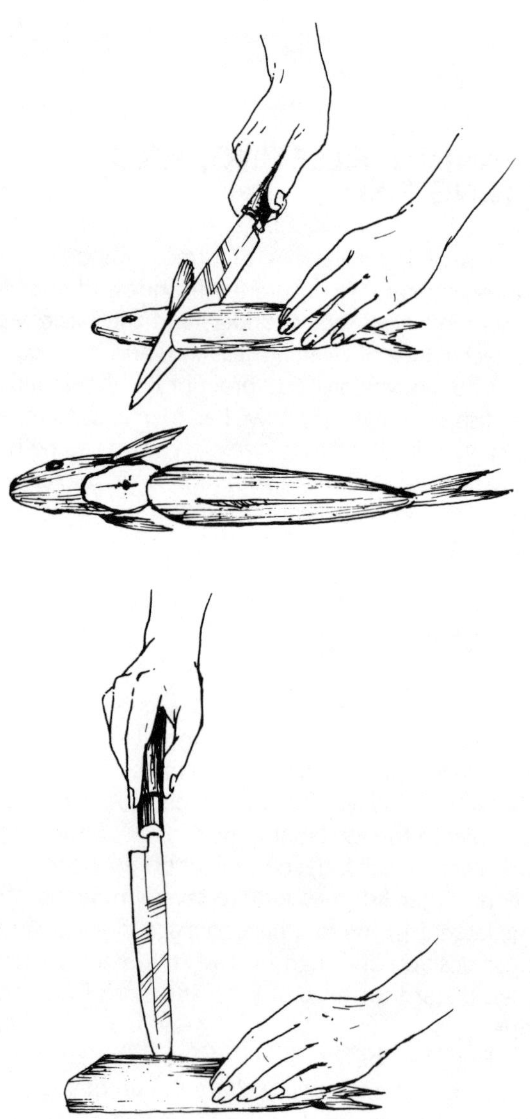

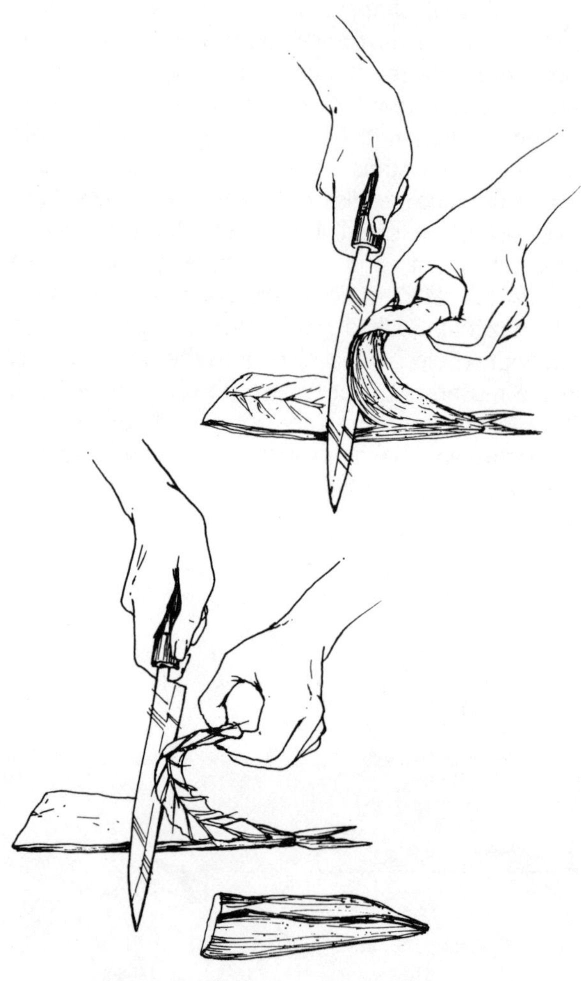

your knife directly under the backbone, again at the neck area, and with the same back-and-forth motion cut the bottom fillet away from the skeleton. You may have to flip a large fish over so that you can remove the second fillet by working from the top.

You now have two fillets. To remove the small triangular patches of bones, use the front third of the blade. Cut from the wide to the narrow part of the patch, directly under the bones.

The fillets with skin are now ready for salting and vinegar washing. You may wish to remove the skin; it can be peeled off (especially in the case of mackerel) or cut off. To peel, place fillets skin side up. From the neck (wider area) to the tail area, carefully pull off the skin with your fingers without losing too much flesh. To cut off skin, place fillets skin side down. Hold your knife in your right hand and the fish tail in your left. Place the blade horizontally between the flesh and skin, and cut using a back-and-forth motion. Carefully pull the skin as you cut. You will now have two skinned fillets. All remaining small bones should be removed with fish tweezers.

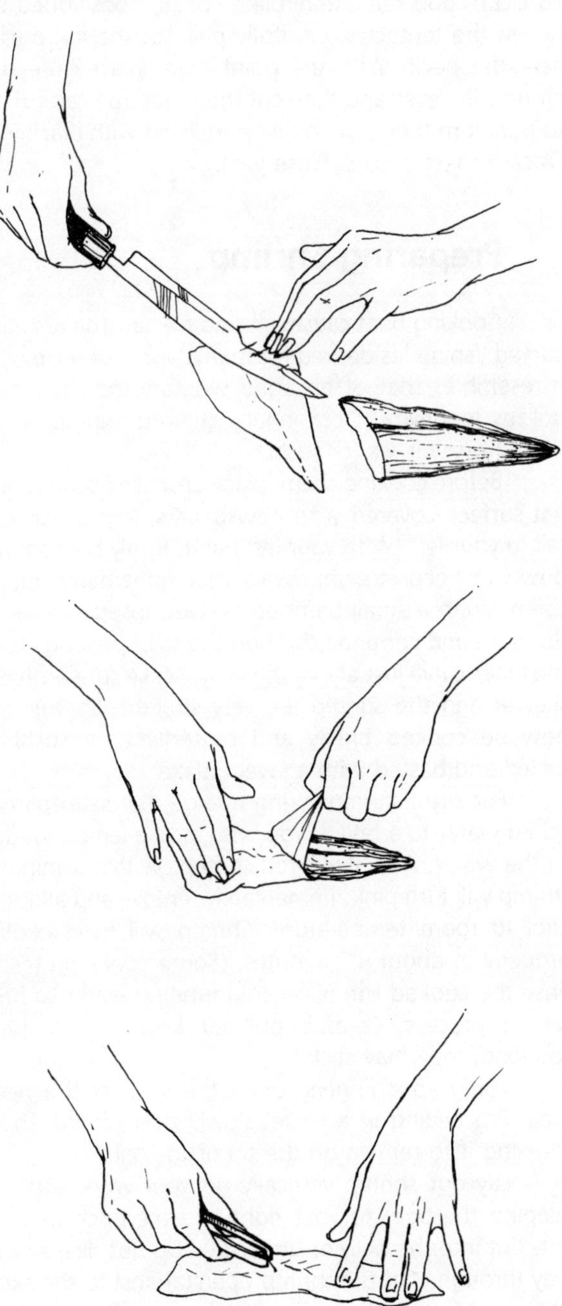

Preparing Squid

Squid, a very popular Japanese food, is generally easily available and inexpensive. Clean them yourself to ensure freshest quality. It is best to clean squid on newspaper near your kitchen sink, with running water handy.

Lay out squid horizontally, with the tentacle end to the right and the tip to the left. Using both hands hold the pointy base end in your left hand, and with your right, hold the tentacle end. Carefully but firmly pull apart. Inside the main part of the body (mantle) is a long, thin, almost transparent backbone, or quill. Hold the mantle with one hand, and with your other pull out this "pen"; remove and discard.

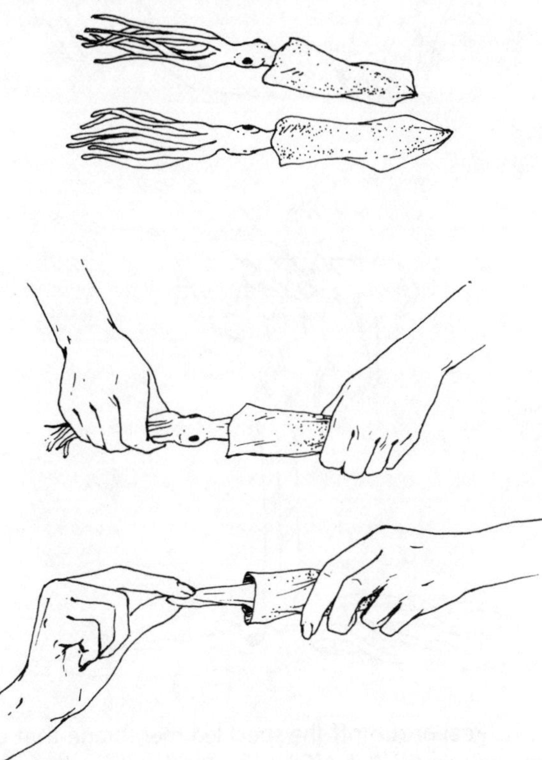

In many cases the squid will have eggs inside the mantle. These are very tasty and can be left inside for recipes calling for simmered squid. Otherwise, scoop them out and discard along with the entrails.

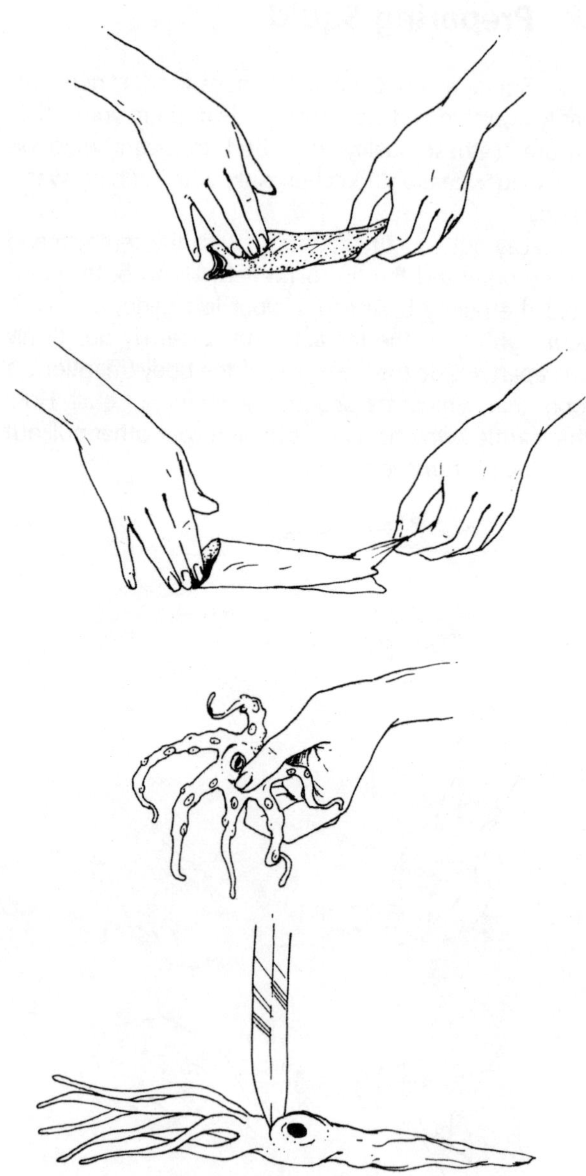

Peel or rub off the speckled membrane that covers the mantle. Pull off the "wings," or "fins," and discard. You may be surprised to find how easily these can be removed. Wash the mantle thoroughly inside and out. The mantle is now ready to be cut into desired lengths or shapes.

The tentacle end is also a prized part of the squid. To clean, pop out the birdlike "beak," positioned between the tentacles. Carefully pull out the ink pocket near the neck. With the point of a sharp knife slice around the eyes and then cut them out. (Be careful not to puncture them, or you'll be squirted with black ink.) Discard these pieces. Rinse well.

Preparing Shrimp

Cooking heat causes shrimp to curl. The resulting curved "spine" is desired for many Japanese recipes, as it resembles that of an aged woman and thus symbolizes longevity. Occasionally straight shrimp is desired, however, as for sushi.

Before cooking them, place unshelled shrimp on a flat surface covered with newspapers, legs down and tail to your left. With your left hand, firmly hold shrimp down to keep straight. With your right hand, pierce shrimp with a small bamboo skewer. Insert skewer at the neck and continue through the tail, spearing along the inner curve just above the belly. Make sure both the skewer and the shrimp are very straight. Shrimp can now be cooked briefly and butterflied for sushi or grilled and basted with a sweet glaze.

For sushi shrimp: Bring a large, flat saucepan of salted water to a boil. If you wish, add a lemon wedge to the water. Add skewered shrimp. Within a minute, shrimp will turn pink; immediately remove and allow to cool to room temperature. Shrimp will have cooled properly in about 15 minutes. (Some cooks prefer to rinse the cooked shrimp in cold running water to hasten this process.) Carefully pull out skewers. If you wait too long, they may stick.

Using your fingers, open the shell at the neck area. Proceeding in a circle, slowly peel off the shell, allowing it to remain on the tip of the tail.

Lay out shrimp vertically on your work surface, keeping the belly to your right and the back to your left. Cut into the belly or underside. Do not slice all the way through. Cut the shrimp open (almost to the skin) until you see the black vein. Do not cut off or separate the tail. Remove the vein. Rinse and wash the opened

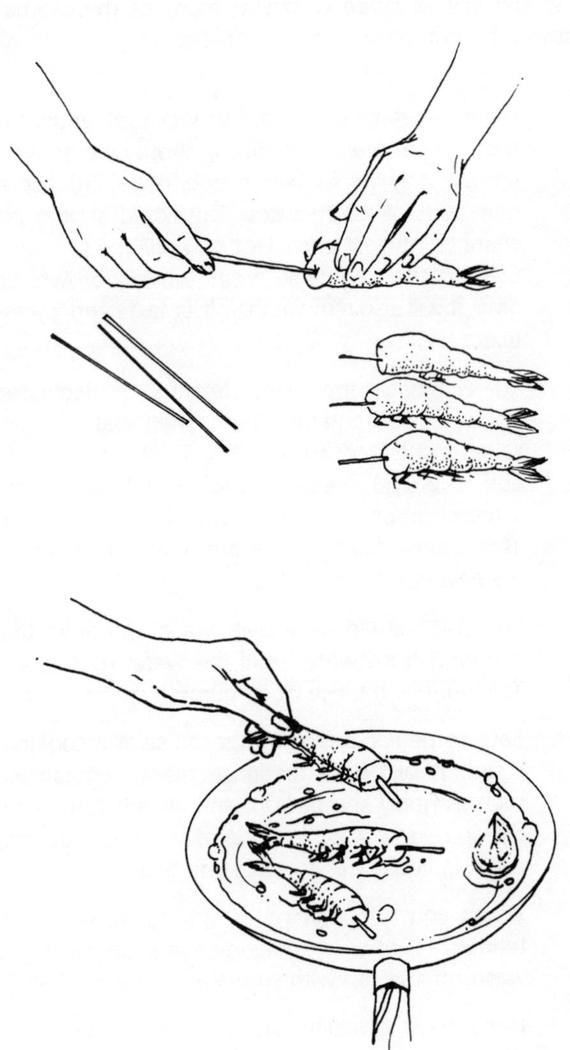

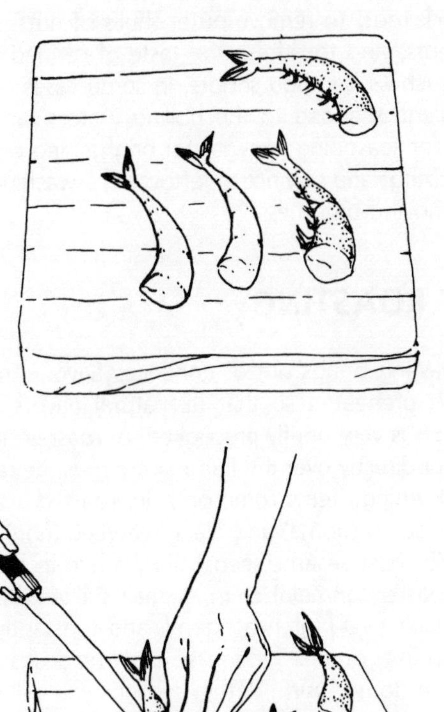

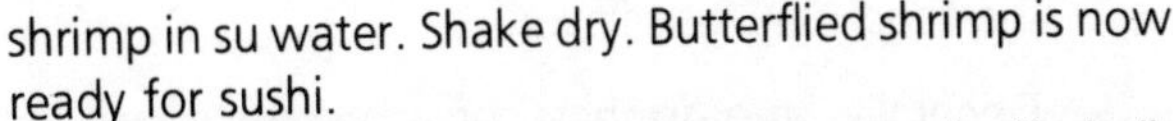

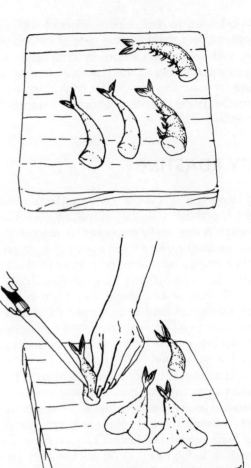

shrimp in su water. Shake dry. Butterflied shrimp is now ready for sushi.

To prepare shrimp for tempura: Peel off shell. Leaving tail on, cut off tip and push out the fantail with the back of your knife. Slightly cut open the back side to take out the black vein. With your knife, make a few short cuts at the inside curve and flatten the shrimp with your fingers. This will prevent the shrimp from curling up when it is deep fried.

PARBOILING AND BLANCHING

Parboiling and blanching, also referred to as two-step or stopped cookery, are essential advance techniques for Japanese cooking. Leafy green vegetables and other green vegetables are briefly cooked (*parboiled*) in boiling water and then rinsed in cold water (*blanched*) and drained in a colander to hold their color. The addition of ice cubes will hasten the setting. Thick or dense vegetables, such as daikon or potatoes, are often parboiled before being added to other ingredients, since their cooking time is longer. Parboiling is also used to remove the bitterness from many vegetables, such as burdock root; to remove outer shells of nuts, such as chestnuts; and to refresh the taste of canned vegetables, such as bamboo shoots. In some cases, another ingredient is added to the boiling water: salt or soy sauce for seasoning; vinegar for brightening color and tenderizing; and raw rice or leftover rice-washing liquid for removing bitterness.

DRY ROASTING

Dry roasting brings out or enhances flavor. An ingredient is preheated so that its natural flavors are released. It is very briefly precooked, or *roasted*, in a dry skillet or directly over the flame. Care must be taken to avoid burning. Items commonly dry roasted are white sesame seeds (goma) and black seaweed (nori).

To roast sesame seeds, place them in a sesame seed toaster (gomairi) or in a small skillet with a lid. Place skillet over high heat; gently and constantly shake the pan in a circular motion so that the seeds pop to toast but do not burn. Within seconds you will smell a wonderful aroma; the seeds are now ready to grind for a sauce or to use as a garnish. Other seeds and nutmeats can be dry roasted in the same manner. To roast black seaweed (nori), carefully hold one corner with your fingers or kitchen tongs. Quickly run the nori over a medium to high flame. You want to crisp the sheet without burning it. The nori should turn a very dark shade of green. Or preheat the oven to 300° F., place nori on an oven rack, and immediately turn off heat. Let stand for 5 to 10 minutes before removing. Roasted nori is more flavorsome for sushi rolls, to cut into small strips to secure sushi "fingers," or to crumble as a garnish for many rice, noodle, and other recipes. (High-quality nori, if kept in a tin or in plastic, may remain fresh and crisp for long periods and may not require this rapid roasting.)

HINTS AND TRICKS

Throughout the introductory part of this book, I have offered many hints to aid in your preparation of Japanese cookery for the American table. At this point, I would like to share with you more of these time-saving, food-improving culinary tricks.

- Many vegetables, such as burdock root, and lotus root, once peeled or sliced, should be soaked immediately in su water (see page 28) for a minimum of 30 minutes. The liquid should be changed at least once. Not only will the su water prevent the vegetable from turning brown or gray, it will also remove the bitter taste and gooey texture.

- To eliminate the slimy texture of Japanese potatoes, peel and slice them. Then soak them in salted water for 30 minutes. Next, drain them and cover with water to which 1 tablespoon and 1 teaspoon of salt have been added, and boil for 10 minutes. Finally, rinse and wash them in su water and rub them clean.

- To cook rice Japanese style, wash and drain the rice with fresh water until the water runs clear. This purifies the rice of its gummy starch.

- Save some rice-rinsing water to use as a cooking liquid. It will help tenderize many vegetables, such as gobo and daikon, and absorb vegetable oils and odors. A tablespoon of raw rice added to cooking liquid will do the same trick.

- When you salt "marinate" fish to freshen and tenderize it prior to cooking or final preparation, wash off the salt with su water.

- Dried food products are best reconstituted in room-temperature liquid. If the liquid is too hot, the food may lose flavor.

- Generally, the freshest of ingredients will be found at the busiest of markets, where you will find the greatest turnover of food products.

- To refresh used cooking oil, strain and return it to the pot. Add a 1-inch chunk of peeled ginger and heat the oil to about 350° F. Fry the ginger until it becomes brown and then discard it. The oil is now ready for reuse. This technique is particularly good for oil that has been used to deep fry fish.

- When slicing a cylindrical vegetable, first cut a thin, flat strip from one side to prevent the vegetable from rolling around.
- Rub fish and chicken with cut lemon to cleanse, freshen, and tenderize it.
- Use scissors to cut nori into thin strips easily.
- To freshen the taste and smell of canned vegetables, pour off the liquid and place the vegetables in boiling water. Let the water return to a boil and then drain and rinse the vegetables.
- When selecting pots and pans, choose nonstick cookware. Many recipes call for a reduction of liquids and sugar to a thick, syrupy sauce, and nonstick surfaces are the easiest to clean.
- Wooden chopsticks make wonderful stirring utensils.
- When testing foods to see if they are tender, carefully pierce them with a bamboo, rather than a metal, skewer.

THE BASIC STOCK: DASHI

If you were to ask me "What is the key recipe in Japanese cooking?" my immediate response would be "Dashi." Almost the essence of Japanese cookery, dashi is the stock upon which most Japanese recipes are built. It is made of seaweed or kelp (kombu), dried bonito flakes (katsuo bushi), and water. The term *dashi* also refers to the entire category of stocks composed of various dried fish and vegetables.

If you are a newcomer to dashi, you may find the aroma and taste rather fishy. For you, I recommend a light hand with the dried bonito flakes. You may even want to substitute your favorite chicken, beef, or vegetable stock or try a half-and-half solution. The results will be tasty, but dishes will not be the same, of course, as those that use dashi as the base.

Dashi can be made easily and quickly. Both the seaweed and the bonito flakes can be stored in your pantry for several months, ready for immediate use. Dashi will keep refrigerated for several days or frozen for weeks. I freeze my excess in ice cube trays so a few teaspoons are always handy. For those in a hurry, premade dashi is available in small packages similar to tea bags, cubes, or crystals (like bouillon), and cans. I have found these convenience products to be great time-savers and perfectly acceptable.

Timing is extremely important: the seaweed should not boil, or the stock will become bitter and cloudy; the bonito flakes must be strained within a few minutes, or the stock will be excessively fishy.

If you've made a mistake in your dashi preparation, do not toss it. Dashi that is too thick or strong tasting can be used as a stock for a simmered recipe. Dashi that is too thin can be used as the base of a clear soup.

SIMPLE DASHI

Yield: 2 cups

This is my basic dashi recipe. You can adjust it to your taste.

1 small piece *kombu* (about 4 to 5 square inches)
2 cups water
1 cup *katsuo bushi*

Place kombu in a pot with the water over low heat. When the liquid comes to a boil, remove kombu. Increase heat and add the katsuo bushi. When the liquid returns to a boil, remove from heat. After the flakes sink, pour liquid through a strainer. Dashi is ready.

Note: For greater quantities of dashi, the basic formula is: Per 1 cup water, use one 2- to 3-square-inch piece kombu and ½ cup katsuo bushi.

There is no need to waste the residual seaweed or bonito flakes. The kombu can be further soaked or simmered and then added to a number of recipes. Thin slices of kombu, simmered in soy sauce and mirin, make an excellent garnish for steamed rice. The katsuo bushi should be put aside until all your cooking is completed. If additional stock is necessary, you can use it for secondary dashi.

Secondary dashi, or dashi 2, has a milder taste since the prime flavor went into the first stock. Yet dashi 2 is excellent for sauces, noodle dishes, vegetables, and simmered recipes. You may wish to add a tablespoon or so of unused bonito flakes to refresh the others.

Kombu dashi, a vegetarian dashi, used for Zen Temple cookery (Shojin Ryori), requires only the kelp. The nutrients from the kombu quickly pass into the warm water, and the stock can be used within minutes. However, for a rich, more flavorsome vegetarian kombu dashi, it is best to bring the kombu and water quickly to a boil and then to reduce it to a low simmer for several hours. A longer period of time is necessary for shiitake dashi, a stock made from water and dried mushrooms. Occasionally the two ingredients are combined for a third vegetarian stock.

Another popular dashi is made from dried small sardines, niboshi dashi. To prevent this stock from becoming bitter, first break off the sardine heads and discard. Add approximately 1 ounce niboshi to 1 quart of cold water or kombu broth. Bring to a boil, then simmer for 4 to 8 minutes, depending upon the desired strength; strain. This strong-tasting stock is popular as a base for miso soup.

A review of dashi-making tips:

- Use approximately one, 4-inch to 5-inch piece of kombu per 2 cups water and 1 cup dried bonito flakes (shavings).
- Allow kombu and water to slowly heat just to the boiling point. Bubbles will appear. Do not boil kombu.
- Add dried bonito flakes. Do not stir. When flakes sink, dashi is ready; strain.
- If you want a more full flavored dashi, add cold water to the kombu broth. Add dried flakes. Slowly reheat liquid just to the boiling point. Remove from heat. When flakes sink, dashi is ready; strain.
- For secondary dashi, bring water with once-used bonito flakes to a boil. Lower heat and simmer about 15 minutes, or until liquid is reduced by about one-third. Remove from heat and allow flakes to sink. Dashi 2 is ready; strain and discard flakes.

Once you've mastered the art of dashi making, you're on your way to soups and stews.

SOUPS AND STEWS

Soups are an intrinsic part of the Japanese diet. They are savored at all meals, including breakfast. Soups can be divided into two classes: (1) an elegant clear broth, and (2) a thick soup, generally with miso. Soups that Americans consider chowders or stews are included in the second group.

A simple broth, suimono, may be served at the beginning of the meal as an appetizer, at a midway point as a refresher, and at the end of the meal with rice as a finale. A proper suimono is composed of three parts: (1) the base, which is the stock (dashi) and a protein, such as fish, chicken, or tofu; (2) a complementary ingredient (tsuma), which is seaweed or a vegetable, such as Japanese onions or spinach; and (3) an outstanding spice, seasoning, or garnish (suikichi), which is seasonal and used for its symbolic appearance or aroma, such as pepper leaves (kinome) or Japanese lemon peel (yuzu). To make a good suimono, freshness is of utmost importance.

The most popular thick soup is miso-shiru, which is a stock (dashi), bits of protein (often tofu), and miso for thickening. Miso-shiru is served for breakfast or lunch and at informal dinners.

Most Japanese soups are served in individual covered lacquer bowls. This lacquer is a protective layer on top of wood and acts as an insulator so that you can hold the bowl with your hands and bring it to your lips to sip. When the lacquer bowl is covered with its lid, a vacuum is created, similar to that of a thermos. If the lid is difficult to remove, carefully press in the sides to break the vacuum. Now, lift off the top. Sip soup directly from the bowl; a spoon is rarely used. Chopsticks are permitted in order to secure the small pieces of protein, vegetables, and starch. Steamed custards and stews may require other utensils.

TOFU SOUP

Yield: 6 to 8 servings

This mild-tasting tofu soup is a favorite in our household.

6 cups fish stock (or *dashi*)
2 cups chicken stock
1 small knob of fresh ginger, peeled
1 tablespoon soy sauce
1 cake *tofu*, cut into 5 slices and dried between paper towels for 30 minutes
1 tablespoon cornstarch, diluted in 2 tablespoons water
2 to 3 scallions, sliced very thinly in small rings
8 sprigs watercress or other leafy green, for garnish

In a large soup pot, heat the two stocks. Bring liquid to a low boil and, using a garlic press, squeeze ginger juice directly into the stock. Add the soy sauce; stir. Cook for a few minutes to combine the flavors. Cut tofu into 1-inch cubes (about 18 pieces altogether). Carefully add the tofu to the soup and continue to cook another 2 to 3 minutes. Stir in the diluted cornstarch. Do not break up the tofu. Continue to cook another 1 to 3 minutes, or until the soup has slightly thickened. Ladle soup into cups and garnish with sliced scallions and watercress.

MISO-DASHI SOUP

Yield: 6 to 8 servings

A traditional Japanese breakfast includes a small bowl of miso soup—a nutritious way to start the day.

4 cups *dashi*
¼ cup *miso* (choose your favorite *miso*; in this recipe, I prefer a light, low-sodium variety)
1 to 2 squares *tofu*, cut into 1-inch squares and dried on paper towels about 30 minutes
1 to 2 green onions, very thinly sliced
Watercress, cilantro, or parsley leaves, for garnish

In a soup pot, heat the dashi. Dissolve the miso in simmering dashi, stirring constantly. Do not let the liquid come to a rapid boil, which would make the miso bitter. Add the tofu and continue to cook at a simmer for a few minutes. Miso will slightly thicken the soup. Ladle soup into individual cups or bowls and garnish with onions and green leaves.

Note: Reconstituted wakame pieces and/or softened yam noodles are an excellent addition to this tasty soup.

CHICKEN AND SWIRLED EGG SOUP

Yield: 6 to 8 servings

Eggs, both raw and cooked, are a common ingredient in Japanese cookery. Many soup recipes suggest that you add eggs at the last minute and allow them to poach or that you stir them with chopsticks so the eggs barely scramble and resemble noodles. I use chicken broth in the following recipe, but feel free to substitute a thin dashi or half dashi and half chicken stock.

1 quart chicken stock
2 cups fresh spinach leaves, sliced into strips
4 *shiitake* mushrooms, soaked for several hours to reconstitute, hard center cores removed and sliced into julienne strips
1 to 2 tablespoons soy sauce
1½ tablespoons cornstarch dissolved in 2 tablespoons water (or leftover mushroom stock)
Salt
2 eggs, lightly beaten

In a medium soup pot, bring the chicken stock to a boil. Add spinach, mushrooms, and soy sauce. Reduce heat and cook at a gentle boil for a few seconds, just until spinach is tender. Add diluted cornstarch, stirring constantly with chopsticks. Salt to taste. Turn off heat and add beaten eggs, stirring constantly with chopsticks until eggs have set slightly. Serve immediately.

Variation: Other ingredients can be added or substituted, such as carrots that have been sliced to resemble flowers. Other favorites include twisted lemon rind, tofu tidbits, shredded cooked chicken, toasted mochi, and thinly sliced tops of green onions.

OSECHI OZONI

Yield: 4 servings

To many Japanese families, New Year's morning would not be complete without a serving of ozoni. Ozoni can be as simple as mochi (pounded rice cake) topped with hot dashi. But most cooks add a number of other ingredients and garnishes—attractively cut into shapes symbolizing longevity, wealth, and good luck in the new year.

SOUP STOCK

4 cups *dashi* (or chicken broth)
1 to 2 teaspoons soy sauce
Salt to taste

FEATURED SOUP INGREDIENTS (*Sumashi*)

Salt to taste
1 chicken breast, boned and cut into thin slivers or julienne strips
1 carrot, peeled and cut into thin rounds
¼ pound *daikon*, peeled and sliced into 4 rounds
½ bunch fresh spinach leaves (approximately ¼ pound)
4 *mochi* (rice cakes), may be frozen
4 slices hot-pink *kamaboko* (approximately 2 ounces) or other colored fish cakes
4 pieces *yuzu* rind (or lemon rind), if desired cut to resemble pine needles (see page 41)

Bring dashi, soy sauce, and salt to a boil, then reduce heat and simmer for a few minutes. Set aside.

Chicken and vegetables can be cooked separately ahead of time and kept at room temperature. To do this, bring a saucepan of lightly salted water to a boil and add the chicken. Boil about 2 minutes or until chicken has turned white. Drain. You can reuse this liquid for another recipe or discard it.

If desired, carrot and/or daikon circles can be further cut into floral or other decorative shapes.

Bring three more pots of lightly salted water to a boil (or use the same pot three separate times). Separately cook the carrot, daikon, and spinach until barely tender. Carrot takes about 8 minutes; daikon, about 10; and spinach, about 1. Drain vegetables, rinsing them in cold water to set the color.

Prior to serving, reheat the soup stock and toast the mochi. You can toast mochi on a stove-top grill or under the broiler, turning to make sure all sides are becoming crisp and browned without burning. You can use frozen mochi (without bean filling) and put directly onto the grill without defrosting. Prick mochi with the tines of a fork.

To assemble: Place one toasted mochi on the bottom of each of four soup bowls. Divide chicken, kamaboko, and vegetables evenly among all bowls.

Carefully pour hot soup stock over all ingredients. Garnish each bowl with lemon rind.

PORK BALLS WITH KINOME SOUP

Yield: 6 first-course or 3 main-course servings

In this beautiful aromatic soup, the unusual peppery taste comes from the kinome leaves. This soup is delightful with chrysanthemum or watercress, depending upon what is available locally.

1 pound ground pork (or chicken, veal, or beef)
1 tablespoon minced fresh ginger
½ teaspoon sugar
1 tablespoon potato starch (or cornstarch)
Dash salt
1 tablespoon *sake*
1 medium egg, lightly beaten
6 cups chicken stock (or *dashi*)
½ pound *kinome* leaves (or chrysanthemum or watercress)
12 ounces *somen*, cooked

Place pork, ginger, sugar, potato starch, salt, sake, and beaten egg in a large mixing bowl. Using your hands, combine ingredients and form into 12 to 15 small balls. Arrange balls on a steamer rack or plate above simmering water; cover and steam for 20 minutes. (See pages 109–110 for steaming instructions.)

In a large soup pot, bring the chicken stock to a boil; then reduce to a simmer while preparing the kinome (or other vegetable).

Bring a saucepan of water to a boil. Add kinome, return water to a boil, and immediately remove kinome; drain excess liquid.

Add the pork balls, kinome, and somen to the simmering stock. Heat everything and serve.

SPECIAL UDON NABE

Yield: 6 servings

There are several hearty Japanese soups, comparable to bouillabaisse, that feature seafood, fish, chicken, vegetables, and noodles, all quickly cooked together in a large pot of stock. Try this for company on a wintry evening.

SOUP STOCK

8 cups *dashi* (or chicken or fish stock)
6 tablespoons soy sauce
¼ cup *sake*
2 tablespoons *mirin*

1 12-ounce package fresh *udon*, cooked according to package directions*
6 clams, shells scrubbed well
1 whole chicken breast, skinned, boned, and cut into bite-size pieces (about ½ pound meat)
⅓ pound scallops (about 8)
1 3-ounce *chikuwa* cake (or *kamaboko*), cut into thick slices
1 bunch scallions (about 6), trimmed, firm part only
4 large fresh mushrooms, cleaned and cut in half (or 8 small *shiitake*, reconstituted)
6 to 8 medium shrimp, shells still on, but heads and legs removed; also, carefully slit open to remove the veins

*To cook the noodles as directed, place them in a pot of boiling water; stir. When the water returns to a boil, add ½ cup cold water. This will stop the boiling process. Allow water to return to a boil, and then add another ½ cup of cold water. Repeat the process 4 more times, which will take about 12 minutes. Rinse noodles well in cold water and drain.

In a large, attractive stove-to-table pot, bring the

soup stock to a boil. I use a large cast-iron wok; an authentic nabe would be excellent. Because of the large quantity of liquid, allow plenty of time for the stock to come to a boil. Meanwhile, bring another large pot of water to a boil for the noodles. While you wait for the liquids to boil, clean and prepare the chicken, seafood, and vegetables. When stock comes to a boil, add clams, chicken, scallops, fish cake, vegetables and shrimp, in that order. The shrimp take the least time; they are cooked when their shells turn pink. Total cooking time is about 10 minutes, or as soon as the clams open wide.

To serve, you can place the noodles in the pot with the stock and chicken-fish-vegetable mixture, or you can spoon noodles into each large soup bowl, in which case each person can top the noodles with desired ingredients; ladle stock on top.

Variations: Using this recipe as a starting point, make changes to suit your taste and the availability of fresh ingredients. Some suggestions: other fish (such as rock cod or salmon), cut into bite-size pieces, stuffed cabbage rolls (see pages 113–114), other vegetables (such as spinach, chrysanthemum leaves, cut carrots, pea pods), tofu cubes, konnyaku, raw egg.

Japanese one-pot dishes cooked at the table are called nabemono. Several of these recipes, such as sukiyaki, mizutaki, and shabu-shabu, bridge the gap between a stew and a sauteed or simmered main dish.

Nabemono recipes are ideal for dinner party entertaining since most of the preparations are completed in advance. Vegetables and meats, including fish and fowl, should be cut into similar sizes. Ingredients that need lengthy cooking should be parboiled. Attractively arrange all ingredients to be cooked on large serving platters. All sauces, condiments, and garnishes should be made in advance. A pot of liquid or a skillet with oil (or suet, depending upon the particular recipe) should be set at tableside. Since the final cooking of these dishes is fairly rapid, the cook should wait until all guests are seated.

SUKIYAKI JAPANESE STYLE

Yield: 4 servings

There are as many different recipes for sukiyaki as there are households, since this is one of the most popular Japanese dishes. You can hold close to the traditional ingredients, or you can select ones that your family most enjoys.

1 to 1½ pounds *sukiyaki* meat*
½ pound fresh spinach, cleaned and trimmed (or chrysanthemum leaves, if available)
4 to 6 Japanese long onions, firm part only (if not available, substitute 10 to 13 green onions)
½ pound fresh bamboo shoots (you may substitute canned, preferably whole and not sliced)
1 9-ounce container fresh *shirataki* noodles (canned or dried)
1 *tofu* cake (select the toasted for easier handling, if desired)
6 to 8 large fresh *shiitake* (you can substitute fresh large mushrooms or large dried *shiitake*)

SUKIYAKI SAUCE
1 cup water (or *dashi* or beef stock)
½ cup soy sauce
½ cup *mirin*
2 tablespoons sugar (or more to taste)

1 tablespoon cooking oil (or about 2 ounces suet)
4 raw eggs (optional)
Cooked rice

*Sukiyaki meat will be easily obtainable at an oriental market. Some markets have it packaged presliced. Otherwise, you can ask the butcher for assistance in the slicing. Request that he or she slice rib eye steak paper thin, similar to extra-thin bacon. To do this at home, place rib eye steak (or roast) in the freezer for an hour or so; then, with an electric slicer or very sharp knife, slice as thin as possible. Place meat on a large serving platter.

Trim spinach leaves. Retain only the tender stems with the leaves, discarding tough stems, and place on serving platter.

Cut green onions at diagonal slants into 3-inch lengths. Place on serving platter.

Cut bamboo shoots into irregular bite-size pieces. The attractive insides should be visible. Wash and place in a small pot of salted boiling water. Return to a boil, then drain, rinse with cold water, and drain again. This process will refresh the bamboo shoots. Place on serving platter.

Place fresh or canned shirataki in a pot of salted boiling water. Allow water to return to a boil. Then drain the noodles, rinse, and drain again. Shirataki should be about 3 to 4 inches in length. If not, cut into these lengths. If using dried noodles, cook longer, until tender. Place on serving platter.

Cut tofu into 1- to 2-inch squares and place on paper towels. Top with paper towels, weight down with a plate, and drain off excess liquid for at least an hour. Place on serving platter.

Place mushrooms on a serving platter. If using soaked, dried mushrooms, drain and, using the tip of a sharp knife, cut crisscrosses into the top. Slightly bend the top of these mushrooms to expose the inner flesh.

The sukiyaki cooking platter can be assembled several hours in advance and refrigerated until needed. Other items can be added, such as pea pods, cabbage, or reconstituted fu.

For easy last-minute cooking, I have found it best to combine the sauce ingredients together in a measuring cup or in another utensil with a pouring spout. As you become proficient in the art of sukiyaki cookery, you may prefer to keep the sauce ingredients in separate containers. Adjust sugar to desired sweetness. Some recipes suggest as much as ½ cup sugar.

The eggs are traditionally served, in individual dishes, to be cracked at the table, then beaten with chopsticks. Each diner dips the cooked food in his or her raw egg before eating, to coat the food slightly.

To make sukiyaki tableside, have all ingredients assembled and your guests seated. Use a hot plate or large electric skillet or chafing dish. Heat the oil or suet. Add half of the meat and cook slightly, stirring meat around with long chopsticks. Add half the onion, and pour a little sukiyaki sauce over the meat and onion. Now add half the remaining vegetables, including the tofu and noodles. Twirl all ingredients around with the chopsticks, pouring additional sauce on top. Try to keep ingredients separated.

Suggest that your guests help themselves to the cooked ingredients. Add ingredients and sauce as needed. Do not overcook. Hot rice should be served in individual bowls. Guests should spoon a little hot sukiyaki sauce over their rice.

SUKIYAKI AMERICAN STYLE

Yield: 4 servings

Here's another version of sukiyaki, made of easy-to-obtain ingredients. Try this recipe and serve family style.

SUKIYAKI SAUCE

1½ cups chicken broth
½ cup sugar
¼ cup *mirin*

¼ to ½ cup cooking oil
1 8-ounce can *shirataki*, drained and parboiled to freshen
½ head Chinese cabbage, shredded to 2-inch lengths
12 scallions, cut into 2-inch lengths
1 large onion, peeled and shredded into 2-inch lengths
4 large fresh mushrooms, sliced thinly

¼ cup thinly sliced bamboo shoots (use canned, refreshed with boiling water)
¼ pound *tofu*, drained and dried
½ pound fresh bean sprouts
½ pound fresh spinach leaves, shredded to 2-inch lengths
1 pound *sukiyaki* beef (or 1 pound top sirloin steak, thinly sliced)

Prepare the sauce in advance: Combine all sukiyaki sauce ingredients in a mixing bowl and pour into a decorative pitcher.

Place all ingredients, except the cooking oil, on a large serving platter, cover with plastic wrap, and refrigerate until cooking time.

Heat 1 tablespoon of oil in an electric skillet or chafing dish over high heat. Slowly add the noodles, cabbage, scallions, onion, mushrooms, bamboo shoots, and tofu, one ingredient at a time, stirring carefully with a pair of chopsticks. Occasionally add more oil. As the vegetables cook, pour in the sauce. Let everything cook over high heat for about 6 to 8 minutes, stirring occasionally. Add the bean sprouts, spinach, and meat. Reduce heat to a simmer and continue to cook for about 5 minutes.

MIZUTAKI (ONE-POT CHICKEN STEW)

Yield: 6 servings

Another tasty member of the nabemono category is mizutaki. Quite similar to boiled chicken or beef and broth, mizutaki is especially popular on a wintry day. The Japanese term *mizutaki* refers to boiling water, and in most cases the cooking liquid for the recipe starts with plain water. By the time the dish is completed, the final liquid is a rich chicken or beef stock.

Originating from Mongolian cookery, mizutaki is cooked and served tableside from a communal pot (donabe). Choose your favorite sauces and condiments.

1 3-pound stewing chicken, washed and patted dry
2 quarts water
Salt
1 small head nappa cabbage (about 1 pound), trimmed of hard end
6 to 8 large *shiitake*, soaked 24 hours to soften, hard core removed
¼ pound *daikon*, peeled and sliced into ½-inch thick circles
1 large carrot, scraped and sliced into ½-inch thick circles
4 medium-thick green onions (about ¼ pound), trimmed
½ bunch watercress, including stems
1 *tofu* cake, drained on paper towels, sliced into 1-inch to 2-inch squares

CONDIMENTS AND SAUCES
Ponzu sauce (lemon-soy sauce; see page 113)
Red maple radish (see page 74)
Minced green onions
Grated *daikon*, squeezed through the palms of your hands to eliminate excess liquid
Grated ginger
Lemon wedges
Powdered red pepper or dried red pepper flakes
Soy sauce

Cooked rice or noodles (optional)

You will need a cleaver to chop up the chicken properly. Chop chicken through the skin and bones into 2-inch pieces. Place chicken in a heavy pot, add water to cover, and bring to a boil; then reduce to a simmer. During the first 5 to 10 minutes, foamy scum will rise. Using a soup skimmer or slotted spoon, remove this and discard. Simmer stock about 30 to 45 minutes, salting to taste. Remove chicken and strain stock through a sieve. Return stock to pot (preferably an attractive cooking and serving pot). Set chicken aside.

Prepare vegetables and tofu: Cut cabbage into 1-inch to 2-inch squares. Using the point of a sharp paring knife, cut a crisscross incision into the outside top of each mushroom and carefully bend to expose the inner flesh. Cut daikon and carrot slices in half to resemble half-moons or use vegetable cutters to shape them into decorative flowers. Cut onions and watercress into bite-size pieces. Arrange all vegetables and tofu on a large serving platter. Other vegetables can be added or substituted, according to your preference.

Prepare condiments and sauces and place in small serving bowls. Everything up to this point can be prepared several hours in advance.

Mizutaki can be completed either tableside or in your kitchen. Return chicken to stock and reheat. Add vegetables and tofu to the pot—the thicker and firmer ingredients first, as they will take longer to cook. As soon as vegetables are heated through and tender, serve; do not overcook.

To serve, place cooked portions in individual bowls, or allow your guests to serve themselves, seasoning to taste with condiments and sauces. The chicken, vegetables, and tofu are traditionally eaten first. Then cooked rice or noodles are added to the broth and eaten next. Or scoop all ingredients together, including the broth, into bowls.

Note: Traditionally, this recipe is made with small pieces of chicken and bones. However, you may wish to make this with larger pieces of chicken, as you would an American-style chicken soup, or to use boned and thinly sliced chicken breasts. Some cooks start with chicken stock instead of water. A small square of kombu can be added to the stock for extra flavor.

SHABU-SHABU

Yield: 4 servings

Related to mizutaki is shabu-shabu, which starts with a flavorsome stock. In a restaurant, the chef might bring a variety of meat, chicken, vegetables, and noodles to the table, instructing diners to cook their own food in a pot of simmering broth and then dip each ingredient into a seasoned sauce before eating. To prepare this recipe at home, you might try using a fondue pot.

1 quart chicken stock
1½ pounds medium shrimp, paper-thin sirloin steak slices, or bite-size pieces of chicken breasts (all raw)
1 bunch watercress
1 bunch spinach leaves
8 small dried *shiitake*, soaked for several hours, drained, and hard center core removed
4 fresh mushrooms, sliced
1 pound Chinese cabbage, shredded into 2-inch lengths
¼ cup bamboo shoots (thick slices)
12 scallions, sliced into 2-inch lengths
4 to 6 ounces *kishimen*, cooked, drained and cut into thirds
4 ounces *tofu*, drained and cut into rectangles about 2 inches long by ¼ inch thick

Citrus-Soy Dipping Sauce*

2 cups soy sauce
1 cup lemon juice
1 cup orange juice
Chopped scallions, for garnish

Sesame-Soy Dipping Sauce

½ cup sesame seeds
2 teaspoons sugar
3 tablespoons *sake*
2 teaspoons soy sauce
Dash freshly ground black pepper

* Ponzu sauce (page 113) may be substituted for the citrus-soy dipping sauce.

Bring chicken broth to a simmer in a fondue pot. Place in center of table.

Arrange shrimp, steak, or chicken, vegetables, and tofu on a serving platter.

Combine ingredients for citrus-soy dipping sauce in a serving bowl. To make the sesame-soy dipping sauce, place seeds in an unoiled, heavy skillet (or in a sesame toaster) and toast over high heat for a few seconds, shaking constantly. Grind toasted seeds into a paste, using a suribachi or mortar and pestle. Combine the seeds with sugar, sake, soy sauce, and black pepper. Place in a serving bowl.

Using chopsticks, each person should dip his or her food into the pot of simmering broth until cooked, then into either of the sauces.

For additional soup and stew recipes, see:

The Basic Stock: Dashi
Simple Dashi
Tofu and Miso
Miso-Shiru with Wakame and Tofu
Rice and Noodles
Tempura Soba
Soba Shop Noodles
Nabeyaki Udon

SASHIMI AND SUSHI

I am a sushi addict. I admit it is a habit that I cannot break, nor do I want to. Sometimes I awake from a sound sleep with my tongue tingling and my stomach growling, craving sushi. The very next day, I indulge myself with sushi for lunch—sometimes for breakfast! I am not alone in this habit. Every week more and more Americans are being "turned on" to sushi. No longer can I go to a sushi bar and immediately be seated and served; now I must wait my turn in line.

My association with sushi began one evening about eight years ago when my husband came home raving about an unusual dinner of raw fish and cold rice. Despite my skepticism, the following day he invited me to lunch at a sushiya (sushi restaurant). I accepted with trepidation. In those days (1974), a woman sitting at a sushi bar was a rare sight. Sushi was macho.

My husband ordered. He started me off with cooked shrimp (ebi) and sweet omelet (tamago)—the beginners' delights—and then progressed to raw tuna (maguro) and halibut (hirame). The seaweed wrappers (nori) had a unique taste and texture. I drank chilled white wine, although most people drink beer or sake with sushi. And, as is common, we bought a drink for the sushi chef, referred to as an itamae or a shokunin, and talked to the other patrons about what was best to order. That afternoon, I became hooked. The next day, I wanted more.

These days, it has become easy to satisfy my craving. Sushi bars are opening all over the United States, particularly in coastal cities and cities with a sizable Japanese population.

Sushi and sashimi date back to about a thousand years ago. Originally, the word *sushi* meant "tart" and "fish." Today, a popular connotation for *sushi* is "happiness" and "purpose." Prior to refrigeration technology, it was customary to clean the fresh-caught fish, place it between layers of salt and rice, weight it, and then allow it to dry in the sun for several weeks. The weights were then removed, the fish covered, and the fish and rice left to ferment for several months before the combination was eaten. Then, during the late fourteenth and early fifteenth centuries, slices of raw fish, like sashimi, became popular fare. At that time, the fish was eaten with wasabi and ginger, not soy sauce. The wasabi was believed to kill parasites and food germs. Finally, in Tokyo during the eighteenth century, a form of fresh fish with seasoned vinegar, which had not had a lengthy fermentation period, was served with cooked rice. This was the first nigiri-style sushi.

The basic difference between sushi and sashimi is the rice. There are several categories of sushi, all of which include a cold vinegar-dressed rice, called sushi meshi or shari. For sushi, the rice and fish are coordinated, whereas for sashimi, the thin slices of fish stand alone.

About the fish: In most cases (though not all) the fish is raw—but don't let the word *raw* mislead you. Properly prepared and sliced, the fish is tender and does not taste fishy. Many species of fish used for sushi and sashimi are precooked. Shrimp can be raw (gray colored) or cooked (pink colored). Crab is usually cooked, as is lobster. Octopus is parboiled. Salmon is salted or smoked. Eel is generally marinated and/or broiled. Mackerel is often marinated and/or cooked.

Both sushi and sashimi are served with several condiments and garnishes (tsuma). I find it interesting that the word for the accompanying garnishes, *tsuma,* means "wife." A small dab of green horseradish paste, wasabi (often called sabi or namida, meaning "tears"), is generally placed between the rice and fish when sushi is made. For sashimi, the wasabi is served on the side. (See page 30 for instructions on reconstituting wasabi.) Shredded daikon that has been crisped in ice water, sweet-pickled ginger (gari), and a small container of soy sauce or special sauce such as ponzu sauce (see page 113) generally accompany both dishes. Other common garnishes or condiments include cucumber, parsley, lettuce or other greens, watercress, red pepper, seaweed, Japanese pickles, minced green onions, or carrot or lemon slices.

PREPARING YOUR FISH

In making sushi or sashimi, it is essential to understand how to cut the fish. In Japan, a sushi chef studies for many years. An apprentice may watch for several years before even allowed to use a knife. To master the art of cutting fish and vegetables, the apprentice may study for ten years! If you wish to slice fish and vegetables as attractively and swiftly as a sushi chef, you'll need practice.

Slightly dampen your knife and cutting board to aid in the slicing. When you slice, use a cutting, not a sawing, motion. Do not tear your fish—you want clean cuts. It is best to use the tip and bottom one-third to two-thirds of your knife blade, occasionally wiping the blade clean with a moist towel.

In most cases, you should cut fish fillets into bite-size pieces, approximately ¼- to ½-inch-thick rectangles. Cut straight down, then pull your knife toward you. Thick loins of fish, such as tuna, can easily be cut in this manner, called hira-zukuri (or hiki-zukuri).

Halibut and other firm white fish are typically cut into very thin, practically transparent, slices, about 1/16 inch thick, called usu-zukuri or sogi-zukuri. These paper-thin slices are often rolled up into a rosette. To cut like this, the blade of your knife must be slanted at an almost-horizontal angle, and you must slice the fish across the grain.

Fish can also be cut into small chunks, about ¾ inch thick, called kako-zukuri, or in threads to be tossed with vegetables; they can also be shaped into flowers, ito-zukuri.

Once you are comfortable with slicing fish, you can serve sashimi at any time. Sashimi makes a wonderful party appetizer. Allow at least five slices of fish per person. Among the most common combinations are tuna, whitefish, and octopus. The thicker rectangular pieces can be placed in a staircase or domino arrangement. Or, you can simply place them side by side. You might try to roll up the thin slices of whitefish into a rosette and garnish the center with salmon roe. Slices of lemon are often attractively placed on the serving dish. This lemon can be garnished with fish roe, or a hollowed-out small lemon half can be used as a cup to hold the fish roe. Other garnishes for sashimi, called sashimi-no-tsuma, include shredded daikon, thin slices of cucumber, carrot, or green onion; and/or shiso leaves, curly lettuce or other greens, parsley. If you are adventuresome with a knife, you might try cutting carrot, daikon, or cucumber into fancy flower or treelike shapes. The basic condiments are pickled ginger slices (to refresh your tastebuds), wasabi (small cone shapes of reconstituted wasabi), and soy sauce (served on individual small plates). Advise your guests to season their soy sauce with wasabi to taste. Other sauces, instead of soy sauce–wasabi mixture, can be served: sanbaizu sauce, a vinegar and bonito stock sauce (available bottled or prepare homemade; see page 77), ponzu sauce (see page 113) or special sauce (ponzu sauce to which you've added dry bonito shavings and a garnish of thinly sliced scallion tops).

STEPS IN SUSHI MAKING

In order to prepare sushi, you must make the special vinegar-dressed rice, called shari or sushi meshi. Sushi rice can be made according to the basic techniques for washing and cooking rice explained in the Noodles and Rice chapter. Some cooks like to add a piece of kombu to the rice during the first few minutes of cooking prior to the water's boiling. Remove kombu before the water boils, or the rice may taste fishy. You can also substitute a few drops of sake or mirin for some water. Or rice can be cooked in dashi rather than water. This subtle advance seasoning is not necessary. It is simply a variation.

The important seasoning for the rice comes from the dressing, called awaze-zu. And the proper marriage of the dressing with the cooked rice is of utmost necessity.

While the rice is cooking, combine the dressing ingredients. A good formula for this dressing is 4–2–½ : 4 parts rice vinegar (su), 2 parts sugar, ½ part salt. To estimate your vinegar needs, calculate approximately 10 percent of the original rice measurement. For 2 generous cups uncooked rice, use ¼ cup su, 2 tablespoons sugar and 1 to 1½ teaspoons salt. Mix the ingredients together in a small bowl, stirring with chopsticks until the sugar has dissolved. Taste the dressing, adjusting the ingredients to taste. (Some people prefer equal parts vinegar and sugar.) A sweet-sour flavor is desired.

After rice has been properly steamed for 15 minutes and then allowed to rest undisturbed for another 15 to 20 minutes, uncover and turn into a wood tub, handai or sushi oke. A glass, porcelain, or plastic bowl will also suffice, but do not use metal because it may interact unfavorably with the vinegar dressing.

Fan rice with a uchiwa (or a sturdy piece of cardboard); cover for 3 minutes to start cooling process. Slowly pour the dressing over the rice. Do not add all the dressing at one time; the rice should absorb the dressing without becoming liquidy (you may even have some leftover dressing).

Use a wooden rice paddle, shamoji, held vertically, and turn the rice over, a small amount at a time, as if you were cutting through the rice from the top to the bottom (a motion similar to that of folding in egg whites). At the same time, continue to cool the rice with the fan so that the rice absorbs the dressing and becomes shiny. This process takes about 10 minutes.

Making sushi rice is not difficult. The only problem you may find is that you run out of hands. It is best to make sushi rice with the aid of another person. My children take turns at fanning the rice. I have seen small electric fans used in sushi bars.

Sushi rice can be made a couple of hours in advance. Cover the mixing container with a damp kitchen tea towel and leave at room temperature. Unfortunately, the seasoned rice does not refrigerate or freeze well, so use it within one day.

There are four basic categories of sushi: (1) fingers or ovals (nigiri-zushi), (2) rolls (maki-zushi), (3) pressed loaves (oshi-zushi), and (4) scattered (chirashi-zushi).

NIGIRI-ZUSHI: FINGER OR OVAL SUSHI

Simplifying matters greatly, take a bite-size slice of sashimi. Place it on top of a finger of vinegared rice with a dab of wasabi inside. Presto. You've got nigiri-zushi, hand-pressed sushi. Step by step:

Set up your ingredients and supplies in an assembly-line manner. You need a bowl of su water for your hands (to prevent rice from sticking), a tub of seasoned rice, wasabi, sashimi slices of fish, and, for some recipes, narrow and medium-size strips of nori.

Dampen your hands with su water by dipping three fingers of one hand into the solution and wiping this hand on your other. (When dining at a sushi bar, you may have heard clapping after an itamae has wet his hands. He is not trying to gain anyone's attention. Instead, he is clapping away the excess su water before putting his hands into the tub of sushi rice.) Pick up a *small* amount of rice, about 2 to 3 teaspoonfuls, with your right hand, placing it at the joints of your fingers. It is better to have too little than too much rice—a piece of sushi is supposed to be one mouthful of food.

Curl your fingers and palm, closing over the rice and shaping it into a small "finger." Do not squeeze your rice fingers tight; leave them loose. While the rice finger is still in your right hand, uncurl your forefinger and get a dab of wasabi on the tip. (Be careful; wasabi is pungent and you do not want it to overpower your sushi. If you do not like wasabi, omit that step.) At the same time, take a slice of sashimi in your left hand, positioning it parallel to the bends of your fingers, and placing it between the first and second joints. Spread wasabi on the center of the slice of fish. Then place the finger of rice on top of the wasabi. With your forefinger of your right hand, firmly and carefully press the rice down so that it adheres to the fish. Positioning your right thumb and forefinger on either side of the sushi, gently squeeze to shape. Roll sushi over in your left hand. Fish is now on top. Again, position your right thumb and forefinger on either side of the sushi and press to firm sides. Take your forefinger and press on top to firm. Turn sushi around to the other side and repeat the parallel pressing, then the top forefinger pressing steps. If you wish to adhere a thin strip of nori around the middle of the fish and rice, do so, and place the seam on the underside. Attractive garnishes, such as a few tiny fish eggs or chopped seaweed, can be carefully placed on top of the fish. Sushi is completed. All of the above steps should be done in a matter of seconds; avoid handling the fish too much.

A variation of nigiri-zushi, sometimes referred to as gunkan-style sushi, involves a small oval or ball of rice instead of the rectangular finger. A wide strip of nori is then wrapped around the circumference of the rice. The nori should come up a bit above the rice, acting as a small vessel or container for the topping (*gunkan* means "boat"). Place a dab of wasabi on the rice. Finally, top with a spoonful of filling, such as fish roe, chopped fish, small shellfish, and/or raw quail egg yolk.

The most popular fish and seafood used for nigiri-zushi are tuna, albacore, yellowtail, bonito, shad, herring, eel, mackerel, sardine, salmon, red snapper, porgy, halibut, sea bass, octopus, squid, shrimp, abalone, clam, scallops, crab, and fish roe. Tamago, sweetened Japanese-style omelet, is a nonfish nigiri favorite.

Nigiri-zushi should be served in pairs, never in one or three pieces. There is a symbolic explanation to this: One slice means "kill" and three, "kill myself." Two connote peace.

Even though there is no written edict on nigiri-zushi consumption, one should follow proper etiquette. Hold sushi with the fingers of your right hand (or, if desired, with chopsticks). Turn sushi over, fish

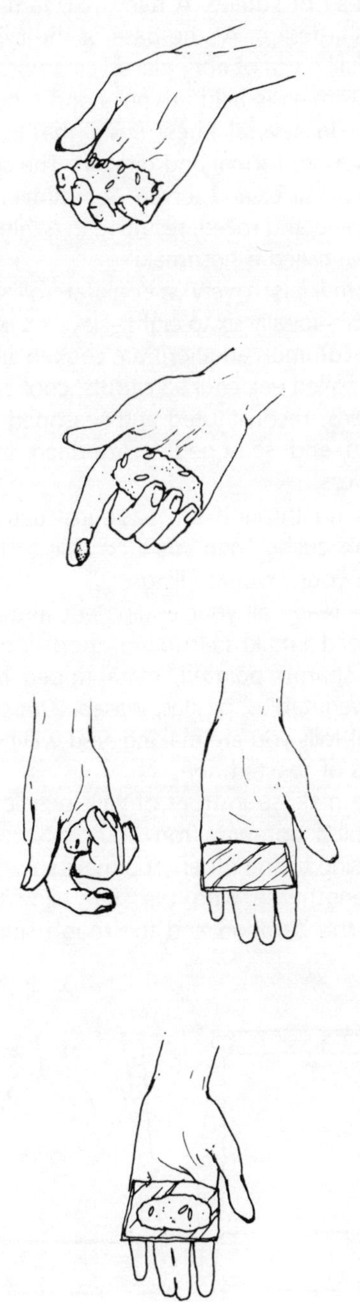

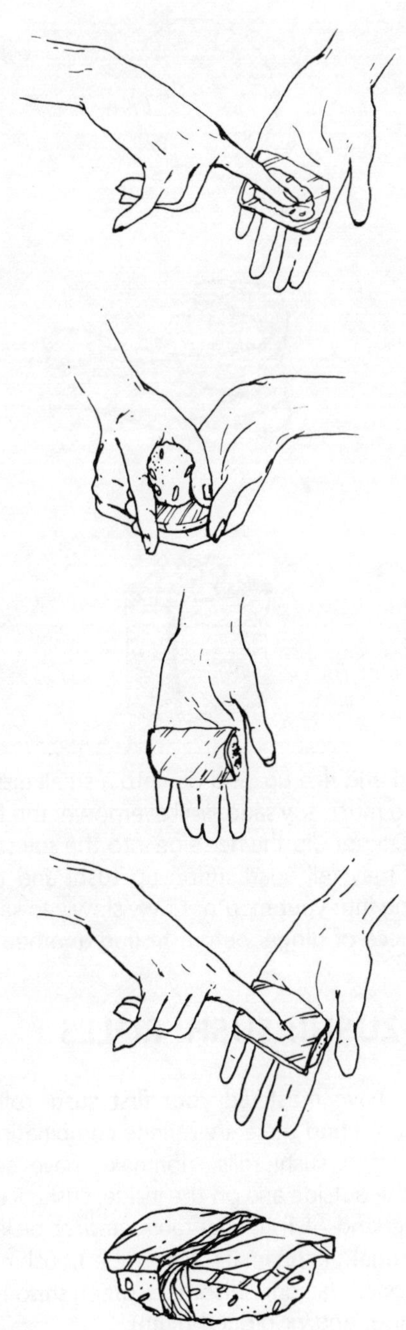

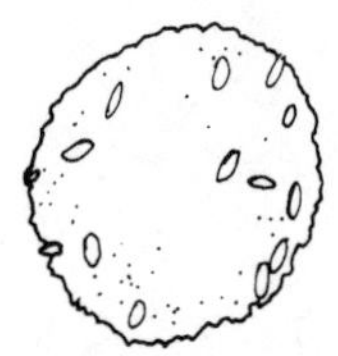

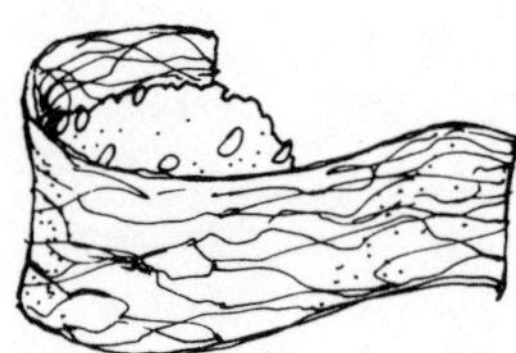

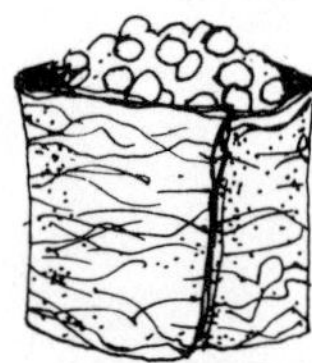

side down and rice up, and dip into a small dish of soy sauce. Too much soy sauce will overpower the flavor of the fish. Do not dip the rice side into the soy sauce, or the sushi may fall apart. Bring up sushi and pop the entire thing into your mouth. Chew slowly to savor. Eat a small piece of ginger before tasting another sushi.

MAKI-ZUSHI: SUSHI ROLLS

Once you have mastered your first sushi roll, maki-zushi, you will find there are infinite combinations. The most common sushi rolls, norimaki, have seaweed (nori) on the outside and on the inside, sushi rice, along with some kind of fish, vegetable, and/or pickle: tekkamaki (tuna), kappamaki (cucumber), oshinkomaki (yellow pickled daikon), shisomaki (green shiso leaf, red pickled shiso, and/or pickled plum).

Maki-zushi can be formed in your hands, as you would roll a cigarette, or it can be formed with the use of a maki-su or sudare. A hand roll, tamaki, is a very casual sushi design. At the base of the cylindrical nori roll is a small piece of nori, placed crosswise to hold the filling in. Tamaki is held in your hand whole, not cut, and eaten in several bites. Sushi that is rolled in a maki-su is more formal and difficult. The stuffed roll is cut into eight slices and served. Sometimes a half sheet of nori is filled and rolled, resulting in a thinner or more slender roll, called a hosomaki.

Futomaki is a very special fat roll with several ingredients—ideally six to eight—layered on top of the rice. Most common additions are cooked and seasoned shiitake, cooked eel, cooked carrots, cooked spinach or other greens, reconstituted and seasoned kanpyo, reconstituted and seasoned freeze-dried tofu, denbu, tamago slices.

Let's go through the basic instructions for preparing maki-zushi. Then you'll be able to follow these steps with your favorite fillings.

Have ready all your equipment and ingredients. You will need a maki-su (sudare), chopsticks (preferably the long, sharply pointed, metal-tipped hashi), sushi rice, fish, vegetables, pickles, wasabi. Depending upon the type of rolls you are making, you will need full and half sheets of toasted nori.

Place maki-su in front of you, positioned so that you can roll it up away from you, not toward you or from one side to the other. Top maki-su with nori, positioned lengthwise with the shiny side (outer side) closest to the bamboo and the rough side up. Leave

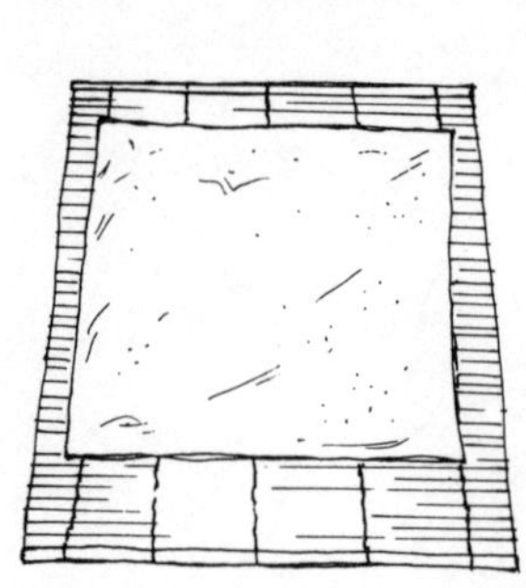

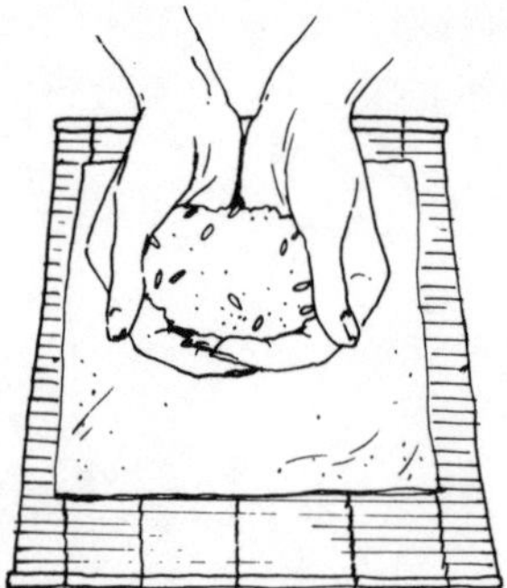

about a ½-inch margin of bamboo with nori at the side closest to you.

Dampen your hands with su water. Place rice in the center of the nori. Carefully and evenly spread it over the nori, pressing it down with your right hand. Do not pat down rice—place it. It should be packed somewhat firmer than for nigiri-zushi. Leave a 1-inch margin of nori at the far end free of rice. Use your left hand to prevent rice from extending beyond the other sides. The quantity of rice depends upon the desired size of your roll, whether you are making a hosomaki with a half sheet of nori, a norimaki with a full sheet of nori, or a futomaki (fat roll). You will need 2 to 3 tablespoons and 1 to 1½ cups of sushi rice.

Spread a dab (⅛ to ½ teaspoon) of wasabi across the center of the rice. Place filling across the center on top of the wasabi. For a simple nori roll, you will need from ½ to 1 ounce of filling. The larger the roll, the more filling you need. If you are making futomaki with a number of fillings, place the bulkier items closer to you so you can prevent them from falling out of position as you roll up the maki-su. Leave a ¼-inch border of rice on either side (left and right) without filling.

To roll the maki-su: Use your thumbs and carefully pick up the mat by the empty ½-inch margin. Hold the filling in place (particularly in the case of futomaki) with your index fingers. (You can use the chopsticks to help.) Partly roll over the mat to enclose the nori with the filling inside. The extra margin of bamboo should be extended flat. With your fingers, press down the mat to shape the roll, and slowly count to five. Open the mat and turn the ½-inch margin under; roll up once again to make sure the sushi is round. Press firmly, and again count to five. Unroll. Move sushi roll from the center to one side of the bamboo mat and pat the side to secure filling. Repeat with second side. Unroll and remove mat. Place sushi, seam side down, on cutting board.

With a slicing, not sawing, action, cut into desired thickness. Sushi rolls are most often cut in half, then the halves are placed parallel and these rolls are cut into thirds or fourths, resulting in six or eight equal pieces. Lay slices flat on serving dish so the beautiful center filling can be seen. Accompany with soy sauce. Wasabi is optional as a condiment, as it is already inside the roll.

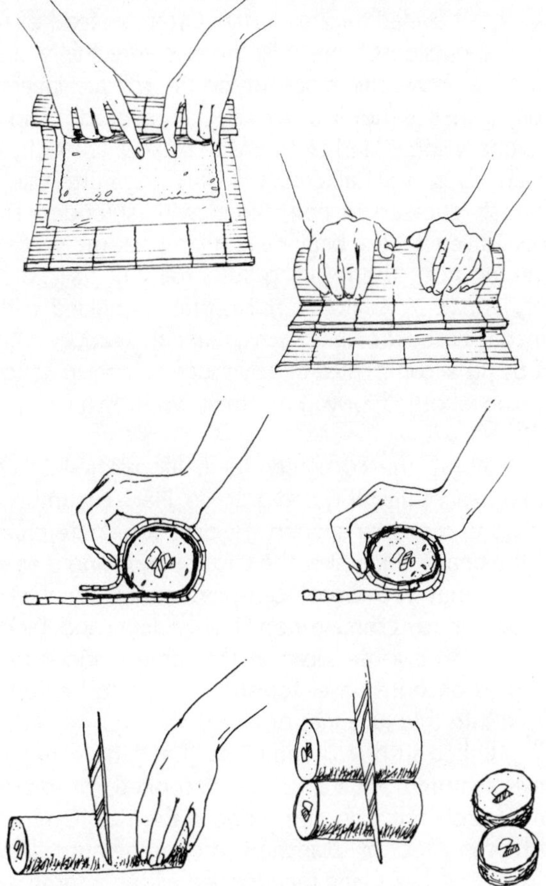

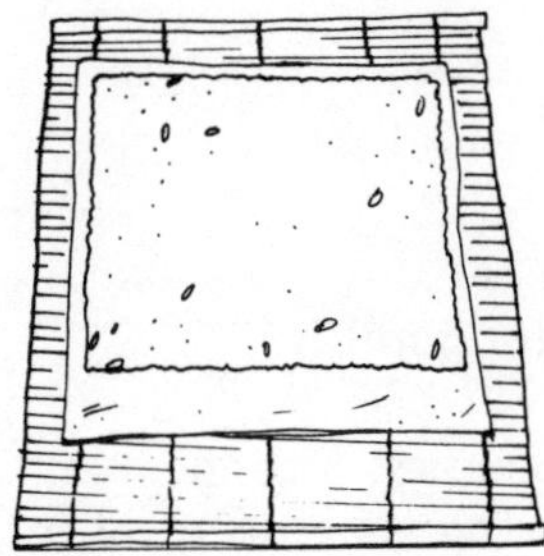

A simple and attractive variation of norimaki has rice instead of nori on the outside, resembling snow. To make this, first place a piece of plastic wrap or cloth on top of the maki-su, as you would usually position the nori. Add half the rice, followed by the sheet of nori, and then the second half of rice. At this point proceed with the recipe, adding the wasabi and filling. When you unroll the maki-su, remove the plastic wrap or cloth and slice. You will find your slices resemble pinwheels. If desired, garnish rice with toasted sesame seeds.

Another variation of norimaki that has recently become popular is called a California roll. This recipe is an excellent example of American influences on the Japanese table as I have heard that this California creation has traveled back to Japan. Often, instead of nori on the outside of the roll, there is very thinly sliced European-style cucumber. Inside the roll are layers of nori, sushi rice (not in all cases), crab, avocado, and occasionally some kind of greens or pickles. I recently enjoyed a beautiful California roll with a cigarette-thin roll of crab encased in nori, along with shredded crab, pickled vegetables, baby daikon, and sesame seeds inside (no rice). The resulting sushi roll when sliced was very artistic. A California roll is often sprinkled with a vinegar-based dressing, such as sanbaizu sauce, instead of being accompanied by soy sauce. Sanbaizu sauce is available bottled, or you can make your own (see page 77).

Slicing the cucumber for California roll takes a great deal of dexterity and practice. Place cucumber on a cutting board for support. Holding your knife parallel to the board, thinly slice the cucumber, rolling it as you cut so that you create one continuous sheet. Trim cucumber to resemble nori. Raw daikon and pickled daikon can also be sliced in the same manner to be used as an outer layer for sushi roll or to be further sliced into thin juliennes or circles.

Other sushi roll variations that I have enjoyed have featured vegetables (raw, cooked, or pickled) and/or fish rolled in nori without the rice. One such dish consisted of blanched chrysanthemum leaves rolled in nori, cut, and then topped with a sesame seed sauce. An unusual nori roll involved layers of salmon skin, flaked crab, and vegetables rolled in nori and then coated with batter and deep fried, tempura style. Another featured pieces of smoked salmon rolled in nori, resembling a cigar. A 2-inch square piece of giant squid was laid out flat and then slit open horizontally to make an open pocket. The salmon was placed through this slit and the excess trimmed off. The top of the squid was scored. Next, the squid was placed into an oven (350° to 375° F.) for 10 minutes. The cooked squid was then cut into four slices in a direction opposite to that of the scoring. The slices were arranged, slightly overlapping, on a platter. The itamae referred to this tasty sushi as "tiger's eye."

INARI (SUSHI-STUFFED TOFU POUCHES)

Yield: 12 stuffed pouches;
3 or 4 servings

An offshoot of the sushi roll is a form of stuffed sushi. Fried tofu pouches, age, are cooked in a seasoned stock, turned inside out, filled with sushi rice, and then turned back into the original shape, completely encasing the rice. The dish, named after a famous Japanese shrine protected by stone foxes, is called inari. Inari are excellent picnic and bento lunch fare.

1 1½-ounce package *tofu* pouches (age)
¼ cup *dashi*
2 to 3 teaspoons sugar
1 tablespoon soy sauce
2 teaspoons *mirin*
1 cup *sushi* rice
Black sesame seeds, for garnish

To prepare the tofu pouches: Slice them in half horizontally and cook in boiling water to cover for a few minutes to get rid of excess oils. During this boiling process, use chopsticks to press tofu under the water and against the sides of the saucepan. (This will help rid the excess oils faster.) Remove tofu and carefully squeeze out excess liquid. Place drained tofu in a saucepan with the dashi, sugar, soy sauce, and mirin. Cook over low heat, stirring to make sure sugar is dissolved and tofu is getting coated with the sauce. Cook over low heat for about 10 minutes, until sauce is absorbed.

Turn pouches inside out to stuff. Wet fingers with su water. Take about 1 tablespoon of sushi rice and form into an oval. Place rice on the inside of one side of a tofu pouch. Wrap tofu around the rice, totally encasing the rice, and turn the pouch around the correct way out. The final shape of the pouch will be almost crescentlike. Repeat process with remaining pouches.

Place pouches on a serving platter and sprinkle with sesame seeds. Serve at room temperature.

Note: I have made inari without simmering the tofu pouches in the seasoned stock. It is still quite good and a much faster recipe. However, I feel the seasoning improves the taste of the final dish.

Variation: Other ingredients can be mixed with the sushi rice before stuffing the pouches. Try cooked mushrooms, peas, bamboo shoots, carrots, fish. Condiments can also be added, such as wasabi, green onions, or ginger.

OSHI-ZUSHI: PRESSED SUSHI LOAVES

Pressed sushi loaves, oshi-zushi, can best be compared to American sandwiches. The vinegar-dressed rice and boiled or marinated fish are layered into molds, pressed, and then unmolded. Rarely are nori or raw fish used in pressed sushi. The sushi loaf is served whole if formed in small molds or cut into bite-size pieces if in large molds. (See page 38 for a discussion of molds, which are called oshiwaku.) Sushi loaves can be made in advance, wrapped in plastic, and refrigerated for several hours until needed. These make perfect picnic fare.

To make oshi-zushi, you should set up your supplies and ingredients in an assembly line manner. Place your mold on top of your cutting board for support. Wet your hands with su water. Place a layer of fish into the mold. Smear with wasabi, if desired. Next add the sushi rice, packing it more firmly than for other styles of sushi. Make sure the corners are well packed. The quantity of rice depends upon the size of the molds—larger ones will hold about one generous cup of sushi rice; smaller ones, from a few teaspoons to tablespoons. Slightly wet the top of the mold and insert over the rice. Press down. Push the sushi loaf out of the mold and turn over so that the fish is on top. Wrap with plastic and refrigerate until needed. You can experiment with these loaves, using tamago sheets instead of fish, topping the fish with an attractive edible garnish, or layering vegetables and rice. When adding layers of other ingredients, such as shredded cucumbers, do not spread them to the edges. The corners should be plain sushi rice so that the final loaf will have the proper shape.

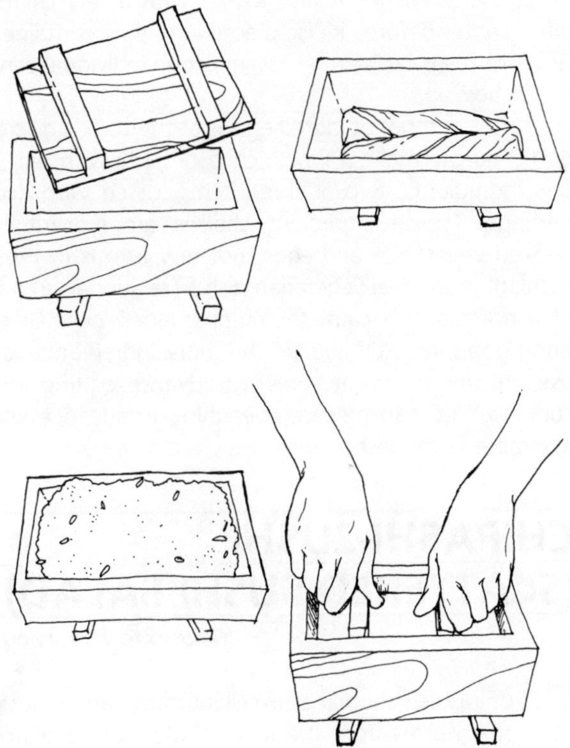

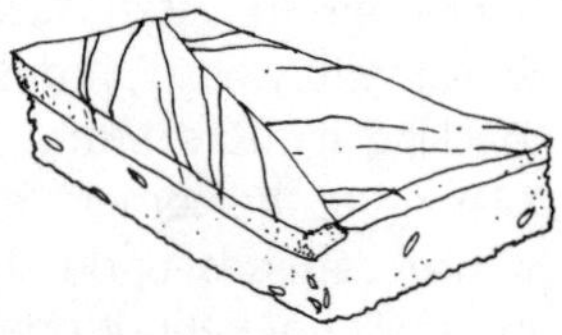

CHIRASHI-ZUSHI: SCATTERED SUSHI

Scattered sushi, chirashi-zushi, while in some ways the simplest form of sushi to assemble, may take the most time to prepare. Instead of fingers, rolls, or loaves, it is a free-form scattering of ingredients (fish and vegetables) on top of the sushi meshi. Sushi rice is first placed in a layer on the bottom of a large platter, bowl, or box. The other ingredients are attractively scattered over the top. Then the garnishes are arranged in the center. Sometimes the sushi rice is first tossed with a few of the ingredients before it is placed in the container. Chirashi-zushi can also be assembled in individual serving dishes.

The number of ingredients is at the cook's discretion. You can make a simple chirashi-zushi with only a few ingredients, two or three items tossed with rice, perhaps. Typical ingredient choices are individually cooked vegetables and eggs, not raw fish as in most sushi. (It is an ideal vegetarian dish.) Traditionally it has nine ingredients because the number nine is believed to bring good luck. Of course, the more ingredients you use, the more time it takes for advance cutting and cooking. You can prepare everything in advance and assemble at the last minute.

CHIRASHI-ZUSHI (SCATTERED SUSHI SALAD)

Yield: 6 to 10 servings

Chirashi-zushi makes excellent party fare. Guests serve themselves from the large platter. Using a rice paddle, they scoop under the rice and place the desired amount in their bowl or dish, much as they might help themselves to pizza. Chirashi-zushi is eaten with chopsticks. A garnish of pink pickled ginger placed on top adds extra color and piquancy.

SHARI MIXTURE (*Sushi* Rice Mixture)

2½ cups hot cooked rice
⅓ cup vinegar
2 tablespoons sugar (or more to taste)
2 teaspoons salt

VEGETABLE MIXTURE

2 ounces pea pods, blanched
2 carrots (about ¼ pound), scraped and slivered into pencil shavings
6 medium fresh mushrooms (about 3 ounces), washed and thinly sliced (dried mushrooms can also be used)
2 whole small *takenoko*, sliced (if canned, wash and parboil to refresh)
½ to 1 ounce *kanpyo* (approximately half the cellophane package), reconstituted
3 ounces (½ cake) *kamaboko*, cut into bite-size pieces (optional)

VEGETABLE SEASONINGS

6 to 8 cups *dashi*
4 tablespoons sugar (or more if desired)
2 tablespoons soy sauce
1 teaspoon salt

POSSIBLE GARNISHES

Crumbled *nori* (about 1 sheet)
Pickled ginger
***Tamago* sheets, thinly sliced**
Minced green onion

Place hot rice in a wood tub or bowl and fan a few seconds to cool slightly. In a small mixing bowl, combine the vinegar, sugar, and salt, stirring until sugar has dissolved. Pour dressing over rice and mix thoroughly. As if cutting the rice with a wooden paddle, turn the rice to blend with the dressing. Continue to fan until cooled.

Vegetables need to be cooked and seasoned separately. I find it best to cook with one large pot, starting with the mildest tasting vegetable. As one vegetable is cooked, remove and repeat process with each remaining vegetable.

Thinly slice pea pods into 2-inch thick matchstick-size juliennes. Place in a pot with 1 cup dashi and 2 tablespoons sugar. Cook until tender and seasoned, about 2 to 3 minutes. Remove pea pods with a slotted spoon and place on a platter. Add carrots and simmer about 3 minutes, until tender, adding dashi as needed. Remove carrots. Add mushrooms, another cup of dashi, 1 tablespoon sugar, 1 tablespoon soy sauce and ½ teaspoon salt. Simmer 5 minutes. Remove. Add takenoko and another cup dashi and remaining sugar, soy sauce, and salt. Simmer about 5 minutes and remove.

Meanwhile, in second pot, boil reconstituted kanpyo in water for about 10 minutes or until almost translucent. Remove and cut up into 1-inch to 2-inch lengths. Place kanpyo in the pot with the remaining seasoned dashi. Add any remaining dashi and simmer about 5 minutes. If desired sweeter, add sugar. Remove and add kamaboko to the pot; simmer a few minutes and remove. If preparing a vegetarian dish, do not include the kamaboko. Also, remember to make the dashi with only the kombu. (See The Basic Stock: Dashi.)

There are two ways to assemble chirashi-zushi, tossed together or scattered. To toss everything together: In a large mixing bowl, combine the sushi rice with all the vegetables. Toss. Or, you can make individual bowls. Garnish the top of the bowl(s) with crumbled nori, pickled ginger, tamago shreds (see page 72), and green onion. To scatter: You can lightly pack the sushi rice on the bottom of a large serving platter or individual bowls and then sprinkle everything on top. Place nori, ginger, tamago, and green onions in the center. You can make this in advance for a party, but you should not add the nori until the last minute because it loses crispness quickly. Or try hosting a make-your-own chirashi-zushi party. Set out a variety of bowls of toppings and garnishes and suggest that your guests top their own sushi rice. Serve at room temperature with additional soy sauce.

Variations: Other ingredients can be added or substituted, such as shiitake, bits of raw and/or cooked seafood, slivered string beans, peas, gobo, cucumber, tofu (plain or freeze-dried or pouches that have been preseasoned and cut up), vinegared celery, or lotus root.

Note: Related to chirashi-zushi is tekka donburi, in which sushi rice is placed in a large bowl (donburi). A few squares of nori are placed on top of the rice, and then tuna sashimi is placed on top of the seaweed. Garnishes of wasabi and pickled ginger are placed in the center. Sometimes these garnishes may be placed underneath the fish.

The rest of this chapter is devoted to some recipes for dishes that patrons of sushi bars have come to expect as standard fare.

MACKEREL AND EEL

Two very popular fish that need advance treatment are mackerel and eel. Follow these sushi bar tips for proper handling:

To prepare mackerel for sushi and sashimi, generously salt the unskinned fillets. Refrigerate for 1 hour. Wipe off salt, and soak for 2 hours in equal parts water and vinegar to cover, to which lemon slices have been added. Drain and serve.

To prepare eel, you can purchase cellophane packages of seasoned eel or, you can start from scratch. In either case, marinate filleted eel in a warm sauce made by combining and briefly heating: 1 cup soy sauce, 1 cup sugar, ¼ cup salt, 1 cup mirin, 2 cups water, and several slices peeled ginger. After eel has marinated, remove and reserve for sushi and sashimi. Sauce should now be simmered over low heat for several hours to thicken—some recommend heating for as long as 6 to 10 hours. To serve eel for sushi or sashimi, put in a hot oven (about 400° F.) for 1 to 2 minutes, brush each piece with about ½ teaspoon of sauce, and sprinkle with toasted sesame seeds. Tare-glazed and grilled eel, called kabayaki, is a favorite Japanese summertime dish. On Ushinohi Day, it is traditionally served on a bed of steamed white rice, not sushi rice; extra tare sauce is poured on top.

As you can see, there is no limit on the variety of sushi dishes you can create. You can try the traditional ideas or experiment with your favorite ingredients. The essentials are understanding the techniques of assembling and shaping, and using only the freshest of ingredients.

TAMAGO YAKI

Yield: 1 roll

Tamago yaki, also referred to as tamago dashimaki, is always present at a sushi bar. From the basic concept of these eggs come several other recipes, such as tamago sheets to be used as "wrappers" or to be sliced into juliennes and added to many other recipes.

This Japanese-style omelet differs from the American in the "batter" and the manner of cooking. With chopsticks—never a beater—eggs are mixed with dashi, mirin, or sake, sugar, soy sauce, and salt. Next, they are strained to improve consistency. In a rectangular or square nonstick pan, a small portion of egg mixture is cooked and rolled, then a little more egg mixture is added to the pan and cooked under and rolled over the first, resulting in layers. The process is continued until all of this liquid "batter" is added to the pan; product resembles a cylinder or thick rectangle. This sweetened egg dish, a favorite among adults and children alike, is then cooled and served in bite-size slices.

4 large eggs
4 tablespoons *dashi*
1 tablespoon sugar (or more to taste)
1 teaspoon *mirin*
½ teaspoon soy sauce (light-colored soy sauce is best)
Salt
Cooking oil

Break eggs into mixing bowl, beating with chopsticks. Add dashi, sugar, mirin, soy sauce, and salt to taste. Mix ingredients with chopsticks until sugar is dissolved. Pour egg mixture through a fine-holed strainer into a glass measuring cup to eliminate any sticky membrane. (The cup's pouring spout will aid in the next steps.)

Place pan over medium heat. Oil well the bottom and sides of the pan. (A trick that my friend and Japanese cooking instructor Matao Uwate uses is to keep a ball of absorbent cotton in a small bowl filled with cooking oil; using chopsticks, pick up cotton ball and rub it all over pan to coat well. A piece of paper towel saturated with cooking oil works well, too.)

Pour a *thin* layer of egg mixture (about ¼ inch) into the pan as if you were making a crepe. Tilt the pan to spread the mixture. When the egg begins to bubble and set, use chopsticks to roll it up, starting at the far side and rolling toward you. Reoil the back of the pan, then push the egg mixture to the back. Reoil the front of the pan. Add another thin layer of egg mixture and slowly push up the cooked egg in the back of the pan so that the new addition spreads completely underneath. This will create a layer. Again, after egg mixture begins to bubble and set, roll up toward you, reoil the back, push the egg mixture to the back. As the quantity of cooked egg begins to increase, push it down to shape into a rectangle or cylinder. Reoil the front. Repeat this process about 4 times, or until all egg mixture is cooked.

I have found using a wooden spatula along with the chopsticks aids in the rolling up, pushing back, and shaping. Also, when rolling up the set egg mixture, taking the pan off the heat will prevent scorching. Scorching can also occur from too high heat, too much dashi, too much sugar, or not enough cooking oil as protection. If part of the egg sticks to the pan, use your oiled cotton or paper to rub it off.

Remove rolled eggs from pan and immediately place on a bamboo mat (maki-su). Roll up as if you were making sushi (see maki-zushi instructions, page 66). Gently squeeze out excess liquid and shape into a cylinder. Keep wrapped in bamboo about 10 to 15 minutes; unwrap.

When the roll is cooled, slice it into circles, rectangles, or decorative pieces resembling bamboo shoots (see page 40). Serve at room temperature or chilled. Garnish, if desired, with black sesame seeds and accompany with soy sauce and grated daikon. You can serve sliced tamago along with sushi and sashimi, as a sweet side course or snack. Since children love it, tamago makes excellent family picnic fare.

Note: To make fatter rolls or rectangles, which you may have seen at sushi bars, it is important to first understand the technique before increasing the quantity. You will also need a larger pan. Then, for every extra egg, you should add 1 tablespoon of dashi. Increase the sugar, mirin, and salt to taste. The sugar creates the shiny outer surface.

Variation 1
TAMAGO YAKI WITH FILLING

If you wish to add other ingredients, such as seafood and precooked vegetables, the 4-egg tamago will hold about ½ cup. Add filling ingredients to egg mixture after it has been strained. For nori layers, place small strips of toasted nori on top of egg mixture as you are rolling it. Layers of nori will be incorporated into the layers of eggs.

Variation 2
THIN EGG SHEETS

Yield: 4 to 6 sheets

4 eggs
1 tablespoon sugar (or more to taste)
½ teaspoon salt
Cooking oil

Beat eggs with sugar and salt and strain as in tamago yaki. Heat skillet and oil well. Pour a small amount of egg mixture (about 1/6 to ¼ of total) into the skillet and tilt pan to spread. When the bottom of the egg mixture has set, in a few seconds to a minute, remove from heat and carefully lift up egg sheet with your fingers and chopsticks, taking care not to tear the sheet. Turn over to second side, return to heat, and cook lightly for a few seconds, until the second side is golden. Carefully remove the egg sheet and place it on paper towels to drain off excess oil. Oil the pan again and repeat the process until all the egg mixture is cooked.

Thin egg sheets can be used for many recipes. They can be rolled up separately like cigars and sliced into thin strips or threads. Use these in norimaki or as a garnish for chirashi-zushi or other recipes. They can also be used to encase sushi rice and fish. Place sheets, one at a time, on a damp towel and spoon a small amount of filling in the center. Filling can also be preshaped into a square or round. With the aid of the towel for shaping, fold up the egg like a drawstring purse and tie with seaweed (chakin-zushi) or like a fabric-wrapped gift (fukusa-zushi).

Note: Because there is no dashi in this recipe, the resulting eggs will be sweeter and less salty. But you may wish to use the basic tamago yaki recipe for thin egg sheets.

Variation 3
THICK EGG SHEET

Yield: 1 sheet

Ingredients are the same as for thin egg sheets. You should have a large tamago pan, about 9 inches square. Oil pan and add all of the egg mixture. Place over very low heat. Cover with foil and cook 5 to 7 minutes; remove from heat and uncover. Using your fingers and chopsticks, very carefully lift up the egg sheet and flip over. Return to low heat, cover, and cook on second side for a few minutes to brown. Lift out and place on paper towel to drain off excess oil. You can slice and serve a thick egg sheet as a side course, use it in sushi recipes, or use it as the "bed" for another recipe featuring vegetables that have been simmered in a seasoned stock.

Variation 4
AMERICANIZED MEDIUM THICK EGG SHEET

Yield: 1 sheet

2 large eggs
2 to 3 teaspoons sugar
¼ teaspoon salt

Beat eggs with sugar and salt. Pour mixture into a well greased 9-by-5-inch loaf pan. Bake in a preheated 300° F. oven for 15 minutes. Carefully flip egg sheet onto paper towels. Let cool and cut into desired shapes or shreds.

VINEGARED GINGER SLICES

Yield: About ¼ cup

Vinegared and pickled ginger is available in many shapes and degrees of pungency. Check out the different varieties at your local market. For a subtle homemade condiment for sushi as well as for other recipes, try this.

2 ounces ginger
¼ cup vinegar
1 tablespoon sugar
Salt

Peel and slice ginger as thin as possible. Combine the vinegar, sugar, and salt to taste. Heat the liquid mixture to a boil, stirring for 1 minute, to make sure the sugar has dissolved. Place ginger in a bowl and pour hot vinegar on top. Cover and allow to cool. Chill before serving.

This recipe will keep refrigerated for several weeks. If you want a deeper pink, add food coloring.

RED MAPLE RADISH (MOMIJI-OROSHI)

Yield: ½ to 1 cup

Red maple radish is a very simple condiment to make, featuring daikon and red peppers. It is delicious grated or sliced and served with sashimi, but be careful—it is very powerful stuff. This condiment is also traditionally served with chicken mizutaki and teppan yaki.

½ pound *daikon*, about 3 inches in length
6 dried red chili peppers

Peel daikon. Using the thicker end of a chopstick, carefully make three holes in the center of the daikon, piercing the daikon vertically. Seed the red peppers, using a sharp knife and carefully opening them without breaking. Place peppers in the daikon holes. Wrap in plastic and refrigerate until needed. If you make this several hours in advance, the flavors of the daikon and the red peppers will have the opportunity to mingle.

At serving time, unwrap daikon and grate into shreds, or slice.

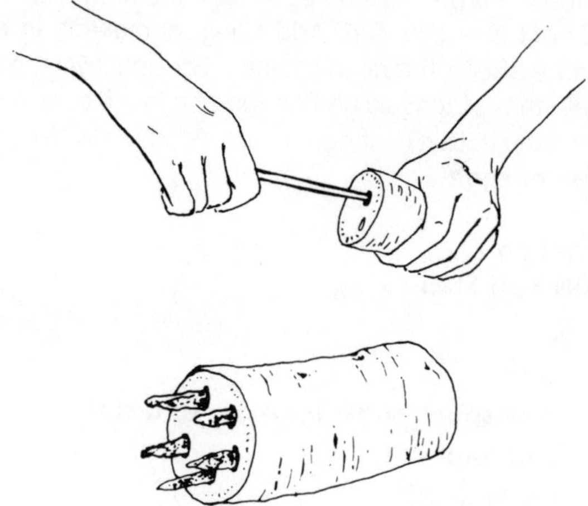

SALADS AND VEGETABLES

Salads and vegetables hold important positions in Japanese cuisine. Japanese salads are a delicate combination of a few well-balanced ingredients, tossed with a vinegar or slightly thickened dressing. Japanese savor pickled foods to refresh the palate. A small dish of pickles is an integral part of the Japanese meal. As for cooked vegetables, I find the American table has long felt the Eastern influence of a preference for vegetables carefully prepared without overcooking. Since dairy products are not inherent to Japanese cuisine, cooked vegetables are not tossed or topped with butter, cream, or cheese. Instead, you will find ginger-and-onion-seasoned oil, soy sauce, tofu, miso, or sesame seeds as the main enhancers.

You may be familiar with sunomono. Meaning ''vinegared things,'' sunomono is similar to salad and is composed of raw or cooked ingredients. Popular items include cucumber, cabbage, lettuce, daikon, carrots, onions, mushrooms, spinach, string beans, pea pods, cauliflower, broccoli, celery, seaweed, seafood, fish, and occasionally fowl, meat, and/or fruit. The common ingredient in all cases is vinegar. Generally the dressing is sweetened with sugar and flavored with mirin, soy sauce, lemon juice, sesame seeds, salt, and/or wasabi.

Small portions of sunomono can be offered to start a meal (instead of a zensai, or appetizer) or to complement an entree.

The second style of flavoring vegetables is aemono, or "dressed things." In this case the dressing is slightly thickened with miso, tofu, and/or ground sesame seeds, resulting in a texture similar to that of a mayonnaise-based dressing.

The Japanese refined the art of pickling during the fourteenth century. *Tsukemono,* the term for pickles, means "soaked things." The base is the pickling agent. It can be as simple as a generous sprinkling of salt, in which case the pickles can be enjoyed after an hour. Or you can go through the steps of using a pickling medium, referred to as the bed, in which you bury the vegetables for several days, weeks, even months. The vegetables should be placed in a deep stoneware, ceramic, glass, or plastic—not metal—crock or a Japanese wood pickling tub (taru), along with the pickling agent, and then covered and weighted down. If you do not own the traditional Japanese equipment, you can improvise by covering your ingredients with several layers of plastic wrap and weighting them down with a brick. The most commonly used pickling agent is miso, and it should be recycled. The miso will become more flavorsome during the pickling process, but also thinner from the vegetable juices. Simply thicken and refresh with additional miso.

Experiment with your favorite vegetables. Cucumbers, cabbage, radishes, and small eggplants are among the most popular. The only fruit traditionally pickled is umeboshi, Japanese plum. But other fruits, such as apples, peaches, and pears, are also delicious pickled.

OSUNOMONO

Yield: 4 to 6 servings

The sweet and sour taste of the dressing poured over crunchy cucumbers makes this a lovely salad or side dish. If you want a touch of spiciness, include the wasabi. The *o* in osunomono alerts the cook that this is an honored recipe. Use this dressing as your basic sunomono recipe for other vegetables. It is especially delicious with chopped cabbage.

2 to 3 cucumbers, peeled and thinly sliced

BASIC SUNOMONO DRESSING

2 to 4 tablespoons sugar
½ cup rice vinegar
¼ cup fresh lemon juice
1 teaspoon salt
1 teaspoon freshly grated ginger
¼ teaspoon *wasabi,* dissolved in 1 teaspoon water (optional)

Place cucumber slices on paper towels to drain excess liquid. Wrap in paper towels and refrigerate until serving time.

Combine dressing ingredients in a small bowl, adding sugar to taste. Stir until sugar and wasabi are dissolved. At serving time, place cucumbers in a bowl, pour on dressing, and toss.

Variation: Try adding ¼ pound (or more) thinly sliced octopus for a delicious cucumber and octopus salad, kyuri tako no sunomono. I serve the wasabi on the side for those people who wish to add it. You might also try garnishing the sunomono with dried bonito shavings.

CUCUMBERS AND SHRIMP SUNOMONO

Yield: 6 servings

Cucumbers and shrimp are an attractive team in the following simple sunomono.

1 large (about 10 ounces) European-style cucumber, or 2 to 3 regular cucumbers

SU-SOY DRESSING

1 tablespoon rice vinegar
1 to 2 tablespoons soy sauce

1 teaspoon sugar
½ teaspoon salt
¼ teaspoon sesame oil

4 ounces cooked baby shrimp

If using European-style cucumber, you do not need to peel. Waxed cucumbers should be peeled. Slice cucumbers thinly and place on paper towels for about 5 to 30 minutes to drain off excess liquid.

Combine the dressing ingredients in a small measuring cup, stirring to dissolve the sugar.

Prior to serving, place cucumbers in a serving bowl and add the shrimp. Pour dressing over them and toss well.

CUCUMBER AND KOMBU SALAD WITH SWEETENED VINEGAR DRESSING

Yield: 4 to 6 servings

Seaweed and cucumbers combined with a sweetened vinegar dressing make a tasty sunomono. You can vary this recipe by substituting other reconstituted seaweed, such as wakame, for the kombu. And you can select another vegetable instead of the cucumber.

1 6-inch European-style cucumber
1 2-inch to 3-inch piece *kombu* (or *wakame*)

SWEETENED VINEGAR DRESSING (*Sanbaizu* Sauce)

2 tablespoons vinegar
1 tablespoon sugar
1½ teaspoons soy sauce
2 to 3 teaspoons *dashi*
Pinch salt

Cut cucumber in half crosswise. If desired, carefully peel. Slice in half lengthwise, scooping out and discarding the seeds. Slice cucumber into matchstick-size juliennes. Place on paper towels to drain off excess liquid. If desired, you can salt the cucumber to help the liquids rise faster. Rinse off salt and pat dry with paper towels before using.

Soak kombu in warm water for about 10 minutes. Rinse. Kombu will become considerably larger. Roll up kombu like a tube and cut into thin slices, about ⅛ to ¼ inch. Slice these shreds into 3-inch lengths. The cucumber and kombu should be similar in size.

Combine the dressing ingredients, stirring until the sugar has dissolved. Toss dressing with cucumbers and kombu.

If substituting reconstituted wakame for the kombu, remove the seaweed from the soaking liquid, douse in fresh hot water, then in cold water. Trim off and discard all hard parts; chop wakame. Place chopped wakame in a kitchen tea towel and squeeze dry. Toss wakame with sliced cucumber, then toss the mixture with the sanbaizu sauce.

CARROTS, GREEN PEPPER, AND CELERY SUNOMONO

Yield: 4 servings

A trio of precooked carrots, peppers, and celery, tossed with a vinegar-based dressing and then garnished with salted black sesame seeds makes a colorful vegetable salad.

2 to 3 carrots, scraped
1 green pepper, cut in half and seeded
2 large stalks celery

SUNOMONO DRESSING

¼ cup vinegar
1 tablespoon sugar (or more to taste)
1 tablespoon *dashi* (or vegetable or chicken broth)

2 teaspoons soy sauce

1 tablespoon salted black sesame seeds, for garnish

Slice vegetables into similar-sized matchstick juliennes. Bring a pot of water to boil and add vegetables. Let water return to a boil and cook vegetables about 1 minute, or until slightly tender. Immediately drain, then rinse with cold water and ice cubes. Thoroughly drain and dry with paper towels. Set aside to cool to room temperature.

Mix the dressing ingredients together in a small bowl or measuring cup, stirring until sugar dissolves. Toss with vegetables.

Garnish top of dressed vegetables with salted black sesame seeds, or with a combination of black sesame seeds and salt to taste. Otherwise, add salt to the dressing (about ½ teaspoon or to taste).

PICKLED UNCOOKED VEGETABLES NAMASU

Yield: 6 to 10 servings

A namasu is similar to a salad. This excellent combination will remind you of a cucumber relish. Serve with the meal as a condiment or at the end of a meal.

1 cucumber (about 10 ounces), peeled and thinly sliced*

½ pound *daikon*, peeled and thinly sliced*

1 small onion, peeled and thinly sliced*

1 carrot, peeled and sliced into julienne shreds*

½ teaspoon minced ginger

NAMASU DRESSING (Cooked)

⅓ cup soy sauce

3 tablespoons vinegar

4 tablespoons sugar (or more to taste)

*Cucumber, daikon, onion, and carrot can all be sliced in a food processor.

Place raw vegetables and ginger in a serving bowl; toss to mix.

Combine soy sauce, vinegar, and sugar in a saucepan. Bring liquid to a boil, stirring constantly, then lower heat and cook about ½ minute. Cool dressing.

Pour cooled dressing over raw vegetables; toss and refrigerate until serving time.

To serve, place small amount of pickled vegetables in individual dishes.

Variation: Other vegetables, such as cabbage and eggplant, can be added or substituted.

CARROT AND CELERY NAMASU

Yield: 4 servings

Here's a simple carrot and celery namasu with a help-yourself garnish.

¼ pound carrots, peeled and sliced into thin matchstick-size juliennes

¼ pound celery stalks, trimmed and sliced into thin matchstick-size juliennes

NAMASU DRESSING (Uncooked)

2 tablespoons vinegar

1 tablespoon *mirin*

½ teaspoon sugar

Dash salt

GARNISHES

Thinly sliced green tops of scallions

Juliennes of reconstituted *kombu*

Dried bonito shavings

Place carrots and celery together in a salad bowl. Combine the namasu dressing ingredients, tasting for sugar and salt. Toss dressing with carrots and celery.

You can serve this immediately or refrigerate for several hours.

To serve: Place garnishes in small, attractive bowls. Guests can top their salad with one or all of the garnishes.

Variation: Julienne slices of daikon can be added. Daikon alone with this dressing is also an excellent namasu.

PICKLED COOKED VEGETABLES AND TOFU WITH GOMA DRESSING NAMASU

Yield: 8 to 10 servings

A sesame seed–based dressing is tossed with several cooked vegetables and tofu pockets for this excellent namasu. Serve small portions as an accompaniment to your meal.

- **3 age (*tofu* pockets), cut in half horizontally**
- **2 pounds *daikon*, peeled and shredded***
- **2 medium (½ pound) carrots, peeled and shredded***
- **2 green onions, firm part only, sliced into thin, matchstick-size juliennes**
- **¼ cup reconstituted *wakame*, thinly sliced with hard parts removed**

NAMASU GOMA DRESSING

- **½ cup sesame seeds, toasted**
- **⅔ cup sugar (or more to taste)**
- **½ cup vinegar**
- **1 tablespoon salt**

*Daikon and carrot can be shredded in a food processor or Japanese shredding utensil.

Place sliced tofu pockets in a pot of boiling water. Cook for 3 minutes to drain off excess oil. Keep pressing the tofu under the water and against the sides of the pot. Drain and cool. Slice tofu into thin shreds. Squeeze dry through the palms of your hands.

Combine daikon, carrot, green onion, tofu, and wakame in a large dry skillet. (You may have to do this in 2 batches.) Cook over high heat for about 2 minutes, stirring constantly until vegetables are wilted. Place vegetables in colander to cool and drain.

When vegetables are cool enough to handle, take small amounts at a time in your hands and squeeze out excess liquid. Place vegetables in a bowl.

In a suribachi, grind the toasted sesame seeds. (You will need a large suribachi or a mortar and pestle. Or you can use a food processor or blender, but take care not to overgrind the sesame seeds so that the paste has no texture.) Grind the seeds with the sugar, vinegar, and salt. Place mixture in a saucepan and bring to a boil. Pour sesame dressing over vegetables and toss. Cover and refrigerate.

Serve salad chilled or at room temperature. This will keep for several days, even weeks, covered in the refrigerator.

SOYBEAN SALAD WITH JAPANESE "VINAIGRETTE" DRESSING

Yield: 4 to 8 servings

Cooked fresh or frozen soybeans tossed with a Japanese-style vinegar dressing make a marvelous legume salad. This dressing is also wonderful to use for other cooked vegetables or as a dipping sauce for tofu recipes.

- **1 16-ounce bag frozen soybeans***

JAPANESE-STYLE VINAIGRETTE

- **1 tablespoon soy sauce**
- **2 tablespoons vinegar**
- **1 teaspoon *mirin***
- **¼ teaspoon grated ginger**

1 medium green onion, firm part only, sliced and separated into thin rings (3 to 4 tablespoons)
Sugar (optional)

Sesame oil

*Frozen soybeans are available at most oriental markets. If fresh soybeans in the pod are available, try them. You might also try this recipe with frozen lima beans or string beans.

Cook soybeans according to package directions in boiling salted water for 5 minutes. Drain. Rinse in cool water. When soybeans have cooled enough to handle, pod. Discard pods. Result is approximately 2 cups soybeans.

Mix together the dressing ingredients. Place soybeans in a bowl. Pour dressing over; toss. Garnish with a few drops of sesame oil.

Variation: For a more Americanized vinaigrette, you may add about ¼ cup salad oil to the dressing.

CARROTS IN VINEGAR

Yield: 2 to 4 servings

Vinegar can be used to dress vegetables after they are cooked or used as the cooking liquid. You might try adding a few tablespoons of vinegar to your water to add flavor and to hold the vegetable's color. Or, as in the following recipe, vinegar alone is used, resulting in a lovely, gently vinegared dish. Try this technique with other root vegetables, such as lotus root, as well as with broccoli and cauliflower.

½ pound carrots, peeled and thinly sliced into circles
⅓ cup vinegar

Place carrots in a small saucepan with the vinegar. Bring vinegar to a boil; cover pan and reduce heat. Cook at a simmer for about 8 to 10 minutes, or until carrots are tender. (Adjust the cooking time for other vegetables.) Uncover and increase heat if necessary, so that carrots have absorbed all liquid.

Serve at room temperature or chilled. If desired, serve with a dressing, such as mayonnaise, or garnish with salted black sesame seeds.

MRS. OZAKI'S OSECHI SALAD

Yield: 4 servings as salad or side dish; 10 servings as part of buffet

This delicious combination of seafood, cucumbers, and noodles is ideal to serve as a salad on New Year's Day since the harusame symbolize good luck and health in the new year.

½ to 1 ounce *harusame*
1 cup canned abalone or fresh raw squid, sliced into strips
1 cucumber, peeled and thinly sliced
2 stalks celery, thinly sliced at an angle
1 carrot, scraped and cut into thin julienne strips

MRS. OZAKI'S SALAD DRESSING
½ cup sugar
¼ cup lemon juice
½ cup rice vinegar
1 tablespoon salt
1 teaspoon grated fresh ginger

Cook harusame in boiling water for 4 to 5 minutes. Drain and cut into 1½-inch lengths. Combine the seafood, cucumber, celery, carrot, and noodles in an attractive serving bowl.

In a small bowl, combine the dressing ingredients; mix well. Pour dressing over the seafood-vegetable combination; toss. Refrigerate until serving time. To serve, toss ingredients once again.

STEAMED CAULIFLOWER WITH MISO SAUCES

Yield: 4 to 6 servings

Steaming a head of cabbage whole and then serving it masked with your choice of miso sauce or serving it with the miso sauce on the side makes a dramatic dressed aemono vegetable dish. This is a basic recipe that can be adapted to practically any steamed vegetable, such as broccoli, cucumbers, string beans, potatoes, carrots, squash, even a mixture of vegetables. You can also boil or broil your vegetables. Broiled eggplant slices are marvelous with these miso sauces. Steamed chicken breasts or white fish also respond extremely well to these sauces.

1 medium head cauliflower (about 1¼ pounds), extra green trimmed off

UNCOOKED MISO SAUCE

¼ cup white *miso*
1 tablespoon red *miso*
¼ cup *dashi* (or leftover liquid from steaming the vegetable)
1 tablespoon *sake*

COOKED MISO SAUCE

¼ cup white *miso*
1 tablespoon red *miso*
¼ cup *sake*
¾ cup *mirin*

GARNISHES
Grated lemon rind
Minced scallions
Slivered fresh ginger
Toasted sesame seeds
Shredded *nori*
Powdered red pepper
Dried bonito shavings

Place whole cauliflower on a steaming rack above 2 inches rapidly simmering water (or other liquid, such as dashi, sake, or chicken stock). Cover pot and steam cauliflower until tender, about 20 minutes. To test for doneness, pierce gently with a skewer; do not overcook. Place cauliflower on a serving platter. Spread miso sauce on top (or serve on the side) and garnish with your choice of condiments.

For the uncooked miso sauce, combine ingredients in a small bowl and stir to blend. Add sugar or honey if desired. You will have approximately ½ cup sauce.

For the cooked miso sauce, combine ingredients in a small saucepan. Gently cook for a few minutes, until the liquid is reduced by about half. If desired, add sugar or honey. You will have approximately ⅔ cup miso.

JAPANESE EGGPLANTS IN MISO DRESSING

Yield: 8 to 10 servings

Miso and toasted sesame seeds ground together make a basic aemono dressing for practically any cooked vegetable. In this recipe, I've used eggplant. Serve as a condiment or as an accompaniment to other dishes.

2 to 3 pounds Japanese eggplants, sliced into fingers
Salt
Cooking oil

MISO–SESAME SEED DRESSING

⅓ cup light *miso*
⅓ cup sesame seeds, toasted
3 tablespoons *mirin*
1 tablespoon vinegar

Place eggplant fingers on paper towels and salt them. Set aside for 10 to 20 minutes to drain off excess liquid, then wipe or wash off excess salt. Brush eggplants with oil and broil for 4 to 6 minutes, turning, or until all sides are wrinkled. Remove eggplants from broiler and keep warm until serving time.

For the dressing: Using a food processor, blender, or suribachi, grind together and blend the miso, sesame seeds, mirin, and vinegar.

To serve: You can either top eggplants with sauce or toss them together. Serve at room temperature.

MISO DENGAKU SAUCE WITH DAIKON

Yield: 4 to 8 servings

Sweetened miso is an excellent topping for your cooked vegetables, in this case, daikon. This sauce can also be used for broiled vegetables. Serve this recipe as an appetizer, side course, or vegetable dish.

1 pound *daikon,* peeled and sliced into ¼-inch thick rounds
Pinch raw rice

MISO DENGAKU SAUCE
2 tablespoons *miso* (choice of flavor)
2 tablespoons *sake*
1 to 2 teaspoons sugar

1 green onion, top only, thinly sliced, for garnish

Place daikon in a pot of boiling water with the pinch of raw rice. Return water to a boil, then reduce and cook gently. As the daikon cooks, the rice will help tenderize it and will absorb offensive aromas. Continue to cook for about 30 minutes, or until tender and slightly transparent. Drain and rinse off the rice.

Meanwhile, combine miso, sake, and sugar in a suribachi and grind to mix thoroughly. Set aside.

Place rinsed daikon in a single layer in a dry, hot skillet. Heat daikon for about 1 minute per side to dry. Place daikon on a serving dish. Top the center of each piece with a small amount (about ¼ to ½ teaspoon) of miso dengaku sauce. Garnish the sauce with the green onion slices.

Daikon can be served warm or can be set aside and served at room temperature.

Variation: This sauce can top other cooked vegetables. For a green dengaku sauce, you can add cooked minced parsley, spinach, daikon, or chrysanthemum leaves to the suribachi when combining the miso, sake, and sugar. (See page 94 for this technique.) Sauce can also be colored red (with beets) or any other color you wish (with a minced vegetable or food coloring).

STRING BEANS WITH TOFU DRESSING SHIRA-AE

Yield: 8 servings

Crumbled tofu serves as the base for a flavorsome and nutritious dressing—similar to a white sauce—to toss with vegetables.

4 pounds string beans
2 tablespoons plus 1 teaspoon vinegar

COOKED TOFU SAUCE
1 ¾-pound cake *tofu,* sliced and placed on paper towels to drain off excess liquid
¼ cup *mirin*
2 tablespoons *sake*
2 tablespoons soy sauce

Trim ends off string beans and cut into 3-inch lengths. Cook in boiling water to which you have added 1 teaspoon vinegar. Allow liquid to return to a boil and cook for a few minutes, just until tender. Immediately drain and add ice cubes to cool.

For the tofu sauce: Mash tofu with a wooden

spoon or push through a sieve. Place tofu in a saucepan with the mirin, sake, and soy sauce. Cook over low heat for a few minutes, stirring. Allow the sauce to cool to room temperature.

Prior to serving, toss string beans with the remaining 2 tablespoons vinegar. Drain off any excess vinegar. Toss string beans with tofu sauce.

NAPPA CABBAGE WITH GOMA SAUCE

Yield: 4 to 8 servings

This sesame seed–based dressing makes a very aromatic and tasty sauce to be spooned over cabbage bundles. It is also excellent on broiled eggplant or green peppers and on blanched spinach, cucumbers, green beans, asparagus, or celery. Try combining a few of your favored cooked vegetables with this dressing.

1 medium head nappa cabbage (about 1½ pounds)

GOMA SAUCE

¼ cup sesame seeds, toasted
1 teaspoon sugar (or more to taste)
1 tablespoon *sake*
2 tablespoons vinegar
1 tablespoon *dashi*

Separate cabbage leaves and wash. Bring a large pot of water to a boil. Add cabbage leaves, the hard bottom and bigger ones first, pushing them into the water as the hard part is lightly cooked and adding the tender, smaller leaves last. Return water to a boil. Cooking time will be about 8 minutes. When the water has returned to a boil and the cabbage leaves are tender, remove with chopsticks, rinse in cold water, and drain thoroughly.

When cabbage is cool enough to handle, place a few leaves (about 3 to 4) together in your hands and carefully squeeze out excess water. At the same time, shape cabbage leaves into small bundles, similar to tiny heads of cabbage. Place cabbage bundles on a serving platter and top with spoonfuls of goma sauce.

For goma sauce: Place toasted seeds in a suribachi and grind for a few minutes. Add sugar and grind together. Add sake, vinegar, and dashi; mix thoroughly. Spoon sauce over vegetables.

SPINACH WITH SESAME DRESSING

Yield: 4 to 8 servings

Sesame seeds, mixed with soy sauce, mirin, and dashi, make a wonderful dressing for any vegetable —most traditionally, spinach, cucumbers, and green beans.

2 bunches spinach (about 1¾ to 2 pounds), washed and trimmed, only tender stems retained
1 tablespoon vinegar

SESAME DRESSING

3 tablespoons sesame seeds, toasted
¼ cup soy sauce
2 tablespoons *mirin*
2 tablespoons *dashi*
Sugar (optional)

Bring a large pot of water to a rapid boil and add the spinach and vinegar. Stir with chopsticks. Cook for only a few seconds, then remove and drain thoroughly.

Place toasted seeds in suribachi and grind to open the seeds, but do not grind enough to make a paste. Mix the seeds with soy sauce, mirin, dashi, and sugar, if desired, to taste.

Place drained spinach on a serving platter. Top with sesame sauce and serve. Or you may hold dish at room temperature for later serving.

SIMPLE SALT-PICKLED SALAD VEGETABLES

Yield: 4 servings

A simple salt-pickled vegetable medley can be ready to eat after half an hour. Or if time allows, let the vegetables pickle for several hours for the flavors to mingle further. Serve these with your meal as a condiment or a side dish. Other vegetables can be processed in a similar method. This is excellent for greens and cabbage.

½ pound red radishes, trimmed (some leaves left on)
1 turnip (approximately ½ pound), peeled
½ pound *daikon,* peeled
½ pound cucumbers
2 tablespoons salt (or to taste)

Coarsely chop radishes and finely chop their leaves. Slice turnips and daikon into thin circles, then cut into quarters. If using European-style cucumbers, simply slice and quarter like the turnip. Other cucumbers will have to be peeled and seeded. Combine all vegetables in a large, fairly low glass, porcelain, or plastic container. Sprinkle with salt. Using your hands, massage salt into the vegetables and set aside. In 30 minutes, drain off all the water that rises. You can serve pickles immediately or allow them to pickle further. If setting aside for later use, place a sheet of wax paper on top of vegetables and weight them down. Keep at room temperature for several hours, checking liquid as it rises, occasionally draining it off. You can enjoy the salt-pickled vegetables as they are, or if you find them too salty, simply rinse in cold water and drain in a colander; dry with paper towels.

MISO TSUKEMONO

Yield: 4 to 6 servings

When miso is used as a pickling agent, it can be compared to a continually replenished sourdough starter. As you remove pungent pickled vegetables from the bed, you replace them with fresh vegetables. Generally, small portions of miso tsukemono are served as a condiment or small accompaniment.

MISO PICKLING SAUCE

½ cup *miso* (your choice)
⅓ cup sugar
¼ cup *sake*
3 tablespoons salt
2 tablespoons vinegar

1 pound assorted raw vegetables, trimmed and sliced (for example, cucumbers, *daikon,* and radishes might be combined)

Combine miso pickling sauce ingredients and place in wide crock. Then add prepared vegetables to the sauce and spoon sauce over top. Place several layers of plastic wrap in crock to top vegetables and weight down with a foil-wrapped brick or other heavy object. Refrigerate for a minimum of 24 hours before tasting. As you consume pickled vegetables, add more sliced vegetables (try green pepper and cauliflower) and miso. Continue the process.

To serve, you may wish to wipe off miso and chop pickled vegetables into small pieces.

SUKI'S KIM CHEE

Yield: 6 to 8 servings

Kim chee recipes, featuring pickled cabbage, demonstrate a Korean influence upon Japanese cuisine.

1 large head cabbage
1 to 2 tablespoons salt
2 cloves garlic, crushed
1 teaspoon finely chopped ginger
2 green onions, finely chopped
2 small raw oysters, finely chopped (optional)

3 tablespoons powdered red pepper (or to taste)
Additional salt

Wash cabbage leaves, discarding hard center core, and cut to 2-inch to 4-inch pieces. Place in a large bowl with 1 to 2 tablespoons salt for 1 hour, turning cabbage over after 30 minutes. Wash cabbage again and drain thoroughly.

Return cabbage to bowl and add garlic, ginger, green onions, optional oysters, and red pepper. Salt to taste. Chill and serve.

FRIED LOTUS ROOT

Yield: 4 servings

I find renkon (lotus root) to be the most interesting of all Japanese vegetables, as hidden under the rootlike surface is a beautiful flowerlike vegetable. Purchase long roots with fair skins. When you peel them, be careful not to go too deep, or you will cut through the canals. Crisp-fried lotus root will remind you of fried potato slices, but the flavor and shape are more interesting. Lotus root slices are also excellent simmered in a seasoned stock or cooked in su water and then soaked in a vinegared dressing.

½ pound lotus root
***Su* water**
¼ to ⅓ cup potato starch (or cornstarch or flour)
Oil for deep frying
Salt (optional)

Wash lotus root and carefully peel the rough outer skin with a vegetable peeler. Slice very thinly and soak in su water to cover for 1 hour, changing the water once or twice.

Remove from su water, rinse, and pat dry. Dust slices with potato starch. Deep fry in hot oil, a third at a time. Drain on paper towels and salt, if desired.

Note: Lotus root can also be fried without a coating. The addition of the starch gives it a lovely color and texture.

GLAZED BELL PEPPERS

Yield: About 10 servings

When I serve glazed bell peppers at a dinner party, newcomers to Japanese cuisine are always impressed with how tasty these vegetables are. They will make an excellent addition to your next buffet.

5 bell peppers (about 3 pounds), halved and seeded
3 tablespoons cooking oil
Knob of ginger, peeled and sliced thinly
4 teaspoons soy sauce
½ teaspoon sugar
Salt to taste

Cut peppers into thick slices, about 12 per pepper. Using a large skillet, heat oil and add the ginger. Stir ginger around for about 1 minute to flavor the oil. Add the peppers, stirring to coat them with the oil, for about a minute. Pour out any excess oil. Add the soy sauce, stirring to coat for another minute. Add the sugar and salt, and stir again. The peppers must cook quickly so that they remain firm. Serve hot or at room temperature.

KIMPIRA GOBO, CARROT, AND CELERY

Yield: 4 servings

An excellent vegetable dish is the combination of the woodsy burdock with carrots and celery. Serve this with a traditional Japanese dinner or as an accompaniment to an American dinner, such as roasted chicken.

6 ounces (3 medium stalks) burdock (*gobo*)
2 tablespoons vinegar
1 large carrot (about 8 ounces)
2 stalks celery (about 8 ounces)
1 tablespoon cooking oil
2 tablespoons soy sauce
2 tablespoons *mirin*
1 tablespoon sugar
Cayenne or chili powder (optional)

Scrub burdock very well and immediately place in a bowl of cold water. Take 1 stalk at a time and slice it into thin, matchstick-size juliennes, about 2 to 3 inches long. Return juliennes to water and repeat process until all burdock is properly sliced. Drain and add fresh water. Pour in 1 tablespoon vinegar. Repeat process in about 15 minutes. Allow burdock to soak about ½ hour.

Peel (or scrub) carrot and slice into thin, matchstick-size juliennes. Wash celery and slice in the same manner.

Drain burdock and combine with the carrots and celery.

Heat oil in a large skillet. Add the vegetables, stirring to coat with the oil. Add the soy sauce, mirin, and sugar. Stir through and simmer about 5 minutes, or until vegetables are tender but still crisp. This recipe will cook faster and more evenly if you are using a dropped lid (see page 33).

For a spicy touch, season to taste with chili powder or cayenne. Serve warm, at room temperature, or chilled.

Note: This recipe will yield more than 4 servings if it is one of many dishes for bento lunch.

FLAVORED SHIITAKE

Yield: 4 to 8 servings

Try serving this recipe as an appetizer (zensai) at your next dinner party.

5 to 10 large dried *shiitake*
⅓ cup *sake*
⅓ cup soy sauce
1 tablespoon sugar

Cover dried mushrooms with warm water and let soak for several hours, preferably 24. To cook, bring mushrooms with soaking liquid to a boil, then slightly reduce heat and continue to cook until all water is absorbed. Add sake, soy sauce, and sugar; stir well to mix ingredients. Continue to cook until all flavorings are absorbed. Let mushrooms cool to handle. Remove center core, if desired. If mushrooms are bite size, serve whole. If they are large, slice into thick strips, about 3 to 4 per mushroom. Serve as hors d'oeuvres.

QUICK-SAUTEED SPECIAL MUSHROOMS

Yield: 4 to 8 servings

The very rare, delicious, and expensive matsutake is a special treat. You may be a little more familiar with the dried variety. During the fall months, these mushrooms are available fresh at many oriental markets. Another mushroom available fresh during these months is the unusual—and less expensive—shimen. For a very special side dish, offer your guests the two mushrooms sauteed together.

¼ pound (2) *matsutake* (or other fresh mushrooms)
1 pound *shimen*
1 teaspoon cooking oil
1 tablespoon soy sauce
1 tablespoon *mirin*
Sugar (optional)

Carefully clean matsutake. (I use a damp mushroom brush.) Trim off only the very bottom. Cut mushrooms in halves or quarters. Clean shimen, cutting off and discarding the root end. Separate these mushrooms.

In a large skillet, heat the oil and add the mushrooms. Stir to coat the mushrooms with the oil. Add soy sauce and mirin and stir through until well coated. Add sugar, if desired, and stir through.

Variation: For a very simple and delicious matsutake recipe, marinate these mushrooms in equal parts soy sauce and mirin. At serving time, quickly grill or broil mushrooms until they are browned and cooked through.

ROLLED KOMBU WITH CARROTS

Yield: 4 to 6 servings

Two simple ingredients, carrots and kombu, make an excellent side dish or appetizer. Serve these with your favorite dipping sauce.

1 large sheet *kombu* (about 5 by 10 inches)
1 large carrot (about 6 ounces)

Soften kombu in a plate with water to cover for 30 to 60 minutes. During this time it will become larger and more pliable. Cut into 5-inch squares. Rinse and pat dry.

Cut carrot into thick juliennes, about 5 inches long. Parboil juliennes in water to soften for about 5 to 8 minutes. Refresh with cold water.

Place carrot juliennes (about 5) at one end of each piece of kombu. Roll up, then cut in half crosswise. Place on a serving dish, seam side down. You can secure these rolls with toothpicks.

Serve with your choice of dipping sauce, such as ponzu, miso, or tofu.

Variation: Other vegetables can also be used with the carrots, including celery, asparagus, or daikon.

FRIED MOUNTAIN POTATOES

Yield: 4 servings

If you're a lover of fried potatoes, you will especially enjoy these Japanese potatoes.

1½ pounds mountain potatoes, peeled and sliced into thick juliennes, about 2 to 3 inches in length
***Su* water**
Salt
Oil for deep frying

Because mountain potatoes are very slimy, they must be soaked in su water and salt water before cooking. The first (su water) soaking should be about 15 to 20 minutes: place potato slices in a pot of water to cover, to which you have added about 2 tablespoons vinegar. For the next 1 or 2 soakings, use salt water. Rinse and dry potatoes.

To cook: Heat a pot of cooking oil for deep frying. Fry potatoes in batches, draining on paper towels. Cooking time is 8 to 10 minutes. Salt to taste.

DASHI-SAKE COOKED SATO IMO

Yield: 4 to 8 servings

On special occasions, Japanese field potatoes are cooked in dashi and sake and served as a most impressive side course. Leftovers are ideal for the following day's bento lunches. These cooked potatoes can also be added to other one-pot-style recipes.

1 pound *sato imo*, peeled and soaked in *su* water*
2½ cups *dashi*

1¼ cups *sake*
2 tablespoons soy sauce

Green onions and/or *nori,* thinly sliced, for garnish

*Peel hairy skin off the small potatoes and soak in su water. Change the water about 3 to 4 times in the period of 1 hour. Wash and dry.

Place potatoes in a pot with 2 cups dashi and 1 cup sake. Bring liquid to a boil, then slightly reduce the heat and cook the potatoes for 30 minutes. (The potatoes should be completely covered by liquid; as necessary, add remaining dashi and sake.) Near the end of the cooking, add the soy sauce. Continue to cook another 5 to 10 minutes. Remove from liquid and serve. If desired, generously garnish with thinly sliced green onions and/or nori.

CANDIED JAPANESE SWEET POTATOES

Yield: 4 to 8 servings

On the outside, Japanese sweet potatoes (yams) look very much like American sweet potatoes. But on the inside they're much lighter in color, resembling yams. Handle them as you would an American yam. Sweetened, they are popular as a New Year's Day buffet recipe, and are also traditionally served on special celebrations and birthdays. You might even serve these for a sweet snack or dessert.

1 pound Japanese sweet potatoes
Salt

SUGAR SYRUP
½ cup sugar
½ cup water

Black sesame seeds, for garnish (optional)

Peel potatoes and slice them into large chunks. Soak in salted cold water for several hours (or a minimum of 30 minutes), changing the salt water several times. Place in boiling salted water and cook until tender, about 10 minutes; drain.

In a saucepan, make a sugar syrup by bringing the sugar and water to a boil, then reducing the heat to a simmer. Cook until golden, about 7 minutes. Add cooked potatoes to the syrup; stir. Place in a serving bowl. Garnish, if desired, with black sesame seeds.

Note: These potatoes can be made in advance and served either at room temperature or chilled.

PARTY VEGETABLE MIXTURE

Yield: 6 to 8 servings

Try simmering a mixture of Japanese vegetables for your next dinner party side dish. If you wish to extend this recipe to a one-pot main dish, you can add a number of ingredients, such as peeled, hard-cooked eggs, cooked chicken, pork, fish, or beef.

½ pound *sato imo,* peeled (or substitute small new potatoes)
Salted water
1 teaspoon vinegar
1 10-ounce package *konnyaku*
3 large carrots, scraped
1 large fresh bamboo shoot (or canned whole or 1 cup sliced)
10 small *shiitake,* soaked in warm water for minimum of 30 minutes, preferably 24 hours, drained
1 tablespoon cooking oil
1 cup chicken stock or *dashi*
3 tablespoons soy sauce
2 tablespoons *mirin*
Sugar (optional)

Soak potatoes for 30 minutes in cold salted water. Then boil in water to cover, to which you have added the vinegar. Cook for 10 minutes, rinse, and drain.

Slice konnyaku and braid (see page 44). Place in a dry skillet over high heat, cooking for 3 to 5 minutes to dry out.

Cut carrots thickly into ½-inch to ¾-inch slices. Cut these slices into decorative shapes (try vegetable cutters to make flowers). Place carrots in a pot of boiling water and boil 5 minutes. Drain.

Rinse fresh bamboo shoot in cold water and cut irregularly. Cook in boiling water about 1 minute; drain.

Remove hard center core from mushrooms.

Pour a thin film of oil into a medium pot and add the carrots and mushrooms. Cook for 5 minutes over low heat, stirring occasionally. Add bamboo shoots and konnyaku, stirring. If necessary, add more oil. Add cooked potatoes, stirring everything together. Add the stock and cook over low heat for 15 minutes. Add soy sauce, mirin, and sugar (if desired) and cook another 10 minutes, stirring occasionally.

For additional salad and vegetable recipes, see:

Sashimi and Sushi
- Chirashi-Zushi
- Vinegared Ginger Slices
- Red Maple Radish

Tofu and Miso
- Bean Curd and Vegetable Salad
- Vegetables with Tofu and Miso Dressing

Grilled, Broiled, Barbecued, and Pan-Fried Foods
- Teppan Yaki
- Pan-Fried Slivered Gobo and Carrot

Steamed and Simmered Foods
- Steamed Pumpkin with Chicken, Vegetables, and Egg Custard
- Steamed Chicken and Tofu Stuffed Cabbage Rolls
- Ground Pork and Pumpkin Nimono
- Simmered Pork and Vegetables
- Soy-Braised Yam Cake
- Japanese Pork Loin Roast and Vegetables
- Winter Nimono

Tempura and Other Deep-Fried Foods
- Fluffy-Fried Chicken and Vegetable Bundles
- Tori Tempura Kushi

Rice and Noodles
- Rice with Fresh Peas
- Rice with Shrimp and Vegetables
- Beans and Rice, Japanese Style
- Ground Meat and Tofu with Vegetables Donburi
- Soba with Zucchini and Mushrooms
- Chilled Noodles with Cucumbers and Mushrooms
- Kudzu Noodles with Peas

Desserts, Confections, and Sweet Snacks
- Sweetened Red Beans
- Yokan

TOFU AND MISO

I have already gone into depth about the importance of tofu and miso to Japanese cookery, and in the Ingredients chapter I discussed the different varieties, their varied uses, and their requirements for preparation.

Entire cookbooks, both Japanese and American, have been dedicated to tofu and to miso. The first Japanese *Book of Tofu,* written in 1782, contains about a hundred tofu recipes. There are even cookbooks dedicated entirely to the subject of miso soup.

Tofu and miso first came to Japan via the Chinese Buddhist priests during the seventh and eighth centuries. It is believed the first Japanese tofu shops were located within the temples and operated by the religious leaders. In the early introductory days, tofu and miso were the foods of the nobility. As the Zen dietary laws were strictly enforced, tofu and miso became more available and were accepted by the common people. By the fourteenth century, tofu and miso were prepared on a daily basis for everyday cookery (katei ryori) as well as the honored tea ceremony cookery (kaiseki ryori) and Zen Temple cookery (shojin ryori).

Today, in twentieth-century Japan, 90 percent of all tofu is used in three basic recipes, of which the greatest use is seen in miso soup. It has been reported that practically three-fourths of the population start their day with a bowl of miso soup.

MISO-SHIRU WITH WAKAME AND TOFU

Yield: 4 servings

In America, we might associate mother's homemade chicken soup, spaghetti sauce, or chocolate chip cookies as symbols of her love and attention to the family. In Japan, miso soup is this symbolic cornerstone of affection. Some rural homemakers always keep a pot of miso on the back burner.

3 cups *dashi*
1 tablespoon soy sauce
3 ounces reconstituted *wakame* (with no hard parts), cut up
½ cake *tofu,* sliced horizontally and drained, then cut into 1-inch squares
3 tablespoons *miso,* softened in ¼ cup *dashi*
1 green onion, thinly sliced, for garnish

In a medium pot, bring the dashi and soy sauce to a boil, then reduce to a simmer and cook for a few minutes. Add the wakame and tofu and continue to simmer for 5 minutes. Stir in the diluted miso and simmer another 1 to 2 minutes. Ladle soup into cups. Garnish with green onion.

PAN-FRIED TOFU

Yield: 2 to 4 servings

One of the simplest and tastiest ways to serve cooked tofu is to quickly pan fry it and garnish with soy sauce, goma, and green onions. These make an excellent breakfast dish (instead of eggs), snack, side dish, or vegetarian entree.

1 cake *tofu,* sliced in half horizontally and vertically, resulting in 4 slices
1 tablespoon cooking oil
1½ tablespoons soy sauce
1 teaspoon toasted sesame seeds
1 green onion, thinly sliced

Dry out tofu on paper towels for about 20 minutes. Slice drained tofu into triangles; you should have 8 equal pieces.

Heat oil in a skillet and add half the tofu; pan fry a few seconds until golden, then flip over and pan fry the other sides. Remove tofu with slotted spoon to a serving platter. Pan fry remaining tofu.

Lightly pour soy sauce over all tofu. Sprinkle with sesame seeds and green onion. Serve immediately.

Variation: Since "raw" tofu is a popular snack and summer food in Japan, follow the same instructions as above, eliminating the pan frying.

FRIED TOFU WITH SEASONED SAUCE

Yield: 4 to 8 servings

By dipping tofu squares in a batter before frying, you get a lovely outer crust. Then simmer the cooked tofu in this well-seasoned sauce for a most flavorsome dish.

1 20-ounce carton *tofu,* drained and cut into ½-inch thick slices
2 eggs
2 tablespoons flour
1 teaspoon cold water
Oil for deep frying
½ cup *dashi* (or chicken or vegetable stock)
1 tablespoon soy sauce
½ tablespoon ginger, grated
½ teaspoon sugar

2 tablespoons green onions, chopped, for garnish

Powdered red pepper (optional garnish)

Cut tofu into 1-inch squares and dry between layers of paper towels.

Combine the eggs, flour, and water to make a batter. Batter should be barely mixed—somewhat lumpy rather than smooth. (See page 123 for further instructions on batter.)

In a deep pot, heat oil. Fry tofu several pieces at a time, turning to brown all sides. Remove to a wire rack to drain off excess oil. Repeat process until all tofu is fried.

In a large skillet, place the dashi, soy sauce, ginger, and sugar. Heat to dissolve the sugar. Place fried tofu in the skillet, spooning sauce on top. Simmer for a few seconds. Place seasoned tofu on a serving platter. Garnish with green onions and, if desired, red pepper.

DEEP-FRIED TOFU

Yield: 4 to 8 servings

Deep-fried small squares of tofu make excellent party hors d'oeuvres. Should you wish to serve them as a first course or luncheon dish, you may prefer to cut them into larger squares or triangles. You can eat them hot with a simple garnish or accompany them with a variety of dipping sauces.

1 20-ounce container *tofu,* drained
¼ cup flour (or potato starch or cornstarch)
Oil for deep frying

GARNISHES
White or black sesame seeds, toasted
Powdered red pepper
Thinly sliced green onion tops
Grated ginger
Grated *daikon*
Crumbled *nori*

Soy sauce
Dab of reconstituted *wasabi*

Slice tofu cakes in half and then into 1-inch squares; you will have approximately 32 squares. Place tofu squares on paper towels and top with towel; set aside to dry out for at least 20 minutes.

Lightly dust tofu with flour (or other coating). Heat oil for deep frying (350° to 375° F.). Add a few squares of tofu at a time, and fry until crisp and golden on all sides. Use a pair of chopsticks to turn tofu around in the hot oil. Drain fried tofu on a wire rack over paper towels. Continue process with remaining tofu. Serve immediately.

Sprinkle fried tofu with your choice of garnishes. Serve soy sauce and wasabi on the side. Instead of garnishes, dipping sauces may be preferred. Try: citrus-soy dipping sauce (page 58), sesame-soy dipping sauce (page 58), ponzu sauce (page 113), namasu goma dressing (page 79), steamed cauliflower with miso sauce (page 81), miso-dengaku sauce (page 82), goma sauce (page 83), sesame dressing (page 83).

TOFU DENGAKU

Yield: 6 servings

Dengaku is a type of recipe in which the main ingredient is skewered, broiled, brushed with miso, and then briefly rebroiled. In Japan, many restaurants specialize in dengaku, and I find that in major American cities, dengaku specialty houses are growing in popularity. Well-drained tofu or vegetables, such as eggplant and zucchini, are perfect; or you might want to try grilling fish or chicken. You can use your favorite flavor of miso for the coating. If desired, you can color it with the addition of pureed vegetables. I have used parsley to color and garnish the miso topping. In Japan, sansho leaves, which are difficult to obtain in America, are used. Remember, when using bamboo skewers for broiling, soaking them overnight in lightly salted water will prevent them from burning.

1 15-ounce container *tofu,* drained

GREEN MISO PASTE

1 cup parsley leaves

2 tablespoons white *miso*

Additional parsley leaves, for garnish

With a sharp knife, carefully cut tofu into rectangles, approximately ½-inch thick and 3 inches by 2 inches; you should have about 12 rectangles. Place tofu on paper towels and top with towels. Weight down with a plate. Set aside for 1 hour, changing the paper towels as they become soaked with liquid.

After tofu has drained, horizontally pierce each rectangle with two skewers (tofu will resemble a lollipop); set aside. Even without skewers you can still proceed: When it is time to turn over and remove tofu, use a spatula.

To make the paste: Cook parsley leaves in boiling water for 1 minute to soften. Drain, rinse in cold water, then squeeze out excess liquid through the palms of your hands. Using a food processor, blender, or suribachi, puree parsley leaves with the miso to make a green paste. You will have about ⅓ cup to ½ cup dengaku sauce.

Place tofu under a broiler and brown on first side, about 3 to 5 minutes. Flip to second side and brown another 3 minutes. Spread dengaku sauce on top and return to broiler. Heat through and remove. Garnish with a few additional parsley leaves.

MISO-GRILLED TOFU CUTLETS

Yield: 1 to 2 servings

Tofu cutlets can be sliced in half horizontally and then grilled with miso for open-faced sandwiches, Japanese style.

1 *tofu* cutlet (5-ounce package)

3 to 4 teaspoons light *miso*

¼ teaspoon toasted sesame seeds

Carefully cut tofu cutlet in half horizontally. Remove interior carefully (a grapefruit spoon is helpful), and discard or save for another recipe (see note below). Pat insides dry with paper towels.

Spread miso on the insides. If desired, cut each half into quarters to make bite-size pieces.

Place on Japanese stove-top broiler to toast the bottoms for a few seconds, or place in a dry skillet over medium heat for a few seconds. Remove and sprinkle with toasted sesame seeds.

Variation: Cutlet halves can be broiled and then placed on top of one another, sandwich style. The outside can then be sprinkled with sesame seeds. Other good fillings are pieces of cooked fish—or even peanut butter and jelly.

Note: If you want to save the inside of the tofu cutlet, you should dry it out. Place on paper towels or in a triple wrapping of dampened cheesecloth, and squeeze through the palms of your hands. You will have about ½ cup.

BEAN CURD AND VEGETABLE SALAD

Yield: 4 to 8 servings

Deep-fried tofu cakes, cubes, and triangles (atsu-age or nama-age) may appear hard and dark on the outside, but inside you'll find them soft and light colored. First, douse them in boiling water and wipe with paper towels to rid of excess oil. Then add them to your favorite recipe, particularly this one for a vegetable salad with soy-sesame dressing.

2 to 3 carrots, scraped

3 celery stalks

¼ cup reconstituted *wakame*

1 5-ounce *tofu* cutlet, doused in boiling water and wiped dry

SOY-SESAME DRESSING

1 tablespoon soy sauce

2 teaspoons sesame oil
1 tablespoon *dashi*
½ teaspoon sugar

Cut carrots, celery, wakame, and tofu cutlet into similar matchstick-size juliennes. In separate pots, parboil the carrots and celery for a few seconds; drain and immediately rinse with cold water and ice to set the color and stop the cooking procedure. Drain and dry. Combine the vegetables, wakame, and tofu in a serving bowl.

Mix together the dressing ingredients, stirring until the sugar has dissolved. Pour dressing over vegetables. Toss and serve.

Note: For an interesting texture and color, you can add a garnish of black sesame seeds.

BEEF AND RICE STUFFED TOFU POUCHES

Yield: 3 to 4 servings

Once you have worked with deep-fried tofu pouches, you will think of dozens of uses. As for other fried tofu, you should first douse or parboil to rid them of excess oil. Experiment with your favorite ingredients—raw or cooked—for other stuffings.

1 1½-ounce package *tofu* pouches (6 pouches)

BEEF AND RICE STUFFING
¼ pound ground beef
1 tablespoon finely chopped onion
Cooking oil
Salt and pepper
2 to 3 tablespoons cooked white rice

SEASONING LIQUID
2 cups water (or *dashi*)
2 tablespoons soy sauce
2 tablespoons *mirin*
1 teaspoon sugar

With a sharp knife, carefully open one end of each pouch. Place in a small pot of boiling water and continue to boil about 5 minutes, pressing tofu pouches under the water and against the sides of the pot to help rid them of excess oil. Drain and cool; squeeze out excess liquid through the palms of your hands.

To make the stuffing, saute beef and onions (add cooking oil if necessary; this will depend upon the fat content of the beef). Cook for a few minutes until they have browned. Season to taste with salt and pepper. Add the rice and stir through to combine ingredients. Place stuffing on paper towels to drain off excess oil. Cool stuffing enough to handle.

Divide stuffing evenly into 6 portions—about 2 to 3 teaspoonfuls per pouch. Carefully stuff each pouch with the mixture, and then close and secure tops of pouches with toothpicks (or tie them with reconstituted kanpyo).

In a saucepan, combine the seasoning-liquid ingredients; bring to a simmer. Place tofu pouches in liquid and cook at a simmer for about 20 minutes, basting tops with the liquid. You will see the pouches puff up beautifully.

Serve warm or at room temperature.

VEGETABLES WITH TOFU AND MISO DRESSING

Yield: 4 to 8 servings

Crumbled tofu combined with miso makes an excellent base as a dressing for vegetables, cooked or raw. Serve this as a summer vegetarian main dish, as a first course, or as a side dish.

¼ pound string beans, blanched and thinly sliced into 2-inch juliennes
2 carrots, peeled and thinly sliced into 2-inch juliennes

8 large nappa cabbage leaves (about 1 pound), hard stem ends trimmed off and leaves thinly sliced horizontally, about 2-inch lengths
8 dried *shiitake,* soaked 24 hours, hard center core removed, squeezed dry of excess liquid, and sliced into matchstick-size juliennes
¼ cup soy sauce
1 teaspoon sugar (or to taste)
½ teaspoon salt

TOFU-MISO DRESSING
1 10-ounce cake *tofu,* sliced and drained on paper towels
3 tablespoons *miso*
1 tablespoon sugar (or to taste)

Combine all vegetables and place them in a large skillet; add soy sauce. Stir over medium heat, adding the sugar and salt. Cook about 3 minutes, or until the cabbage has wilted. Place in a colander to cool and drain of excess liquid.

Meanwhile, crumble the tofu and mix with the miso and sugar. I find it is best to combine these ingredients in a suribachi rather than in a food processor or blender. If you do not use a suribachi, be careful to avoid overblending so as not to make a paste. The final texture should remain lumpy. Place cooled vegetables in a serving bowl and toss with the tofu-miso dressing.

Variation: An excellent salad can be made by slicing raw vegetables, such as tomatoes, and placing them on small, individual dishes. Then spoon a dollop of tofu-miso dressing in the center and garnish with thinly sliced green onion tops.

MISO-MARINATED CHICKEN WINGS

Yield: 2 to 3 servings

Although traditional Japanese recipes do not specify lengthy marination, I find that soaking chicken wings in a miso-based marinade for several hours or days results in wonderful flavors. You might also try this recipe with fish fillets. Serve these as hors d'oeuvres, a first course, or an entree. Leftovers are excellent for bento lunch or picnics.

6 chicken wings (about 1½ pounds)
½ cut lemon
½ cup *miso*
2 tablespoons *sake*
Dash of additional soy sauce and *sake*

Rub chicken wings with the lemon. Combine the miso and sake. Spread a little of the thinned miso on the bottom of a glass dish. Top with chicken wings and spread remaining miso all over the wings. Refrigerate and marinate until needed.

Wipe off excess miso from the chicken wings. Place on a broiler tray or a stove-top broiler. Splash a few drops of soy sauce and sake over the chicken. Broil on all sides until done, about 6 minutes per side.

Notes: Recipe can easily be increased. Use a large dish for marinating, so that chicken is in one layer only. If you desire a sweeter flavor, substitute mirin for the sake.

RED SNAPPER PICKLED IN MISO

Yield: 2 to 4 servings

Miso is often used as a pickling agent for vegetables, as well as for fish fillets. This recipe demonstrates an important technique for miso pickling, followed by broiling. Other fish fillets can be used, preferably white or pink-colored fillets. Leftovers are excellent for bento lunch or breakfast protein.

¾ pound snapper fillets, boned and washed

MISO PICKLING SAUCE
½ cup light *miso*

¼ **cup *mirin***
Lemon slices

Wrap each fish fillet separately in a piece of damp cheesecloth. Thin the miso with the mirin. Spread half the sauce on the bottom of a glass dish. Place fish on top and smooth remaining miso sauce over fish. Refrigerate for several days. Remove fish and wipe off miso sauce. Place fish under a broiler or on a stove-top broiler, and broil on both sides, about 3 minutes per side. Time will depend upon the thickness of the fillets.

Serve with lemon slices.

For additional tofu and miso recipes, see:

Soups and Stews
- Tofu Soup
- Miso-Dashi Soup
- Sukiyaki Japanese Style
- Sukiyaki American Style
- Mizutaki
- Shabu-Shabu

Sashimi and Sushi
- Inari (Sushi-Stuffed Tofu Pouches)

Salads and Vegetables
- Pickled Cooked Vegetables and Tofu with Goma Dressing Namasu
- Steamed Cauliflower with Miso Sauces
- Japanese Eggplants in Miso Dressing
- Miso Dengaku Sauce with Daikon
- String Beans with Tofu Dressing Shira-ae
- Miso Tsukemono

Steamed and Simmered Foods
- Steamed Chicken and Tofu-Stuffed Cabbage Rolls

Tempura and Other Deep-Fried Foods
- Tofu-Miso Age

Rice and Noodles
- Ground Meat and Tofu with Vegetables Donburi

GRILLED, BROILED, BARBECUED, AND PAN-FRIED FOODS

One of the most varied categories of Japanese cookery is yakimono—*yaki* meaning "to sear with heat"—as this includes many styles of cooking as well as many diverse ingredients. A number of recipes that fall into this category have already become well accepted on the American table.

Yakimono recipes include grilled, broiled, barbecued, and pan-fried foods. In yakimono, the ingredients are quickly cooked at a high temperature. Practically all foods can be prepared in this style. Most likely you are already familiar with teri*yaki*, teppan*yaki* and suki*yaki*. In sukiyaki, the meat and vegetables are first seared in a hot skillet before seasoned sauce is added. (See Soups and Stews chapter.)

American cooks are very comfortable with yakimono recipes. I find the major difference in our two cuisines is in the manner of seasoning the ingredients. While Americans often use generous amounts of spices, sauces, and marinades, traditional Japanese yakimono recipes call for little advance seasoning. Americans prefer lengthy marination and frequent basting during the final cooking. Japanese recipes, on the other hand, suggest very brief, if any, marinating, and basting is used to glaze foods with a thickened, sweetened soy-based sauce. In the recipes that follow, I have combined the best of both worlds, suggesting seasoning and cooking styles with American preferences in mind. The resulting foods should be somewhat crisp on the outside yet always tender and moist on the inside.

Within the extensive category of yakimono is a major subdivision, shioyaki, meaning salt-grilled. No sauce is used, and salt alone is the seasoning. This is one of the oldest methods of Japanese cookery. Coarse salt (I use sea salt) is generously sprinkled on the food—usually fish or chicken—and then it is put aside for about 30 minutes before final cooking. Shioyaki ingredients are placed under a broiler or over very hot coals, skin side up, until the skin turns a golden brown. Situated under the skin is a layer of fat, which bastes the food as it melts. Shioyaki recipes are accompanied by simple dipping sauces. Sushi bar devotees are probably very familiar with fish cheeks and backs, delicacies that are cooked to order in this manner.

Besides the salt-grilling method, several yakimono recipes feature a brief period of marinating for extra flavoring. This is generally a light coating of soy sauce, sake, and mirin, in which the food marinates for 15 to 30 minutes, or longer if time permits. Sweetened miso is sometimes used as a marinade. The foods are first cut up into bite-size pieces, and it is believed that the seasonings penetrate very quickly because of this uniform size.

Ingredients in yakimono cookery are generally threaded on skewers. This technique keeps the food attractive and aids in the turning, glazing, and serving. Foods are sometimes skewered to attain a special shape. For example, shrimp and lobster are often curled around a skewer; so curved, they are thought to resemble the spine of an old woman and thus symbolize longevity.

One of the most popular skewered and broiled recipes is yakitori. Bite-size pieces of chicken (tori) are laced on skewers. The best parts of the chicken for this dish are the legs, thighs, wings, livers, and skin. Often, vegetables, such as green onions, green peppers, mushrooms, and/or gingko nuts or tofu are added. You can add fish, seafood, or meat to the chicken. The skewered ingredients can be assembled several hours in advance and then grilled at the last minute with a sauce. Yakitori recipes make excellent party appetizers or buffet food, since most of the work can be completed prior to your guests' arrival.

One of the most Americanized of all Japanese recipes is teriyaki. The sweet sauce has become so noted throughout our country that even fast-food restaurants sell their versions of teriyaki burgers. Bottled and dehydrated teriyaki sauces and marinades are easily obtainable at local markets. In America, *teriyaki* has come to refer to food that is marinated for several hours or days and then barbecued, grilled, or broiled. In Japan, however, teriyaki originally represented a type of sweetened soy sauce–based glaze that is brushed on foods as a final touch.

SALTED TROUT SHIOYAKI

Yield: 4 servings

The basic technique used in this salted trout recipe can be adapted to other whole fish.

4 small, pan-size trout
2 to 4 tablespoons salt (preferably coarse salt)

SHIOYAKI DIPPING SAUCE
½ cup *dashi*
2 tablespoons soy sauce
¼ cup vinegar
Chopped scallions, for garnish

Wash trout and pat dry. Salt heavily and let sit for 30 minutes. Prior to cooking, resalt trout, massaging salt into the skin and under the fins. Skewer trout, using three small oiled metal or wet bamboo skewers per fish. Skewers will aid you to turn the fish as well as to keep the trout from curling. Broil or barbecue about 3 minutes per side, or until barely done. Serve with sauce. To make shioyaki dipping sauce: Combine dashi, soy sauce, and vinegar in a saucepan; heat to reduce by half. If you prefer a sweeter sauce, add sugar to taste. Garnish sauce with chopped scallions.

SALMON SHIOYAKI

Yield: 3 to 4 servings

When you rub your fish or chicken with salt and lemon juice before broiling, the resulting dish is especially fresh and tender.

1½ pounds salmon parts (necks, collars)*
2 teaspoons salt (preferably coarse salt)
¼ cup fresh lemon juice
2 tablespoons *sake* (optional)

*Salmon parts can be purchased at most oriental fish markets. Ask your local fishmonger to save these parts for you. If not available, be sure to try other parts of fish, such as fillets.

Place salmon parts on a platter and sprinkle with salt, lemon juice, and sake. Massage marinade into salmon and let rest for 30 minutes.

Broil salmon, skin side up, for a few minutes, just until the outside becomes crisp and the inside barely flakes.

Variation: For those people who follow a salt-free diet or who prefer the taste of lemon to salt, reduce the salt and increase the lemon juice to taste (the dish will then be called salmon lemon yaki). Season this dish to taste with grated fresh ginger. (Chicken breasts can be marinated and cooked in the same manner.)

BROILED BREAKFAST FISH

Yield: 2 to 4 servings

Fish for breakfast? At first, this may sound peculiar. But haven't you ever eaten lox and bagels with cream cheese, or smoked whitefish or salted cod? A simple Japanese-style breakfast can feature broiled, salted, half-dried aji (Spanish mackerel), steamed rice, and miso soup. The aji, already cleaned, butterflied and salted, is easily available at most oriental fish markets.

2 salted, half-dried *aji* (approximately 1 pound)
Juice of ¼ lemon
1 teaspoon soy sauce
½ teaspoon toasted sesame seeds, for garnish
Additional soy sauce
Reconstituted *wasabi* (optional)

Wipe aji with a damp paper towel to clean. Place on broiler tray and squeeze lemon juice on top. Allow to sit for 5 minutes. Brush with soy sauce. Place under a broiler for about 1 minute; turn over and brush with soy sauce. Return to broiler for about 1 more minute. The fish should be cooked until it is crisp and parts of the skin begin to blister. Remove from broiler. Garnish with sesame seeds, and serve with additional soy sauce and wasabi, if desired.

SCALLOPS YAKI

Yield: 3 to 6 servings

Skewered and broiled seafood or fish chunks make a fabulous first course. Chicken pieces, liver, beef, pork, or vegetables such as eggplant and zucchini can be added or substituted.

½ pound scallops (or other seafood or bite-size pieces of fish)

YAKI MARINADE

2 tablespoons *sake*
1 tablespoon lemon juice
½ teaspoon soy sauce

YAKI BASTING SAUCE (Special *Tare*)

2 tablespoons soy sauce
2 tablespoons *sake*
2 tablespoons *mirin*

1 tablespoon lemon juice
2 Japanese green onions (about ½ pound), trimmed of excess green stems
1 green pepper, halved and seeded (or 6 Japanese green peppers)

Place scallops in a bowl with marinade ingredients. Mix well with your fingers and massage sauce into the scallops. Set aside for 30 minutes.

In a saucepan, combine the yaki basting sauce ingredients. Bring to a boil, then reduce about one-third, or until thickened.

Slice each green onion into fourths. Cut each green pepper half in thirds; you will have 6 thick slices. Using metal or bamboo skewers, attractively pierce scallops, onions, and green peppers. Broil or grill, basting with sauce and turning until all ingredients have browned nicely, for about 5 to 8 minutes.

Note: Japanese green onions are considerably longer and thicker than scallions and are very mild. If substituting scallions, you will need at least 8; slice scallions in half crosswise.

YAKITORI CHICKEN LIVERS AND SCALLIONS

Yield: 4 appetizers; 2 main dishes

Yakitori chicken livers make a perfect party appetizer or a delicious main dish to serve along with Japanese rice and peas. Another time, try substituting other vegetables for the scallions. Try beef, pork, or fish instead of the chicken.

½ pound chicken livers
4 medium scallions, firm part only, sliced into about 3-inch lengths

YAKITORI BASTING SAUCE 2

¼ cup soy sauce
1 tablespoon lemon juice
1 tablespoon *mirin*
Dash sugar

Grated *daikon* and grated ginger

Place chicken livers in a pot of boiling water for a few seconds. This will firm up the livers so you can easily skewer them along with the scallions. Intersperse livers and scallions on skewers. Combine basting sauce ingredients. You can use them as is, or you can heat them in a saucepan to thicken slightly. Brush livers and scallions with sauce. Place under broiler (or on stove-top broiler) and cook, about 2 to 3 minutes per side, basting with sauce.

Serve with grated daikon and grated fresh ginger as condiments.

BASIC GLAZING SAUCE

Yield: About ¾ cup

It is helpful to keep a container of this basic glazing sauce always handy in your refrigerator. I use it for chicken, game birds such as doves, and fish. It's marvelous with eel!

½ cup soy sauce
¼ cup *mirin*
¼ cup *sake*
1½ tablespoons sugar (or to taste)

Combine ingredients in a saucepan and bring to a boil. Slightly lower heat and cook for about 10 minutes, stirring often, until sugar has dissolved. Reduce liquid by almost one-half.

SIMPLE BASTING SAUCE

Yield: ½ to ¾ cup

Since mirin can often be substituted for sake and sugar, you will find this basting sauce a snap to make. Use a nonstick pot, since the sauce becomes very thick and sticky as the liquid evaporates. Try this when broiling or barbecuing fish. It's also excellent as a dipping sauce for grilled vegetables.

½ cup soy sauce
½ cup *mirin*

Bring soy sauce and mirin to a boil in a saucepan. Slightly lower heat and continue to cook about 3 minutes until the sauce has thickened, stirring occasionally. Allow to cool.

Refrigerate leftovers.

TORI-TAMAGO YAKI (CHICKEN BROILED WITH EGG GLAZE)

Yield: 3 to 4 servings

An egg yolk glaze makes an attractive and nutritious topping for chicken breasts. You might want to experiment with this recipe by substituting thick white fish fillets or your favorite vegetables for the chicken breasts.

1½ pounds boneless whole chicken breasts (3 whole breasts or 6 halves), skin still on
Salt
2 egg yolks
2 teaspoons *mirin*
1 teaspoon *sake*
½ teaspoon soy sauce
1 scallion, finely sliced

Place chicken breasts, skin side up, in one layer on a foil-covered cookie sheet. Pierce breasts well with the tines of a fork and salt them.

In a small mixing bowl, combine the egg yolks, mirin, sake, soy sauce, and a dash of salt.

Place chicken under the broiler for about 5 to 7 minutes, or until a light golden color. With a pastry brush, spread yolk mixture all over the top of the chicken. Return to broiler. Continue to broil another 3 to 5 minutes, or until nicely glazed and golden.

Garnish chicken with scallions and serve. If you wish to serve bite-size pieces, slice very thinly and reshape.

SIMPLE TERIYAKI SAUCE

Yield: 3 cups

It is so easy to make this simple teriyaki sauce that you may never again purchase a bottle of prepared sauce.

1 cup *mirin*
1 cup chicken stock (or dashi)
1 cup soy sauce

In a mixing bowl, combine the mirin, stock, and soy sauce. Pour into a bottle and refrigerate until needed. It will keep for several weeks.

SIMPLE TERIYAKI GLAZE

Yield: About ¼ cup

Using the preceding teriyaki sauce recipe, you can make an excellent glaze to brush on your broiling or barbecuing foods at the last minute.

¼ cup *teriyaki* sauce
1 tablespoon sugar
1 tablespoon dry mustard
2 teaspoons cornstarch, dissolved in 1 tablespoon water

Place a small saucepan over low heat and add all ingredients, stirring constantly until sugar has dissolved and glaze has somewhat thickened. Refrigerate leftovers in a covered container.

AMERICAN-JAPANESE TERIYAKI MARINADE

Yield: About 1½ cups

This is my family's favorite Americanized teriyaki marinade. I faithfully use it on steaks, ribs, or chicken for barbecuing.

1 cup *teriyaki* sauce (homemade or bottled)
½ cup pineapple juice
1 to 2 teaspoons garlic powder (or 1 tablespoon minced fresh garlic)
Dash black pepper

Combine all ingredients, stirring until garlic powder has dissolved.

FLANK STEAK WITH TERIYAKI MARINADE

Yield: 4 servings

The addition of fresh ginger and garlic to this uncooked teriyaki marinade gives a lovely fresh taste to the resulting broiled steak slices. You might also try this with wafer-thin pork chops.

1½ pounds flank steak (or London broil or top sirloin)

UNCOOKED TERIYAKI MARINADE

1 knob ginger, peeled
1 clove garlic
¼ cup soy sauce
1 tablespoon *mirin*
1 teaspoon sugar

Slice flank steak against the grain into about 14 very thin but long slices, similar to those for sukiyaki.

Squeeze the ginger and garlic through a garlic press into a mixing bowl. Add the soy sauce, mirin, and sugar, stirring until sugar has dissolved. Place meat in this bowl and marinate in the refrigerator for several hours.

Bring meat to room temperature and remove from marinade. Place meat on broiler trays (or on hibachi or stove-top broiler). Broil meat about 3 minutes per side.

SPECIAL TERIYAKI FISH

Yield: 4 servings

This is an aromatic way to prepare a family-size fish. Remember to keep the fish whole: According to Japanese legend, a headless fish may bring bad luck.

1 2-pound whole fish (bass, halibut, and rock cod are best)
½ lemon
1 teaspoon grated ginger
Salt and pepper
1 tablespoon thinly sliced ginger
2 scallions, chopped
¼ cup *mirin*
¼ cup soy sauce
2 tablespoons *sake*

TERIYAKI GLAZE

5 tablespoons *mirin*
5 tablespoons soy sauce
2 teaspoons lemon juice
1 teaspoon sugar (or more to taste)

Lemon slices, for garnish

Slit the belly open the full length and thoroughly clean the fish, leaving the fish whole, with head and tail intact. Wash and pat dry. Rub fish inside and out with the cut lemon, grated ginger, and salt and pepper to taste.

Place fish on a sheet of foil and bend foil up a

little to hold in the liquid. Place sliced ginger and chopped scallions in the belly. Pour the mirin, soy sauce, and sake all over the inside and top of the fish. Set aside to marinate for 1 hour.

Combine the glaze ingredients together in a small saucepan. Heat to a boil, stirring, and reduce by half. Set glaze aside to cool.

At cooking time, place fish under broiler or on a barbecue. (Fish can also be steamed in the foil "boat.") Broiling will take about 10 to 15 minutes, varying with the thickness of the fish. A good rule of thumb is to allow 10 minutes per inch thickness of fish. Your fish should be moist and tender, just barely cooked. During the last 5 minutes of broiling, brush fish with glaze inside and out. Remove fish and garnish with lemon slices.

TORIYAKI WITH GOMA SAUCE

Yield: 4 servings

A sauce made of toasted sesame seeds makes an excellent baste for broiled chicken, pork, or fish.

4 chicken breasts (halves), boned

SESAME SEED SAUCE

¼ cup toasted sesame seeds
2 tablespoons soy sauce
¼ cup *sake*
1 tablespoon *mirin*

Lemon slices (optional)

Place chicken on broiler tray. Grind toasted sesame seeds in a suribachi or mortar and pestle to open them slightly and release the flavor. Combine seeds with soy sauce, sake, and mirin. Brush sauce over chicken and let rest for 30 minutes.

Place chicken under a broiler and cook for about 15 minutes, or until chicken breasts are fully cooked and the tops begin to blister and spot. Spoon sauce over chicken while it is broiling.

To serve: Slice chicken breasts into bite-size strips, then arrange them in original shape. Garnish with lemon slices, if desired.

Note: If you are substituting sliced pork, combine the sauce ingredients in a bowl and add the pork; toss and marinate for 30 minutes.

TONKATSU-MAKI (PORK CUTLETS ROLLED AROUND STRING BEANS)

Yield: 3 to 4 servings

Though pork cutlets are most often fried and served with a sauce, I find these boneless fillets of pork to be perfect for rolling around vegetables and then pan frying and glazing.

½ pound string beans (or asparagus), parboiled about 2 minutes, drained, and rinsed with cold water
6 to 8 pork cutlets (about 1½ pounds)
1 to 2 tablespoons cooking oil
¼ cup *mirin*
½ cup *sake*
¼ cup soy sauce

When string beans have cooled, trim off ends and cut in half crosswise. All beans should be similar in length and about as long as the pork cutlets are wide.

Divide string beans equally among pork cutlets and place them at the widest end of each cutlet. Roll up the cutlets from the widest end to the narrow end. If you wish to secure the cutlets, you may use toothpicks, small skewers, or tie with reconstituted kanpyo.

Add cooking oil to a large skillet and heat. Place rolled pork, seam side down, in the oil. Brown rolls on all sides, carefully turning with chopsticks and a spatula and being careful to maintain the shape of the rolls.

After all pork rolls are browned, either completely drain off excess oil or remove rolls to a clean, hot skillet, being sure to place them, again, seam side down. Pour mirin over all rolls and cook, carefully turning them, for about 3 minutes. Add sake and soy sauce. If it becomes difficult to turn rolls in the sauce, you may find it easier to spoon sauce over the tops. Continue to simmer pork rolls for another 3 to 4 minutes. Do not overcook; the pork should be tender and the string beans still firm and green. The cutlets will absorb the sauce as it thickens.

TEPPAN YAKI

Yield: 4 to 6 servings

Turn your kitchen counter into a teppan bar for your next Japanese dinner party. Have trays of attractively arranged meat, chicken, seafood, and vegetables set out alongside an electric skillet or griddle. When the guests are ready for dinner, start cooking. Teppan-style cooked vegetables (without the meat, chicken, seafood) make an excellent hearty side dish for any meal. Or for vegetarian teppan yaki, substitute tofu for the meat.

¾ pound spencer steak, cut across the grain into ¼-inch thick slices
13 medium shrimp (about ⅓ pound), shelled and deveined
6 to 8 large mushrooms, trimmed and halved
1 medium zucchini (about ½ pound), sliced into ½-inch thick circles
1 large green pepper, halved, seeded, and cut into eighths
1 1 pound eggplant, cut into ½-inch thick slices (with skin), placed on paper towels, and sprinkled with salt to drain off excess liquid
1 large onion, peeled and cut into ¼-inch to ½-inch thick slices
½ pound bean sprouts
¼ to ½ cup cooking oil
Salt
¼ to ½ cup *sake* (optional)
Ponzu sauce (see page 113)

Grated *daikon* sprinkled with cayenne pepper
Cooked rice

Attractively arrange steak, shrimp, and vegetables on a large platter. Have cooking oil and sake handy in pouring cups. Place ponzu sauce and daikon in small serving bowls.

Heat skillet or griddle and add about 1 to 2 tablespoons of oil. Add meat and shrimp first, searing the outsides. Then start adding the vegetables, saving the bean sprouts until last. As cooking oil is absorbed, add more. Salt to taste. If desired, add sake to the cooking vegetables. Have guests help themselves as foods are cooked.

Serve with ponzu sauce for dipping, grated daikon, and cooked rice.

Variation: Other ingredients can be added or substituted, such as boned chicken pieces, lobster, teriyaki-marinated steak, and cabbage. Vegetables can also be sprinkled with sesame seeds.

MASAME'S PAN-FRIED CURRIED SQUID

Yield: 2 to 4 servings

Curry seasoning has recently become very popular in Japanese cuisine. Simmered curry sauce dishes are often eaten over noodles or rice. Pan-fried fish or fowl is perked up with curry, as in this recipe for curried squid. This makes a delicious appetizer, snack, or bento lunch dish.

2 pounds small squid
2 tablespoons cooking oil

⅛ teaspoon curry powder
Salt and pepper
Soy sauce

Clean squid according to directions on pages 43–44. This recipe uses only the main part of the body, the mantle. (Reserve the tentacles for another recipe or discard.)

Cut squid into bite-size squares and score the tops. Cook squid in a skillet in hot oil until almost translucent, or about 2 minutes. The squid will curl like tubes of pasta. When squid is almost cooked, sprinkle with curry powder, salt, and pepper. Continue to cook another minute. Serve with soy sauce.

PAN-FRIED SARDINE SNACKS

Yield: 1 cup

You can munch on dried mini sardines straight out of the cellophane package, or you can quickly season them further with a little soy sauce and sake. They're great to enjoy in front of the TV. Try serving with beer for football munchies. They're habit-forming.

1 cup dried mini sardines (*niboshi*)
2 tablespoons soy sauce
1 tablespoon *sake*
½ to 1 teaspoon lemon juice

Dry roast or "toast" the sardines for a few seconds to bring out their flavor. Shake the pan constantly or stir with chopsticks to prevent sticking. Combine the soy sauce, sake, and lemon juice and immediately pour this mixture over the fish. Cook a few seconds further until sardines have absorbed the sauce.

Note: If you desire them sweeter, substitute mirin for the sake, or add sugar and omit the lemon juice.

PAN-FRIED SLIVERED GOBO AND CARROT

Yield: 4 to 8 servings

Your favorite vegetables can be pan fried with a little cooking oil and then quickly glazed with seasoned soy sauce. This method is a form of yasai-itame cookery. In this recipe, pencil shavings of woody burdock and carrot are teamed up. Leftovers are excellent for next day's bento lunch.

½ pound (about 8) *gobo,* scrubbed and sliced into pencil shavings
***Su* water**
½ pound (about 2 medium) carrots, scrubbed and sliced into pencil shavings
2 tablespoons cooking oil
2 tablespoons soy sauce
2 tablespoons *mirin*
1 tablespoon *sake*
2 teaspoons toasted sesame seeds, for garnish

Soak gobo in su water for about 20 minutes, or until ready to use in recipe; drain, rinse, and drain again. Soak carrots in plain water until ready for use; drain.

In a large skillet, heat the oil and add the gobo and carrots. Cook over high heat, stirring, for about 2 to 3 minutes. Glaze gobo and carrots by adding the soy sauce, mirin, and sake. Continue to cook another 4 to 5 minutes, stirring everything together. As the sauce reduces, the vegetables will glaze. Place vegetables on a serving platter and garnish with sesame seeds.

For additional grilled, broiled, barbecued, and pan-fried recipes, see:

Soups and Stews
Sukiyaki Japanese Style
Sukiyaki American Style

Sashimi and Sushi
- Tamago Yaki

Salads and Vegetables
- Japanese Eggplants in Miso Dressing
- Glazed Bell Peppers
- Quick-Sauteed Special Mushrooms

Tofu and Miso
- Pan-Fried Tofu
- Tofu Dengaku
- Miso-Grilled Tofu Cutlets
- Miso-Marinated Chicken Wings

STEAMED AND SIMMERED FOODS

I have grouped steaming (mushimono) and simmering (nimono) together in this chapter, because both techniques involve a gentle heating and cooking with a liquid. Foods to be steamed are mixed, placed on a rack over a simmering liquid, and then cooked. The food should never touch the liquid. With simmered recipes, the ingredients are placed directly into the saucepan with the liquids and then cooked over a low heat. Sometimes a lid is dropped on top of the simmering foods.

In the Equipment chapter, I discuss the equipment needed for steaming. Since it is very easy to transform everyday American pots into steamers, there is no need to rush out and buy a Japanese steamer. You can improvise by using a cookie rack or empty 8-ounce tuna fish cans (tops and bottoms removed) as your bases. It is wise to first place ingredients on an upside-down, heat-proof platter (such as a pie plate). This will keep your ingredients from dropping into the hot liquid. Another way to steam is to wrap bite-size ingredients in aluminum foil, so that they resemble individual boats, and to place these on a rack. These attractive bundles should be brought to the table for your guests to unwrap.

The steaming liquid, most often plain water, must be watched, both at the top and at the bottom. To prevent bubbles of hot liquid from bouncing onto your steaming foods, wrap a kitchen tea towel under, around, and on top of your lid. Secure the cloth tightly on top (I use a safety pin) so that it doesn't fall on to the stove's heating element. The simmering liquid should never be so high as to touch the steaming food or so low as to evaporate.

Foods to be simmered are gently cooked directly in the seasoned stock or sauce. The basic flavorings used for nimono are dashi, soy sauce, sake, mirin, vinegar, and miso. In most cases, the ingredients are mixed together in one large, heavy pot, the seasonings are added, and then the foods are cooked at a simmer until the flavorings are absorbed. The ingredients are often covered with a dropped lid so that they will simmer evenly without breaking up. Recipes may occasionally call for ingredients to be simmered separately and then combined at the last minute. Some tough or bitter-tasting ingredients may need to be parboiled separately before being added to the major pot.

Nimono recipes are considered basic, everyday fare. Generally, at a Japanese meal, at least one dish is simmered. This technique is ideal for the busy cook as these recipes can be made in advance and reheated at mealtime. Leftovers are frequently used for bento lunches.

STEAMED EGG CUSTARD

Yield: 6 to 10 servings

Steamed egg custard, a nondessert custard, can be served as a snack or first course. Because it resembles tofu in appearance, it is sometimes referred to as egg tofu—even though there's no tofu in it. If you have never before steamed eggs, you will find the liquid's setting up is an exciting culinary adventure. Serve squares of the custard warm or chilled with simple condiments or a sauce.

6 large eggs
2 cups *dashi*
1 tablespoon *sake*
2 teaspoons sugar (or to taste)
Pinch salt

GARNISHES
Black sesame seeds
Sliced green onions
Grated ginger
Soy sauce

EGG CUSTARD SAUCE
2 tablespoons soy sauce
2 teaspoons *sake*
2 teaspoons *mirin*
¼ teaspoon grated ginger
Green onions, sliced, for garnish

Combine the eggs, dashi, sake, sugar, and salt in a bowl. Beat lightly with chopsticks and pour through a strainer into a wet mold. (A Japanese two-piece square mold is best. Otherwise, use an 8-inch pan or heatproof glass dish, and take special care when removing the slices.) Discard any thick egg that remains in the strainer.

Bring water in the bottom of a steamer or Dutch oven to a boil. Place mold containing egg mixture on top of the steamer rack or cookie sheet. Wrap steamer or pot lid with kitchen towel and secure on top. Cover pot and reduce heat. You should steam the eggs, not boil them. Steam for about 20 minutes, or until eggs have set up like a custard. Remove mold from pot and allow to cool at room temperature before refrigerating. If you prefer to eat custard while still hot, let cool a few minutes before slicing.

At serving time, carefully unmold and slice into 2-inch squares. Serve with your choice of garnishes or sauce. To make the egg custard sauce, mix together ingredients in a small bowl and garnish with green onion.

STEAMED PUMPKIN WITH CHICKEN, VEGETABLE, AND EGG CUSTARD

Yield: 2 to 4 servings

The concept of using a vegetable as an edible cooking container is wonderful. Japanese pumpkins are considerably smaller than American ones. Therefore, they make excellent cooking containers, as well as handsome individual servings. If these are not available, try this recipe with small acorn squash. Or use one small American pumpkin and prepare this recipe family style.

You can use this recipe as a springboard for many other dishes. Try adding shrimp, crab, or whitefish. Spinach, tofu, and zucchini are also wonderful. Treat this recipe as you might a quiche, and experiment. Serve as an unusual luncheon or brunch dish. Leftovers are excellent chilled.

2 small Japanese pumpkins (about 1 to 1¼ pounds each)
Salt
1 tablespoon *sake*
½ pound boned and skinned chicken pieces (1 whole breast), cut into bite-size pieces
1 carrot, diced into pieces the size of peas, parboiled 1 minute, rinsed, and drained
¼ cup fresh peas, parboiled, or frozen peas, defrosted
2 to 3 tablespoons finely chopped green onions
6 small dried oriental mushrooms, soaked overnight, then sliced into juliennes

EGG CUSTARD
4 large eggs
1 tablespoon soy sauce
2 tablespoons *mirin*
1 tablespoon *sake*
4 pea pods, for garnish

The pumpkins can be prepared several hours before the final cooking. Cut off the top part (about 2 inches) of the pumpkins. Carefully scoop out and discard the seeds and strings (a grapefruit spoon is an effective tool). You can keep the pumpkin tops as lids for the pumpkins, or you can discard them and cover the pumpkins with foil. Using a sharp knife, carefully remove most of the side skin from the pumpkins. Leave the bottom skin intact. Generously sprinkle pumpkins with salt and set upside down for an hour to drain off excess liquid. At cooking time, rinse pumpkins and pat dry. Sprinkle insides with 1 tablespoon sake and let stand for 10 minutes.

In a large steamer or a Dutch oven, partially cook the pumpkins for about 6 minutes over very low heat. Be very careful when steaming pumpkins that the heat is not so high that they will crack. If this happens, they won't hold the egg custard later.

Combine the chicken, carrot, peas, green onions, and mushrooms in a small bowl. Combine the egg, soy sauce, mirin, and sake for the custard in another bowl. Lightly beat with chopsticks, then pour through a strainer directly into the bowl with the chicken and vegetables. Pour chicken and egg mixture into the pumpkins. Garnish liquid custard with pea pods, and cover with reserved pumpkin lids or foil.

Place filled pumpkins on steamer rack and gently steam for about 20 minutes, or until eggs have set. (Any extra custard can be poured into small heat-proof glass cups and steamed alongside the pumpkins.) Uncover, remove lid or foil, and serve.

KAMABOKO

Yield: 1 to 2 rolls;
18 to 20 slices 1/2 inch thick;
6 to 10 servings

Kamaboko, steamed fish cakes, can best be compared to sausages, with their availability of various styles, fillings, and seasonings. These homemade

Japanese fish "sausages" are easy to do, and they make excellent picnic fare or appetizers.

- **10 ounces firm whitefish, without bones or skin**
- **2 egg whites**
- **¼ cup *sake***
- **2 tablespoons sugar**
- **1 teaspoon salt**
- **⅛ teaspoon pepper (preferably white pepper)**
- **⅓ cup cornstarch dissolved in ½ cup *dashi***

EGG WASH

- **1 egg yolk**
- **1 teaspoon *sake***
- **Pinch of sugar**

- **Soy sauce**
- ***Wasabi***
- **Sliced lemons**

It is simplest to prepare the fish mixture by using a food processor or blender. Cut up fish and place in the body of a processor that has been fitted with the steel chopping blade. Process quickly to chop. Through the funnel, pour in the egg whites, continuing to process. In a small dish, mix the sake with the sugar until the sugar is dissolved; then pour into the fish mixture. Season with salt and pepper. Slowly add the diluted cornstarch, continuing to process until everything is smooth and well mixed.

Lay out a maki-su and place a piece of cloth (kitchen tea towel) or several layers of cheesecloth on top; trim cloth to size of maki-su.

Spread fish mixture over half the cloth (the horizontal half closest to you), allowing a 1-inch to 2-inch free border at both sides and bottom nearest you. You may wish to make two smaller fish cakes rather than one large roll. The smaller ones are easier to roll, although the thicker, larger roll is more impressive. Roll up maki-su, completely encasing the fish paste with the cloth. Squeeze firmly to shape. Unroll and remove maki-su, but leave cloth on to help shape the fish. Seal ends by folding in. If preparing two fish cakes, repeat above steps with a second cloth. (For a discussion of the use of a maki-su, see Sashimi and Sushi chapter.)

Place fish roll(s) seam side down on a steamer rack. Gently steam above simmering water for 30 minutes. Check the water level after 15 minutes to make sure there is sufficient water.

Remove fish roll(s) from the steamer and allow to cool on a rack, about 30 to 60 minutes, before removing the cloth. Fish will firm up during this cooling, and the bottoms may have flattened.

Prepare the egg wash by mixing the egg yolk, sake, and sugar, stirring to dissolve the sugar. Keep fish roll(s) on wire rack and place rack on a foil-lined cookie sheet. Using a pastry brush, spread egg wash on top and sides, as if glazing a loaf of homemade bread.

Place cookie sheet under broiler, a few inches away from the heat. Broil a few seconds until golden. Watch carefully so that fish does not burn.

Allow to cool to room temperature before slicing. Serve at room temperature or chilled. Kamaboko can be made in advance and refrigerated until needed. Slice at serving time. Accompany with soy sauce, wasabi, and sliced lemons.

Variation: Other ingredients can be added to the fish mixture, such as chopped, cooked shiitake, carrots, pea pods, green onions, and/or nori flakes.

STEAMED SAKE-MARINATED CHICKEN BREASTS

Yield: 10 to 14 servings

These very simple sake-marinated steamed chicken breasts will be a favorite party appetizer at your house. Or serve slices upon shredded lettuce or cabbage for an unusual salad course. The ponzu sauce makes a tangy dressing.

10 to 15 boned chicken breasts (halves), pierced well with tines of fork
1 to 2 teaspoons salt
¼ cup *sake*
Juice of 1 lemon
Shredded lettuce or cabbage (optional)

PONZU SAUCE
⅔ cup soy sauce
Juice of 4 lemons (or ⅔ cup fresh lemon juice)

Sprinkle chicken with salt and then sake, massaging them into chicken. Place chicken on platter and sprinkle lemon juice on top. Let sit for 30 to 60 minutes.

Place chicken in a single layer on a rack or platter in a steamer. Cover and steam for 15 to 20 minutes. Let chicken cool completely prior to slicing.

To serve: Slice chicken into bite-size pieces. Reshape slices into the original breast forms. Place on bed of shredded lettuce or cabbage, or garnish platter with lettuce leaves. Combine soy sauce and lemon juice to make ponzu sauce. Serve chicken at room temperature with sauce.

Note: For a spicy dip, accompany chicken with soy sauce and reconstituted wasabi. Also, thinly sliced tops of scallions make a tasty and attractive garnish.

LEMON AND SAKE STEAMED CHICKEN ROLLS

Yield: 2 to 4 servings

By interrupting the steaming process and adding lemon juice, the rolled chicken fillets become especially moist and zesty. These rolled chicken fillets are especially delicious when served with a spicy sauce. You might try combining cuisines, accompanying chicken with a Mexican salsa.

4 boned chicken breasts (halves)
¼ cup *sake*
4 large scallions
1 to 2 lemons
Salt

Place chicken breasts on a platter and pour sake over. Rub sake onto breasts and let them rest about 30 minutes to marinate. Trim scallions to the same length as the length of the chicken breasts. Place 1 scallion in the center of each breast. Roll up breasts into tubes, encasing the scallions. Secure with toothpicks or reconstituted kanpyo. Squeeze lemon juice over the outsides, and salt to taste.

Using a bamboo steamer, metal steamer, or improvised steamer place rolled breasts on rack over 2 inches of simmering water. Cover and steam until tender, about 15 minutes. Halfway through the steaming, uncover and squeeze lemon juice over all breasts; carefully turn breasts over. To test for doneness, make a small incision with a sharp knife; when the chicken is no longer raw pink, it is finished.

Note: Other vegetables can be substituted for the scallions. I have tried asparagus, string beans, and zucchini fingers. Fish fillets can be handled in the same manner.

STEAMED CHICKEN AND TOFU-STUFFED CABBAGE ROLLS

Yield: 4 to 6 servings

Cabbage leaves are ideal for encasing other ingredients to be steamed. This recipe stands alone as a tasty dish, or it can be added to any number of simmered dishes or soups.

12 large nappa cabbage leaves (outer leaves of large cabbage, approximately 1½ to 2 pounds of leaves)

4 small chicken breasts (halves)
1 teaspoon salt
1 tablespoon *sake*
1 tablespoon grated ginger (optional)
1 10-ounce cake *tofu,* drained
Soy sauce with reconstituted *wasabi* and/or *ponzu* sauce, for dipping sauce

Bring a large pot of water to a boil. Holding cabbage leaves in your hands by the soft sections, place the firm core ends in the water for about 30 to 60 seconds to soften. Then gently add the leafy ends. Carefully push into boiling water and cook until tender, about 15 to 30 seconds. Do not overcook; they should be just tender enough to roll. Immediately drain cabbage, rinse with cold water and ice cubes to stop the cooking and hold the color, and completely drain before stuffing.

Bone chicken breasts and slice each into thirds, resulting in 12 "fingers." Sprinkle chicken with salt, sake, and optional ginger. Massage seasonings into chicken and set aside.

Cut tofu into 4 slices and place on paper towels. Cover with paper towels and allow to drain of excess liquid for at least 30 minutes. Cut slices in thirds, resulting in 12 "fingers," similar in size to the chicken.

To assemble: Lay out cabbage leaf. Place 1 piece of chicken at the core end and top with tofu. Carefully roll up from the wide to the narrow end, folding in and around the sides to completely encase the filling. If desired, you can secure cabbage with softened kanpyo, which will make the bundles very attractive; tie little knots on top, so that bundles suggest packages.

Place cabbage bundles seam sides down on the rack of a steamer, and steam over simmering water until tender, about 20 minutes; remove.

To serve: Steamed chicken and tofu-stuffed cabbage rolls can be served simply with soy sauce and reconstituted wasabi or with ponzu sauce.

Variations: Instead of water, you can simmer rolls in a dashi-soy-mirin stock. You might also add other ingredients to the filling, such as minced scallions, garlic, mushrooms, peas, string beans, or carrots. Minced or ground fish, seafood, pork, or beef can be substituted for the chicken.

Note: If you have any leftovers of steamed cabbage rolls, here's an Americanized recipe for another meal: Place the stuffed cabbage rolls in a baking dish. Top with tomato sauce, season with dried herbs, salt, and pepper. Generously sprinkle grated Parmesan cheese on top, and bake in a 350° F. oven for about 30 to 40 minutes, basting once or twice.

GROUND PORK AND PUMPKIN NIMONO

Yield: 6 servings

Your family will enjoy this home-style recipe for ground pork and Japanese pumpkin.

1 1½ to 2 pound Japanese pumpkin (you can substitute acorn squash)
½ teaspoon salt
2 tablespoons *sake*
1 teaspoon vinegar
1 to 3 teaspoons sugar (or to taste)
1 tablespoon cooking oil
1 pound lean ground pork (or ground beef, chicken, or turkey)
1 teaspoon minced ginger
2 scallions (white only), chopped
¼ cup soy sauce
¼ cup *mirin*
1 to 3 teaspoons additional sugar
2 teaspoons potato starch (or cornstarch), dissolved in 2 tablespoons water
½ cup fresh peas, blanched, or frozen peas, defrosted

Cut pumpkin into large pieces; remove seeds and most of the skin. Place pumpkin in a pot with water to cover; add salt, sake, vinegar, and sugar. Bring water to a boil and cook pumpkin until tender, for about 20 minutes. (Pumpkin can also be steamed.) Remove pumpkin and reserve cooking liquid.

In a large skillet, heat the cooking oil and add the meat, ginger, and scallions. Cook over fairly high heat for 1 minute, stirring to break up the meat. Reduce heat and add soy sauce, mirin, and sugar. Stir through and continue to cook for 5 minutes, or until liquid is absorbed. Add pumpkin to meat mixture.

Pour 1 cup reserved liquid in a small pot. Add diluted potato starch and heat to a boil. Cook for a few seconds until liquid is thickened.

Pour sauce into pan with meat and pumpkin. Stir through and heat gently for about 1 minute, until everything is well mixed. Turn mixture into serving dish. Garnish with cooked peas.

SIMMERED PORK AND VEGETABLES

Yield: 4 to 8 servings

The meaty farmer-style pork ribs are especially flavorsome when simmered with Japanese vegetables and seasonings.

- **3 pounds farmer-style pork ribs**
- **1 to 2 tablespoons cooking oil**
- **1 tablespoon grated fresh ginger**
- **1 large *daikon* (about ¼ pound), peeled, cut into rings, then cut into flower shapes**
- **2 to 3 large carrots, peeled, cut into rings, then cut into flower shapes**
- **1 cup *sake***
- **1½ cups water (or stock)**
- **3 tablespoons soy sauce**
- **½ cup frozen peas, defrosted, or fresh peas, blanched**

Cut ribs into bite-size pieces. (You might ask your butcher to do this for you.) Pour oil in a heavy pot or Dutch oven and brown pork on all sides. Pour out any excess oil. Add ginger, daikon, and carrots, and stir to mix. Pour in sake, water, and soy sauce, and stir through. Bring liquid to a boil; cover and reduce heat to a simmer. Simmer for 45 to 60 minutes. Uncover and adjust seasonings to taste. Return to a boil, uncovered, stirring occasionally, until meat absorbs sauce. Add peas immediately before serving, tossing through to heat.

Note: This recipe can be made in advance, but do not add the peas until serving time. Other vegetables can be added, such as potatoes, burdock, bamboo shoots, lotus root, and/or konnyaku. If you desire the sauce sweeter, add sugar to taste.

HARD-COOKED EGGS SUKIYAKI

Yield: 8 to 24 appetizer portions

Hard-cooked eggs are a commonly used Japanese ingredient. They are popular eaten plain for lunch. For Japanese-style stuffed eggs, you might try mashing the yolks with soy sauce and wasabi and restuffing them. I like to wrap thinly sliced beef around my peeled, hard-cooked eggs, simmer them in a seasoned liquid, and serve slices as an unusual party appetizer or picnic treat. You can eat them warm as a first course or refrigerate for later use.

- **8 hard-cooked eggs, carefully peeled**
- **½ pound *sukiyaki* meat (I use rib eye steak and slice paper thin)**
- **½ cup *sake***
- **⅔ cup soy sauce**
- **2 tablespoons sugar**
- **4 thin slices ginger**

Wrap eggs with sukiyaki meat, encasing them completely. If eggs and meat are cold, the meat will adhere easily.

In a large skillet, combine the sake, soy sauce,

sugar, and ginger. Cook at low heat, stirring, until sugar has dissolved. Place the meat-covered eggs in the sauce. Cook gently for about 10 minutes, spooning sauce over the eggs. Remove.

To cool, place cooked eggs on a rack over wax paper. Excess liquid will drain off. Slice cooled eggs in halves or thirds, so that each slice has some egg yolk.

SOY-BRAISED YAM CAKE

Yield: 6 to 8 servings

Konnyaku, yam starch cake, can be sliced and cooked as a vegetable to be eaten by itself or as one of many ingredients. Once you've worked with konnyaku, you will want to add it to many simmered or stewed recipes. Slices should be heated at a high temperature in an empty skillet to dry them out. In this recipe, they are threaded and simmered in a special sauce. The appearance of threaded konnyaku is most impressive.

1 *konnyaku* cake (about 10 ounces), washed and sliced thinly (about ⅛ inch thick) into about 20 pieces
2 cups *dashi*
¼ cup soy sauce
2 tablespoons *mirin*
Dash fresh lemon juice
Toasted sesame seeds, for garnish

Take each konnyaku slice and turn it flat. With the tip of your knife, slice a horizontal slit in the center, without penetrating either side. Thread one outside end through the slit, and the konnyaku will twist and appear braided. Proceed with remaining konnyaku. Place konnyaku in a dry skillet over high heat and cook to dry out, about 3 minutes.

To the skillet with the konnyaku add the dashi, soy sauce, mirin, and lemon juice. Bring liquid to a boil and cook for about 10 minutes, or until konnyaku has absorbed the sauce. Place on a serving dish and garnish with sesame seeds.

SIMMERED SQUID

Yield: 4 to 10 servings

Squid can be eaten either raw or cooked in innumerable ways. With certain methods, the squid will curl, making for a most attractive dish. If you slice open the cleaned body, lay it flat, and cut the squid into thin strips or small squares (scoring the top), when you cook it in water or stock it will curl into rings suggesting small pinecones. If you keep the cleaned body, or mantle, in the tube shape and cut it into rings, these rings will shrink slightly and become attractive circles. Squid rings are wonderful for deep frying; first coat them in beaten egg yolk and then in bread crumbs or tempura batter.

4 small squid, cleaned (see pages 43–44) and cut into rings
2 tablespoons soy sauce
2 tablespoons *sake*
1 to 2 tablespoons fresh lemon juice
Sugar (optional)

Place rings of squid in a saucepan with the soy sauce, sake, lemon juice, and sugar. Simmer for about 5 minutes. Serve as a tasty—and very inexpensive—hors d'oeuvre.

JAPANESE MEATBALLS (DANGO)

Yield: 4 servings; more as appetizer

Children adore meatballs, and these Japanese-style simmered meatballs are always a tremendous success in our household.

1 pound ground meat
1 teaspoon soy sauce

1 teaspoon ginger juice (1 small knob pressed through a garlic press)
1 clove garlic, pressed through a garlic press
½ medium onion, grated
Cooking oil

JAPANESE MEATBALL SAUCE
¾ cup stock (beef, chicken, vegetable, or *dashi*)
¼ cup soy sauce
¼ cup *mirin*
1 tablespoon vinegar
Sugar (optional)

Combine meat, soy sauce, ginger juice, garlic, and onion in a mixing bowl. Shape into small balls the size of walnuts.

Heat a 2-inch to 4-inch layer of cooking oil in a heavy pot. Fry meatballs, about 6 at a time, in the oil; remove and drain on paper towels. Discard the oil and add the sauce ingredients; stir to combine. Return meatballs to the pot. Bring liquid to a boil, then reduce to a simmer, continuing to cook a few minutes.

SOY SIMMERED KAMABOKO

Yield: 4 to 6 servings

For a snack, you can eat fish cakes straight out of their plastic wrappers. Better yet, slice and simmer them in a seasoned sauce. You might try purchasing a variety of fish cakes to experiment with different tastes and colors.

1 5½-ounce package *kamaboko* ("*narutomaki*")
1 6-ounce package *kamaboko* ("*tempura*")
2 tablespoons cooking oil
½ onion, thinly sliced into strips
3 tablespoons soy sauce
1 to 2 teaspoons toasted sesame seeds, for garnish

Slice fish cakes into thin juliennes or rounds. Heat cooking oil in a large skillet. Cook the onion until softened and coated with oil. Add the fish cakes, stirring to coat them with the onion and oil. Add the soy sauce and heat through, about 3 minutes to glaze. Place in a serving dish and garnish with sesame seeds. Serve warm, at room temperature, or chilled.

HALIBUT SIMMERED IN GINGER BROTH

Yield: 2 to 3 servings

The predominant flavor in this simmering broth is ginger. It's an excellent seasoning for mild-tasting fish and chicken. Leftovers are excellent for a bento lunch.

1 ¾-pound halibut fillet (1 inch thick)
Salt
Vinegar

SIMMERING LIQUID
2 cups water
½ cup *sake*
¼ cup *mirin*
1 medium knob ginger, peeled and sliced
2 tablespoons *mirin*
2 tablespoons soy sauce

***Mitsuba* or cilantro leaves or other attractive green leaves, for garnish**

Remove all bones and skin from halibut and sprinkle with salt; set aside for 30 minutes. Rinse off salt, sprinkle with vinegar, and wash under running water. Dry completely. Cut fillet in half or thirds.

In a medium saucepan, combine the water, sake, mirin, and ginger. Bring to a boil, then reduce heat to simmer for 5 minutes. Place halibut pieces in the simmering liquid and cook the fish for about 15 minutes, or until tender. With a slotted spoon, remove any scum (foamy skin) that rises to the surface. Remove halibut to a platter and cover to keep warm.

Return saucepan of liquid to a boil. Boil for about 10 minutes, or until liquid is reduced by half. Add mirin and soy sauce and continue to boil until liquid is further reduced to a thicker sauce. Spoon gingered sauce over halibut pieces. Garnish with mitsuba or cilantro leaves.

JAPANESE PORK LOIN ROAST AND VEGETABLES

Yield: 8 to 10 servings

My guests have been most impressed by this Japanese-style pot roast with vegetables. I have offered this dish both hot and chilled. You can strain the pan juices to use as a base for a sauce or as a "soup" for cooked noodles. If you prepare the recipe early in the day, slice the meat after it has cooled and serve it along with a ponzu sauce. The bundles of vegetables should accompany the sliced pork. After you have enjoyed the appearance and taste of these kanpyo-tied vegetables, you will likely want to braise your vegetables in this manner often. You might even try this technique for other cuisines—how about French-style simmered asparagus.

2 1½ to 2 pound boned pork loin roasts (have butcher bone and tie with string)
2 to 3 tablespoons cooking oil
16 slices ginger (large knob)
3 cups chicken stock
1 cup *sake*
½ cup soy sauce

VEGETABLE BUNDLES

½ package of *kanpyo,* washed, reconstituted, and cut into 4-inch lengths
24 scallions (primarily white and firm green parts), trimmed
3 to 4 large carrots, cut into thick julienne strips
4 large celery stalks, cut into julienne strips

Bring pork loin roasts to room temperature. Heat oil in a large Dutch oven and add half the ginger to flavor the oil. When the ginger is browned, remove and discard. Brown pork loin roasts on all sides in the flavored oil. Discard excess oil. Add stock, sake, and soy sauce; stir around. Add remaining ginger.

Meanwhile, tie bundles of vegetables with kanpyo: The scallions, carrots, and celery should be similar in length. Place about 3 vegetables together and tie in an attractive knot with the kanpyo. I prefer to keep each type of vegetable separate, since they vary in cooking time.

Add carrot and celery bundles to the pot; cover and reduce heat to a simmer. Cook about 30 minutes, then add the scallions to the pot and cover again. Cook another 15 minutes, or until pork is tender. (Pork should register about 160° F. on a meat thermometer.) Baste pork and vegetables often.

Allow pork to cool before slicing. Serve sliced pork with vegetable bundles. If desired, accompany with ponzu sauce.

WINTER NIMONO

Yield: 4 to 6 servings

For a successful nimono-style recipe, do not skimp on the dashi ingredients. A full-bodied dashi flavored with soy sauce, sake, and mirin is an excellent stock in which to simmer whatever vegetables are on hand. In this case, winter root vegetables were most attractive. You might also add potatoes, bamboo shoots, shiitake, konnyaku, sliced fish cakes, stuffed cabbage rolls (see page 113), peeled hard-cooked eggs, and/or your favorite fried or freeze-dried tofu. (For a springtime nimono, you might prefer asparagus, zucchini, and cucumber.) The more ingredients you add, the bigger the pot and the more stock you'll need. If you include all the ingredients I've mentioned, you'll end up with a marvelous Japanese one-pot winter stew, known as oden. Allow your oden to simmer for several hours, adding stock as needed.

¾ pound *daikon,* peeled and sliced into 1-inch-thick circles
2 to 3 tablespoons vinegar
1½ cups *dashi*
⅔ cup soy sauce
⅓ cup *sake*
1 tablespoon *mirin*
Sugar (optional)
½ pound carrots, peeled and sliced into 1-inch to 2-inch lengths
1 medium turnip, peeled and sliced into ½-inch circles
8 green onions, firm white part only

Cut a crisscross into one side of the daikon to resemble a flower. Place on a platter and pour vinegar over. Let stand for 15 minutes, turning once. Rinse and pat dry.

In a large skillet, combine the dashi, soy sauce, sake, and mirin. If you prefer a sweeter stock, add sugar to taste. Place daikon, carrots, turnip, and onions in the simmering stock. Cook at a simmer for 30 minutes, or until vegetables are tender. Leftover stock can be refrigerated and reused.

For additional steamed and simmered food recipes, see:

Soups and Stews
Pork Balls with Kinome Soup
Mizutaki (One-Pot Chicken Stew)
Shabu-Shabu
Salads and Vegetables
Carrots in Vinegar
Steamed Cauliflower with Miso Sauces
Party Vegetable Mixture
Tofu and Miso
Beef and Rice Stuffed Tofu Pouches
Rice and Noodles
Chicken Donburi
Kayoko's Oyako Donburi
Ground Meat and Tofu with Vegetables Donburi
Desserts, Confections, and Sweet Snacks
Candied Chestnuts (Kuri No Kanro)
Manju (Dumplings with Sweet Bean Filling)
Egg Sweets

TEMPURA AND OTHER DEEP-FRIED FOODS

Deep frying in hot oil is found in practically every cuisine. Fried foods are often thought to be heavy, greasy, and fattening. Yet in Japanese cooking, fried foods, agemono, are delicate in texture, light in taste, and almost grease free.

There are three basic techniques to Japanese-style deep frying: (1) Batter-frying, koromo-age, includes the well-known tempura recipes. These batters should remain a little lumpy, as a smooth batter generally becomes heavy and gummy. (2) Starch or flour frying, kara-age, involves a light dusting with potato starch, cornstarch, kudzu, or flour. (3) Plain frying, su-age, refers to deep frying with no outer coating. It is often used for root vegetables, such as lotus root and potatoes, and for green beans and small inland fish, all of which are first washed with vinegar (su).

Seasoning for deep-fried foods can be handled in a number of ways. You can marinate your ingredients before frying; you can even bathe them in a marinade or sauce after they are fried. Some batters include seasonings. And foods are very often simply fried and garnished with a few citrus slices or other seasonal fruit or vegetable.

The most commonly recommended oil is vegetable oil, perhaps blended with a few drops of sesame oil for enrichment. Some agemono chefs prepare their own combination of oils, including peanut, corn, sesame, olive, and cottonseed.

If you are a newcomer to deep frying, you may be surprised by the quantity, and therefore the cost, of the required cooking oil. Fortunately, to balance this expense, cooking oil can be reused. Some Japanese food authorities even believe the oil gains flavors and improves with reuse. To save your oil, allow it to cool after use, skim off and discard any burned particles, then reheat to warm (not hot), stir, and carefully pour through a filter (or layers of cheesecloth) into a plastic or glass container with an airtight seal. Keep in a dark, cool place, but not in the refrigerator. When reusing, add some new cooking oil to refresh the taste. The combination of used oil and new oil gives a beautiful golden-brown finish to the fried foods.

So that foods fry without absorbing grease, the oil must be at the proper temperature. When adding your ingredients to the oil, quickly sear their exterior. I test my oil by dropping in a pinch of batter or a salad crouton. If my tester sinks, then rises, and next begins to sizzle, the oil is fine. If the tester sinks and stays put, wait a few more seconds. If it sizzles immediately, lower the heat and allow the oil to slightly cool before using. Generally, vegetables are cooked at a lower temperature than are meat, fowl, and fish. In the majority of deep-frying recipes, the best temperature range is from 350° to 375° F.

Do not crowd your pot with foods. Use chopsticks to turn frying foods in the oil. Skim off any particles of food or batter that may form in the hot oil—it is *very* important to keep your oil clean. A slotted spoon is fine, and a Japanese mesh strainer (tempura ami) is even better for this job.

Foods that have been deep fried should first be placed on a wire or bamboo rack to drain off excess oil and then served immediately while still hot.

Tempura is the most famous of all Japanese deep-fried foods. Portuguese missionaries are credited with introducing deep frying to the Japanese during the sixteenth century. Since then, the Japanese have modified and refined the original idea, using a lighter batter and a lighter oil and incorporating characteristic Japanese foods.

Today many Japanese restaurants have tempura bars where you sit while foods are cooked to order in front of you. Further proof of tempura's popularity are the packaged, dried batter mixes that are easy to obtain in American markets and just as easy to make. By following my tempura tricks, you will find the batter a snap to assemble with dry goods you have on hand.

TEMPURA TRICKS

- Make batter just before use. Do not let it sit for too long.
- Water should be icy cold.
- Do not over mix batter to make it smooth. It should be lumpy.
- You can control the thickness of your coating by the amount of ice water added to your batter. For a thin coating, the batter should be thin, so add more ice water. For a thick coating, you need a thick batter, so add less ice water.
- Ingredients to be deep fried should be at room temperature and completely dry.
- Lightly dust your ingredients with flour first and then coat with batter. Batter will adhere better.
- Set up your deep-frying area like an assembly line. Have handy your ingredients to be deep fried, a bowl of flour for dusting, a bowl of batter, a pot with hot oil, chopsticks for turning and adding ingredients, a skimmer for removing floating batter, a rack for draining excess oil (some tempura nabes have these attached), and a serving platter.
- Test your oil before adding ingredients to make sure it is at the proper temperature.
- Vegetables should be added to the pot first, since they require a lower cooking temperature than does seafood, meat, or fowl.

The tempura dipping sauce, tentsuyu, should be made and poured into small individual serving bowls.

Use these instructions to ready your ingredients for tempura-style cooking.

PREPARING INGREDIENTS FOR TEMPURA

Vegetables for tempura must be washed, trimmed, and dried completely. Some vegetables require special attention. Mountain potatoes and yams should be peeled, cut into desired shapes, and soaked in su water for at least 30 minutes, the water changed at least once. "American" potatoes, such as russets, need not be peeled—just scrubbed—but they do benefit from soaking in ice water. Lotus root should be peeled, sliced into ½-inch circles, and then soaked in su water for at least 20 minutes. Parsley should be washed, then carefully divided into bundles; stems should then be tied into knots. Carrots are best scrubbed and then sliced into large diagonals, about ¼ inch to ½ inch thick. Scallions need trimming; use primarily the firm white part.

Other ingredients that are wonderful for tempura include: spinach leaves (with stems for easier handling), pea pods, eggplant (slices or fingers), cucumber, asparagus, onion slices, celery, gobo, squash (especially zucchini), broccoli, mushrooms, cauliflower, green pepper, shiso, sorrel, basil, nori, seafood and fish (particularly shrimp, squid, and bite-size chunks of whitefish), fowl, meat, noodles, fruit, even ice cream.

To clean your shrimp, hold it by the tail and carefully peel and pull off the shell, leaving the tail intact. The shell can remain on the tail. Using the tip of a sharp knife, remove the black vein from the back side, then butterfly the shrimp along this side. Wash and pat dry; continue with tempura recipe. To clean your squid, refer to pages 43–44. Then slice mantles, or hoods, crosswise into ¼-inch to ½-inch rings. Rinse rings and bodies, and pat dry. Continue with tempura recipe.

One of my favorite fruits cooked tempura-style is apples: Slice and core but do not peel, and drop in acidulated water (lemon water) to hold the color. Pears are excellent as well. In Japan, tangerines, mikan, are often prepared tempura style.

Ice cream balls are a bit tricky: The ice cream must first be shaped into balls and then refrozen to make sure they are very cold and solid. You can coat the ice cream with a regular tempura batter, or you can sweeten batter with sugar and use a little soy flour, kinako, or sweet rice flour, mochiko, with the flour.

TEMPURA BATTER

Yield: About 1 cup

In the following tempura batter, I have included an egg yolk, so that it is richer and more golden than a batter made only of flour and ice water. If you desire a lacier effect, omit the egg yolk.

1 egg yolk
¾ to 1 cup cold water
1 cup flour
Extra flour

Gently mix together the egg yolk and water. The amount of water will be determined by your preference for a thick or thin batter. Sift the flour directly into the mixture, combining gently with chopsticks.

Note: To prepare as much as possible in advance, the egg yolk can be held in a small dish. The water can be measured and kept refrigerated. The flour can be measured and kept in a separate bowl. The dusting flour can be placed in another bowl. All ingredients to be deep fried can be washed, trimmed, dried, and arranged on a platter.

TENTSUYU SAUCE

Yield: About 1 cup

Tempura dipping sauce, tentsuyu, is available canned or bottled in concentrated form and only needs water-diluting. However, you can easily make this sauce, and it keeps for several days in the refrigerator.

Traditionally, the sauce is served warm and is used for dipping tempura and other fried dishes, such as Tonkatsu, Fried Pork Cutlets.

1 cup *dashi*
⅓ cup soy sauce
⅓ cup *mirin* (or to taste)
Grated *daikon* and ginger (optional)

Combine dashi, soy sauce, and mirin in a small saucepan. Adjust the amount of mirin to obtain desired sweetness. Heat to a boil, then reduce to a simmer for about 1 minute. Set aside. This sauce is often accompanied by grated daikon and ginger.

FLUFFY FRIED CHICKEN AND VEGETABLE BUNDLES

Yield: 8 to 10 bundles; 3 to 5 servings, depending on number of courses

Almost like a mixed bag of tempura goodies, these fluffy fried chicken and vegetable bundles make delicious appetizers or entrees. You can change the ingredients to your taste. Just make sure you have a variety of textures, from soft to crunchy. These bundles make wonderful and unusual additions to a large platter of tempura.

1 whole chicken breast, skinned, boned, and cut into bite-size pieces (about 10 ounces of meat)
1 tablespoon *sake*
1 medium stalk *gobo* (about 3 ounces)
***Su* water**
3 medium scallions, firm part only, chopped
12 small pea pods
2 egg whites
½ to ¾ cup potato starch
Cooking oil for deep frying
Warm *tentsuyu* sauce

Place chicken pieces in a large bowl; add the sake and massage into the chicken to flavor it. Scrub gobo, cutting off and discarding the tough stem ends. Have a bowl of su water handy (approximately 1 tablespoon vinegar to 1 quart water). Cut gobo into thirds and place 2 of the pieces in the su water. Coarsely chop the third piece and place in the su water. Repeat process with other 2 pieces. Set gobo aside for about 30 minutes, changing water once. Drain and dry gobo and add to the chicken. Add chopped scallions and pea pods. (If pea pods are large, chop into smaller sizes.) Mix in the egg whites. At this point, you can refrigerate the mixture for later use.

At cooking time, mix potato starch into the bowl with the chicken and vegetables. The mixture should be pasty.

In a large heavy pot (I use my wok), heat oil for deep frying. Drop several bundles of chicken mixture (each about 2 tablespoons) into the oil. Deep fry until they are a nice golden color and crisp on the outside. Drain and continue process until all bundles are cooked.

Serve with warm tentsuyu (tempura) sauce.

Variation: Substitute shrimp for the chicken, or use both. Other vegetables can be added, such as peas, carrots, bamboo shoots, green peppers.

TORI TEMPURA KUSHI

Yield: 3 main-dish servings; 6 appetizers

Bite-size pieces of food can be skewered and dipped in a tempura batter, then deep fried for a delicious main dish or party appetizer. Select your favorite ingredients and attractively alternate them, piercing with small bamboo skewers, kushi.

1½ pounds chicken breasts, skinned and boned
1 3½-ounce can *gingko* nuts (24 nuts), drained and parboiled to refresh
4 green onions, sliced into thirds
1 green pepper, seeded and cut into 12 bite-size pieces
Flour, for dusting
1 cup *tempura* batter
Cooking oil for deep frying

Cut chicken into 36 bite-size pieces. Attractively place chicken, nuts, and vegetables on 12 small bamboo skewers. (At this point, skewered ingredients can be refrigerated for several hours until needed.)

Dust skewered ingredients with flour. Combine tempura batter ingredients and dip one skewer at a time in the mixture. Deep fry about 4 skewers at a time in the hot oil, until batter is golden. Drain and immediately serve. If desired, serve with tempura sauce.

TONKATSU

Yield: 4 to 8 servings, depending on number of courses

A simple dusting of flour, then eggs, and finally Japanese-style bread crumbs makes the beautiful outer surface for this home-style recipe for fried pork chops. At Japanese markets, you can purchase tonkatsu-cut pork chops, boneless pork loin cutlets. If this cut is not readily available at your market, ask your butcher to slice a boneless pork loin roast into ½-inch pieces.

8 pork cutlets (about 1½ pounds)
2 to 3 tablespoons flour
Salt and pepper
2 eggs, beaten with 2 tablespoons *sake*
1½ cups Japanese bread crumbs, *panko* (or homemade bread crumbs)
Cooking oil for deep frying
Shredded cabbage or lettuce
Lemon wedges, for garnish
***Tentsuyu, tonkatsu*, or Worcestershire sauce**

Dust pork cutlets with flour, then season to taste with salt and pepper. Dip one cutlet at a time in beaten eggs, then dredge lightly in bread crumbs. It is best to coat pork cutlets at least 30 minutes in advance and refrigerate them so that the crust has time to set before frying.

Heat oil in a heavy pot or wok to a medium temperature, about 350° F. Fry a few pork cutlets at a time for about 6 to 8 minutes, or until the pork is fully cooked and the coating reaches a lovely golden color. Drain on paper towels and continue until all pork is cooked. Keep cutlets warm.

Place cooked pork cutlets on a bed of shredded cabbage or lettuce. For easier handling at the table, you may want to first cut each cutlet into bite-size strips and then reshape into original form. Garnish platter with lemon wedges. Serve with your choice of tentsuyu, tonkatsu (a bottled sauce), or Worcestershire sauce.

SOY-MIRIN-MARINATED FRIED CHICKEN

Yield: 3 to 4 main-dish servings; more if used as appetizers

The following recipe's steps result in an unusual crunchy texture. The chicken is first coated with egg and starch and then deep fried. Next, it is marinated in a simple sauce and then coated once again before it is refried. Try it with pork also.

4 chicken breasts (halves), boned and cut into bite-size pieces (approximately ¾ pound)
1 egg, beaten
½ cup potato starch (or cornstarch or flour)
Cooking oil for deep frying
1 tablespoon sesame oil (optional)

¼ cup soy sauce
2 tablespoons *mirin*
1 cup Japanese bread crumbs
Spicy mustard (optional)

Place about one-fourth of the chicken at a time into a bowl with the egg. Then dip the chicken into a second bowl containing the potato starch. Remove coated chicken to a sheet of wax paper. Continue until all chicken is coated. (This can be done several hours in advance.)

Combine the cooking oil and the sesame oil in a deep pot and heat. The oil should not be too hot; the best temperature is about 300° to 325° F., so that the chicken will cook without becoming too crisp or darkening too fast. Fry about one-fourth of the chicken pieces at a time, for about 3 to 5 minutes. Remove to drain off excess oil (wire rack or paper-lined colander). If oil becomes too hot, add more oil to lower the temperature.

Combine the soy sauce and mirin in a bowl. Add the fried chicken and let the chicken soak in the liquid. Toss with your fingers. Let rest for 5 to 15 minutes.

Coat chicken with the bread crumbs. Return chicken to hot oil and quickly refry to crispen, for about 2 minutes. Drain and serve immediately.

Serve with spicy mustard as an appetizer, snack, or main dish.

FRIED PORK BALLS (DANGO)

Yield: 12 to 20 balls; 3 to 8 servings, depending on number of courses

Serve this as an appetizer with a spicy mustard, or with soy sauce mixed with a dash of wasabi. Instead of the pork, you can use ground chicken, turkey, veal, fish, beef—or any combination of these ingredients.

1 pound lean ground pork
1 medium knob ginger, grated (about ½ teaspoon)
2 medium scallions, firm parts only, chopped (about 2 tablespoons)
½ teaspoon soy sauce
2 egg yolks, beaten
2 teaspoons *sake* or *dashi*
1 cup potato starch (or cornstarch or flour)
Cooking oil for deep frying
Soy sauce with *wasabi,* or spicy mustard

In a mixing bowl, combine the pork, ginger, scallions, and soy sauce. Shape mixture into small balls, about the size of walnuts. In a small bowl, beat the egg yolks lightly with the sake or dashi. In another bowl, place the potato starch. Dip pork balls first in the egg and then in the potato starch.

Heat oil for deep frying to about 340° or 350° F. Do not allow the oil to become too hot, or the meat will brown before it is fully cooked.

Fry a few pork balls at a time in the oil, for about 5 minutes. Remove with a slotted spoon and drain on paper towels. Continue until all pork balls are cooked.

Serve with soy sauce mixed with wasabi to taste, or with spicy mustard.

SPICY MARINATED CHICKEN

Yield: 2 main-dish servings; 4 to 6 appetizers

In this recipe, the chicken is first marinated and then deep fried. Although the Japanese do not traditionally marinate chicken, I find it adds terrific flavors to this recipe. You might also try this technique with boneless fish chunks—it's delicious, too.

1 whole chicken breast (2 halves), cut into bite-size pieces, through the bones and skin

SPICY MARINADE

4 small dried red peppers, seeded
2 tablespoons *mirin*

4 teaspoons soy sauce
2 teaspoons sugar
½ to 1 teaspoon salt
3 large scallions, cut diagonally (firm part only)

½ to ¾ cup potato starch (or cornstarch)
Cooking oil for deep frying

Place chicken in a large glass bowl. Combine marinade ingredients and toss with chicken. Marinate for several hours, or days, in the refrigerator. Occasionally, spoon juices and vegetables over chicken.

At cooking time, bring chicken to room temperature and remove from marinade; dry with paper towels. If desired, green onions can also be dried and deep fried.

Place potato starch in a dish and coat the chicken and scallions. In a large heavy pot, heat the cooking oil. Add chicken and scallions, a few pieces at a time, to the hot oil.

Variation: Chicken or fish can first be deep fried and then marinated in this spicy marinade for a few days. In this case, the chicken or fish should be eaten cold.

PARTY FLANK STEAK STRIPS

Yield: 4 to 10 servings, depending on number of courses

This recipe for fried steak strips with a special coating of green onions makes a perfect party appetizer, dish for a buffet table, or picnic treat, since it is made several hours in advance. It's simple, delicious, and you will receive many compliments from your guests.

1 flank steak (about 1½ to 1¾ pounds)
½ cup soy sauce
¼ cup *mirin*
1 tablespoon sugar (or to taste)
2 scallions, finely chopped
¼ cup flour
1 egg, well beaten
Extra flour
Cooking oil for deep frying

Pierce flank steak all over with the tines of a fork. This will help tenderize the meat and allow the marinade to penetrate. Combine soy sauce, mirin, and sugar, stirring until the sugar is dissolved. Marinate steak in this mixture for 30 to 60 minutes.

Combine the scallions and the ¼ cup flour. Spread on a sheet of wax paper or a large plate. Place beaten egg in another large plate.

Remove steak from marinade and pat dry with paper towel. Lightly dust with the extra flour. Place steak in scallion-flour mixture, pressing coating onto the meat with your fingers. Dip steak into egg and then again into the scallion-flour mixture. Again, press coating into the steak.

In a large skillet, heat cooking oil for deep frying. There should be a minimum of 2 inches—the height of the oil must extend above the steak. Deep fry the steak in the hot oil. Fry a few minutes on each side. Do not overcook; meat should be rare.

Remove steak and drain off any excess oil. Slice steak as thin as possible into long strips. Place on serving platter and allow to cool. Serve at room temperature or chilled, with additional soy sauce if desired.

TOFU-MISO AGE

Yield: About 28 balls; 4 to 10 servings, depending on number of courses

Tofu responds handsomely to deep frying. Whether plain cubes, with or without coating, or a more complicated mixture of ingredients, the result is a firm outer surface with a soft, warm, almost cheeselike, inner surface. You might want to try these American style, with tomato sauce and spaghetti.

1 20-ounce container *tofu*, drained
¼ cup *miso*
2 tablespoons sugar (or to taste)
½ cup potato starch (or cornstarch)
Cooking oil for deep frying

Slice tofu and drain on paper towels for about 1 hour. Combine tofu, miso, and sugar in a food processor or blender to make a paste. (Tofu and miso can also be pureed with a suribachi.) Mold mixture into small balls, about the size of walnuts. Lightly dust with potato starch.

Heat oil for deep frying and add 6 balls at a time. When balls are golden, remove, drain, and add more tofu-miso balls. Continue until all balls are deep fried. Serve warm with your favorite sauce, if desired.

For more tempura and deep-fried food recipes, see:

Salads and Vegetables
Fried Lotus Root
Fried Mountain Potatoes
Tofu and Miso
Fried Tofu with Seasoned Sauce
Deep-Fried Tofu
Noodles and Rice
Tempura Soba
Desserts, Confections, and Sweet Snacks
Senbei

RICE AND NOODLES

Rice and noodles are the mainstay of the Japanese diet. Meals are properly accompanied by a bowl of steamed rice. And for people on the run, a big bowl of noodles or rice with broth, topped with any number of food items (donburi), is the usual fare. Picnic choices might be sushi or cold somen, again featuring rice or noodles.

RICE

To the Japanese, rice is considered the more prestigious of the two staples. Reverence for rice can be observed in the country's celebrations. During the spring and autumn months, the rice god, Inari, and the food goddess, Ukemochi-no kami, are honored at festivals in appreciation for the fertility of the soil and the bounty of the harvest.

Cooked polished rice (gohan), even if plainly steamed for everyday cookery, is highly revered. To prepare short-grain rice in the Japanese manner, wash it with fresh water until the water runs clear (see Ingredients chapter). The purpose of washing the rice is to rid it of the starchy powder (sometimes talc) and to prevent the final dish from becoming gummy. Once the rice is washed to your preference, if time permits it should be soaked in its cooking water for 30 to 60 minutes before heating. Most Japanese do not measure the quantity of water needed by the cup but instead check the height of the water level above the rice layer, the ideal being about 1 inch. However, to be safe, allow 1 cup of water for every 1 cup of rice. If you prefer your rice drier, decrease the amount of water. For added flavor and nutrition, rice can also be cooked in dashi or in the liquid from a previously cooked or reconstituted vegetable, such as shiitake. A few tablespoons of mirin, sake, or soy sauce can be substituted for some of the water as well.

If using an automatic electric rice cooker, proceed with the rinsing and draining steps as with the standard method. Add rice and water to the pot and cover. The thermostatic control unit will reduce and turn off the heat at the proper times. Rice will be kept warm until needed.

If you do not use a modern rice steamer, cook rice in a heavy metal pot with a tight-fitting lid. For softer rice, you may wish to allow an extra ¼ cup water for every 6 cups rice. Some cooks feel you should bring the rice and water to a boil, then quickly cover it. Others prefer to cover first, then bring to a boil. Craters begin to appear on the surface of the rice after it has properly boiled for 1 minute. Next, reduce the heat to low and continue to cook for another 15 minutes. Do not uncover the pot during this time. If you find that your lid is not heavy enough and it allows steam to escape, weight it down. After cooking is completed, turn off heat and let rice rest for 15 to 20 minutes. Uncover. The rice is properly cooked if little holes appear on the surface. Using a wooden rice paddle, fluff up your rice and cover until needed. Serve rice in small bowls, and if desired, garnish with black sesame seeds, shredded nori, minced scallions, or ginger—or any other favorite ingredient. Rice is also ready to be used for other dishes, such as sushi. Incidentally, should any hard, crusty rice form around the sides or bottom of the pot, reserve this rice, called koge rice, to enjoy with a little soy sauce or in a soup.

NOODLES

The noodle family is called menrui. There are several different varieties of Japanese noodles available fresh in the refrigerator and freezer sections of most major markets and oriental food stores and dried in cellophane wrappers in the pasta or oriental food shelves. (Refer to Ingredients chapter for specific products.) Though less prestigious than rice, noodles—both hot and cold—are a favorite everyday Japanese food.

The Japanese technique for cooking noodles greatly differs from that known to American cookery. Several steps of interrupted cooking are used, in which fresh cold water is added to the pot of boiling water. With this method of cooking, known as sashimizu, a large pot is filled ¾ full with water. The water is brought to a boil, the noodles are added, and when the water returns to a boil, another cup of water is added. When it again returns to a boil, another cup of cold water is added. Generally, somen needs only 2 additions during a boiling period of about 3 minutes; soba, 2 or 3 additions during a boiling period of about 4 minutes; and udon, 2 or 3 additions during a boiling period of about 5 minutes.

If you do not have the time or inclination to cook your noodles with these additional cups of water, then prepare them American style in a large pot of water without interruptions. (I do not find a great difference in the final product.) The important rule is: Do not overcook noodles. Drain and proceed with your selected recipe.

Japanese noodle etiquette differs considerably from American. Noodles are slightly twirled, with a great deal of dexterity, around the bottom of the chopsticks. The chopsticks are brought to the mouth with several inches of noodles still hanging from them. It is acceptable to make noisy, slurping sounds while ingesting these noodles. When noodles are combined with a broth, the noodles are generally eaten first, then the broth is sipped directly from the cup or bowl.

RICE WITH FRESH PEAS

Yield: 6 servings

For an excellent accompaniment to any main dish, rice can be cooked with your choice of vegetable. One of the most commonly enjoyed combinations is rice with peas.

1 pound fresh peas
1 cup rice, washed
1 cup water
2 tablespoons *mirin* (optional)

Pod fresh peas; you should have about 1 generous cup of peas. Place peas in a pot of boiling water, return water to a boil, and cook for 30 seconds to 1 minute. Do not overcook. Immediately drain and rinse in cold water to stop the cooking and set the color. Set aside. (The water used to cook the peas can be reserved, cooled, and used for the rice.)

Wash rice by soaking in water and draining through a fine sieve or your fingers. Repeat until water is clear. If time permits, let rice soak in 1 cup water for 30 to 60 minutes. (You can use reserved pea-cooking liquid for this soaking, too, adding, as well, 2 tablespoons of mirin, but the total liquid measure should equal 1 cup.)

Bring pot of rice and liquid to a boil. Cover; cook for about 1 minute, then reduce heat for 15 minutes. Turn off heat; keep covered for 20 minutes. Uncover and stir peas through to warm them. Cover until serving time.

Variation: A very simple variation uses 1 cup defrosted frozen peas. Pour boiling water over top of peas and drain immediately. Let sit, if desired, in a bowl with 2 tablespoons of mirin to flavor. Toss hot cooked rice with peas; cover a few minutes to warm through.

RICE WITH SHRIMP AND VEGETABLES

Yield: 6 to 8 servings

Rice with shrimp and vegetables is another delicious side dish. If you want to serve it as a main dish, donburi style, increase the quantity and the size of the shrimp. You can also add or substitute small pieces of cooked chicken, meat, pork, tamago, and/or seaweed.

2 cups rice, washed
2 cups water
1 tablespoon soy sauce
1 tablespoon *sake*
1 cup cooked baby shrimp, washed and rinsed with salt to refresh
4 *shiitake,* soaked several hours, then drained and sliced into thin shreds
1 to 2 carrots, sliced into ⅛-inch rounds, then cut into flower shapes, parboiled for 5 minutes, and rinsed
½ cup frozen peas, defrosted
Soy sauce

In a covered pot, bring to boil the rice, water, soy sauce, sake, shrimp, mushrooms, carrots, and peas. After about 2 minutes, reduce the heat and simmer for about 15 to 18 minutes. Remove pot from heat and let rest for 15 minutes. Uncover and fluff up (add any extra ingredients, such as tamago or nori). Cover and let stand until needed. Serve with soy sauce for seasoning.

CHESTNUTS AND RICE

Yield: 6 to 8 servings

The combination of fresh chestnuts and rice is commonly seen during the autumn months and is a special dish to serve when guests come to dinner. The firm texture of the chestnuts is wonderful when contrasted with the softer texture of the cooked rice.

½ pound chestnuts (about 15)
2 cups rice, washed

To peel chestnuts, use a sharp knife and cut an X into the flat side of each nut. Then use your fingers (or the knife) to peel off the hard outer skin. Place chestnuts in a small saucepan of boiling water and allow to boil about 5 minutes. Drain and rinse with water to cool for handling. With your fingers, rub off the bitter inner skin of the chestnuts. (Refer to page 142 for additional discussion of peeling chestnuts.)

Place washed rice in a medium pot with the chestnuts. Add 2⅛ cups water; cover pot and cook according to basic rice instructions given earlier in this chapter.

Serve with soy sauce for seasoning.

BEANS AND RICE, JAPANESE STYLE

Yield: 8 to 10 servings

The colors red and white are revered as lucky. This recipe for red azuki beans and sweet rice is customarily served on happy occasions, such as birthdays and weddings. Traditionally, the cooked beans and rice are further steamed together, and a substantial amount of sugar is added during the cooking process. In Japan and in the United States, oriental confectionery shops often sell packages of these sweet beans and rice, called sekihan.

I have shortened the steps in this recipe for beans and rice and have eliminated the sugar according to American taste. The resulting dish is highly nutritious as a side course, instead of as a dessert, since the rice and beans complement each other. However, I find the flavor rather too subtle and therefore much improved with the addition of a sprinkling of red pepper, hot sauce, or Mexican salsa prior to serving.

1 12-ounce bag *azuki* beans, soaked in water a minimum of 4 hours, better overnight
1 cup rice (preferably sweet rice), washed
2 tablespoons *mirin* (optional)

Drain liquid from beans and use to cook rice, adding water, if necessary, so that liquid measures 1 cup. The bean liquid will color the rice slightly. Cook according to basic rice instructions given earlier in this chapter.

Cook beans in fresh water to cover. Bring to a boil, cover, and lower heat, simmering for about 1½ hours. Occasionally stir and check that the beans are cooking properly and not sticking to the pot.

When rice and beans are cooked, combine together in a large pot. For added sweetening, you may wish to pour in 2 tablespoons mirin. Stir to combine and heat through. Cover and let stand for 15 minutes. Serve warm or cool.

If desired, prior to serving stir in 1 cup red Mexican salsa.

Variation: For a simpler version, substitute a 32-ounce can of red beans and liquid for the cooked beans.

ONIGIRI

Yield: 20 to 24 rice balls;
5 to 12 servings, depending
on number of courses

Cold rice balls, onigiri, are perfect for a picnic or boxed lunch, or as party hors d'oeuvres. Children like them, too. You can serve them with a simple sprinkling of salted black sesame seeds or you can hide a pinch of filling inside or on top.

3 cups cooked rice

ASSORTED FILLINGS AND WRAPPINGS
Black sesame seeds, salted*
***Nori,* toasted and cut into strips**

***Kombu*, chopped and mixed with soy sauce (about 2 tablespoons *kombu* to 1 tablespoon soy sauce)**
Fish, broiled and seasoned
Fermented soy beans
Pickled plum
Crushed pineapple (canned is fine) or other fruit
Sweetened and pureed *azuki* beans

*Salted black sesame seeds can be purchased in small bottles. If you wish to make this item yourself, equal amounts of coarse salt and black sesame seeds are a good proportion for American tastes. The bottled mixture has considerably more salt.

Use rice that is still very hot, since after it has cooled it is difficult to shape. Have a bowl of salted water (or su water) handy to dip your hands into; it will be easier to shape rice into ovals and balls.

Place about 1 tablespoon rice in the palm of your hands and shape. If a filling is desired, press into the center of the rice ball as you are shaping it. If filling is placed on top, press a fingerprint on the rice ball. If desired, balls may be wrapped with strips of nori.

Serve at room temperature, with soy sauce if desired. Leftovers can be stored at room temperature for several hours.

CHAZUKE

Yield: 4 to 6 servings

I find it most interesting how some simple customs develop into standard recipes. Ochazuke, Tea over Rice, is one of these cases. Originally, because it is bad manners to leave rice in one's bowl, people would pour tea over their remaining rice and drink this combination at the end of the meal. Since both items are highly revered, this dish became popular, sometimes even enjoyed as the main part of the meal. A square of nori and a sprig of trefoil are commonly used as garnishes. Today dashi is frequently substituted as the liquid. Other toppings may be included: sashimi tuna (maguro chazuke) with wasabi, pickled vegetables (tsukemono chazuke), salted salmon (sake chazuke), or whitefish (tai or fugu chazuke). This rice dish is now eaten with chopsticks rather than drunk.

2 to 3 cups hot steamed white rice
2 cups hot tea
1 teaspoon black sesame seeds
1 sheet toasted *nori*, crumbled or cut into slivers
1 tablespoon chopped pickled ginger and *shiso* mixture (or other Japanese pickles available refrigerated in most major markets and oriental markets)

Spoon rice into one large bowl or into individual bowls. Pour hot tea over rice. Sprinkle rice with sesame seeds and garnish with nori. Place pickles in the center.

CHICKEN DONBURI

Yield: 4 to 6 servings

Donburi recipes are for foods served in a large donburi (big bowl) on top of a bed of cooked rice or noodles. Generally, meat, fish, chicken, tofu, and/or vegetables are cooked, then beaten eggs are added at the last minute.

1 cup bite-size pieces of chicken breasts
1½ cups chicken broth (or other stock)
3 tablespoons soy sauce
¼ cup *mirin* (or ¼ cup *sake* and 2 tablespoons sugar)
Salt
4 small *shiitake*, soaked in warm water to reconstitute, hard center core removed
2 ounces *kamaboko* (¼ fish cake), sliced thinly, preferably pink
3 ounces bamboo shoots, preferably whole bamboo shoots attractively cut into irregular shapes, refreshed in boiling water, and drained

½ cup fresh peas, blanched, or frozen peas, defrosted
3 large eggs, beaten
3 cups hot cooked rice
Sliced scallions, for garnish

In a large pot, cook the chicken in the broth seasoned with soy sauce, mirin, and salt to taste. Bring liquid to a simmer and cook about 10 minutes until tender. Add the mushrooms, sliced kamaboko, bamboo shoots, and peas. Continue to simmer another 10 minutes. (At this point, you can set the ingredients aside and complete recipe just prior to serving time.)

A few minutes before serving time, bring liquid to a boil. Add the beaten eggs. When the eggs have set, the dish is completed.

Place rice in the bottom of an attractive serving bowl. Spoon chicken and vegetables on top. Garnish with scallions.

KAYOKO'S OYAKO DONBURI

Yield: 4 to 6 servings

This family-style dish features chicken and egg on top of hot cooked noodles.

3 split chicken breasts, boned and cut into bite-size pieces
2 teaspoons cooking oil
4 green onions, chopped coarsely
2 *shiitake,* reconstituted in warm water, drained, tough center core removed, and sliced into matchstick-size shreds

DONBURI SAUCE

½ cup chicken broth (or *dashi*)
2 tablespoons *mirin*
4 tablespoons soy sauce
1 teaspoon sugar
½ teaspoon salt

4 eggs, lightly beaten
4 cups hot cooked noodles or rice

In a large skillet, saute the chicken pieces in the cooking oil. When chicken is lightly browned on all sides, add onions and mushrooms and combine well.

Combine donburi sauce ingredients in a small bowl; pour into skillet with chicken and vegetables. Cook over low heat for 10 minutes.

Just before serving, bring liquid to a simmer; add the beaten eggs, stirring constantly until they solidify. Serve immediately over hot cooked noodles or rice.

GROUND MEAT AND TOFU WITH VEGETABLES DONBURI

Yield: 4 to 6 servings

Donburi recipes, such as this one with ground beef, tofu, and vegetables over cooked rice, are a tasty and inexpensive family-style meal. Children sometimes enjoy pan-fried crispy noodles instead of rice. Leftovers are excellent as stuffing for tofu pouches (see page 95).

1 pound ground beef
1 medium onion, chopped
2 medium carrots, chopped
1 teaspoon minced ginger
1 tablespoon cooking oil
Salt
¼ cup soy sauce
¼ cup *sake*
1 cake *tofu,* drained, parboiled for 5 minutes (to rid of excess liquids), and drained again

½ cup fresh peas, blanched, or frozen peas, defrosted
4 cups hot cooked rice or pan-fried noodles

In a large skillet, saute the meat with the onion, carrots, and ginger in the oil at a high temperature for 2 minutes, stirring often. When meat becomes crumbly, lower heat to a simmer; salt to taste. When vegetables have somewhat softened, after about 5 minutes, add soy sauce and sake; stir through. Continue to simmer about 8 minutes, stirring occasionally, until almost all sauce is absorbed.

When tofu is cool enough to handle, place in tea towel and squeeze out all excess liquid. Set aside.

After sauce is almost completely absorbed, add the tofu, breaking it up with a wooden spoon. Continue to simmer another 2 to 3 minutes, or until tofu is completely mixed in. Add the peas, cook another minute, and spoon mixture over rice.

HOMEMADE UDON

Yield: 4 to 8 servings, depending on number of courses

Fresh Japanese noodles are fairly easy to locate at major supermarkets and oriental foods stores in the refrigerator or freezer sections. But if you should wish to try your hand at homemade noodles, udon made from all-purpose flour is the simplest. Cooked udon can be used in most noodle recipes and is often a substitute for soba.

4 cups all-purpose flour (or whole-wheat flour)
1 teaspoon salt
1 egg yolk
Cold water
Additional flour

Sift the flour and salt together into a large bowl. Add egg yolk and enough water to make a stiff paste. Knead thoroughly. Cover the dough with a damp kitchen towel, and let it stand for 30 minutes. Sprinkle board and rolling pin with additional flour. Roll out dough until it is paper-thin. Fold into a long roll and cut into strips, about 1/10 inch wide. When unrolled, the dough strips should be at least 12 inches long. Cook 3 to 4 minutes in boiling salted water.

KUDZU NOODLES

Yield: 1½ to 2 cups; 4 to 6 servings

For hundreds of years, the Japanese have appreciated the medicinal value as well as the food value of kudzu. A simple broth of dissolved kudzu is thought to aid digestion and to calm the nerves. Kudzu is also used to make sweets and a gelatinlike noodle similar to shirataki. You can purchase packages of kudzu noodles, or you might try your hand at making them at home.

The following process is quite different from the mixing and kneading employed in making flour-based noodles, and the boiling and simmering of the powder with water is quite interesting to watch. Sharing this with children makes for a fun kitchen experiment.

⅔ cup *kudzu*
2 cups water

Kudzu straight out of the box is generally very lumpy. You will have to turn it into a fine powder before you can dissolve it in the water. To do so, either push through a strainer or a flour sifter—or faster yet, process in a food processor or blender until light and powdery.

Place kudzu in a saucepan and add water; stir with chopsticks or a wooden spoon to dissolve into a milky liquid. Over medium heat, bring to a boil; immediately reduce heat to a simmer, stirring constantly. The liquid will almost immediately become gummy. Simmer, continuing to stir, for about 3 minutes, or until mixture is thick and transparent.

Turn kudzu into a wet 9-inch square 2-part Japanese mold or a baking dish. With a spatula, spread the mixture evenly. Refrigerate for about 30 minutes to cool enough for easy cutting.

Remove sheet of kudzu from the mold onto a dampened cutting board. If using a baking dish, wet your hands, then carefully pull up and slightly roll kudzu, flipping it over onto the wet cutting board.

To slice kudzu, I find it simplest to work by the kitchen sink with running water. Otherwise, keep a large glass of cold water handy. Wet the blade of a sharp knife and slice kudzu as thinly as possible into snakelike strands. For easier handling, keep your hands damp. Carefully pick up the noodles and place them in a bowl of cold water with ice cubes. Refrigerate antil needed.

Homemade kudzu noodles are excellent in sukiyaki, one-pot simmered recipes, and soups or stews. They are also terrific served chilled with vegetables and a mixture of vinegar and soy sauce. Use your imagination in working with these most unusual noodles.

Kudzu noodles can also be cut into larger shapes, such as rectangles, circles, or flowers. Use your decorative vegetable cutters. For very thin noodles, put kudzu through a potato ricer.

BASIC JAPANESE NOODLE BROTH

Yield: Approximately 3 cups

The basic broth used for many noodle dishes is made of dashi, soy sauce, and sugar. From the original broth, hundreds of sauces are devised.

3 cups *dashi*
4 tablespoons soy sauce
1 tablespoon sugar (or to taste)

In a large saucepan, simmer together the dashi, soy sauce, and sugar. Use broth immediately to flavor cooked noodles or other dishes. Or place in a covered container and refrigerate for later use.

TEMPURA SOBA

Yield: 4 servings as first course;
8 servings as main dish

A favorite Japanese lunch dish is tempura soba, in which fresh noodles are cooked in hot broth, drained into individual large soup bowls, and topped with a piece of tempura shrimp, chicken, or vegetable. A similar recipe with a base of rice instead of noodles is called ten don. Sometimes a small amount of cooked spinach is added for color. I have eaten deluxe bowls of tempura soba, to which pieces of chicken, scallions, and a raw egg have been added.

1 recipe *tempura* batter (see page 123)
Oil for deep frying
4 to 8 very large prawns, cleaned (see pages 44–45)
1 quart chicken stock (or *dashi*)
1 pound fresh cooked *soba*

Prepare tempura batter according to instructions at that recipe.

In a large pot, heat the cooking oil to 375° F. Coat, one prawn at a time, in the batter. Deep fry one coated prawn at a time until golden; remove and keep warm as you continue the process.

Meanwhile, heat chicken stock in a large pot. Add the fresh noodles, cooking for a few minutes until tender. Remove the noodles to individual soup bowls, top each with one cooked prawn, and carefully pour the broth into the bowls. Or if you prefer your shrimp tempura to remain crisp, add the noodles and stock to the bowls, then top with prawns.

SOBA SHOP NOODLES

Yield: 4 servings

Hot noodles, appropriate to cold weather, are served with combinations of fish, meat, and vegetables. If traveling in Japan, you might hear the noodle vendor's horn on the street. In a soba shop, you will find lacquer bowls filled with a variety of condiments, such as sliced scallions, nori, dried bonito flakes, grated daikon, and crushed nuts. A covered bowl of hot buckwheat noodles and broth are served. Then you select the garnishes that appeal to you.

1 cup thinly sliced raw chicken breasts
2 teaspoons *sake*
1 teaspoon minced fresh ginger
1 teaspoon potato starch (or cornstarch)

SOBA BROTH
3 cups *dashi*
½ cup soy sauce
2 tablespoons sugar
1 tablespoon cooking oil
3 tablespoons *sake*
1 teaspoon salt

1 tablespoon cooking oil
½ pound *soba* noodles, boiled until tender, drained, and rinsed in cold water

CONDIMENTS
½ cup ground walnuts or toasted sesame seeds
½ cup chopped scallions
½ cup crumbled *nori*
½ cup dried bonito flakes

Place chicken in a small bowl with the sake; mix well with your fingers to coat. Add the ginger and potato starch; combine well and marinate for about 30 minutes.

Combine the soba broth ingredients in a large pot. Bring to a boil and reduce heat to a simmer for 5 minutes.

Heat oil in a skillet and quickly cook the chicken with its marinade, stirring for 2 minutes.

Add noodles to the simmering soba broth. When noodles are heated through, pour with broth into individual serving bowls. Top with chicken and serve with small bowls of condiments.

NABEYAKI UDON

Yield: 1 generous serving

One of my favorite hearty dishes is nabeyaki udon, featuring udon and stock and several toppings, including chicken, seafood, fish, vegetables, and a barely cooked egg. This delicious recipe was shared by the Mifune Restaurant, Los Angeles.

⅔ pound *udon*
1 chicken breast or thigh
2 shrimp
2 *shiitake,* soaked in water a minimum of 12 hours
4 slices *kamaboko* (approximately 2 ounces)
1 egg
¼ cup finely sliced green onion
2 to 3 fresh spinach leaves, parboiled in boiling water with ½ teaspoon sugar

UDON SOUP STOCK
1½ cups *dashi*
1 tablespoon *sake*
½ teaspoon sugar
2 tablespoons soy sauce

Thin strip *nori,* for garnish
Sprinkling of *shichimi* (7-spice hot pepper), for garnish (optional)

There are two methods for cooking udon for this recipe.

Method 1: Bring to boil a large pot of water. Add udon and stir with chopsticks so noodles do not stick. After water returns to a boil (in about 5 minutes), shut off heat, cover pot, and let noodles stand for 10 minutes. Noodles should be cooked but not soft. Rinse noodles in cold water and put in a strainer to drain completely. Noodles should be completely dry before they are added to soup.

Method 2: Bring to boil a large pot of water. Add udon. Boil udon uncovered, stirring with chopsticks. When liquid returns to a boil, add 1 cup cold water. When water returns to a boil again, turn off heat. Cover noodles and let stand for 10 minutes. Rinse in cold water, drain, and set aside to drain completely.

Bone chicken and slice as if making sashimi. Shell and devein shrimp. Remove shiitake from soaking liquid and slice crisscrosses into the tops to expose the inner flesh. Have kamaboko, egg, and green onion handy. Rinse parboiled spinach in cold water and drain. Cut into 1-inch lengths.

Using a donabe or saucepan, heat the dashi. Add sake, sugar, and soy sauce just before dashi comes to a boil. To refresh udon, take from colander and dip quickly into boiling water to warm, shake, and drain completely before adding to soup stock. Top noodles with chicken, shrimp, shiitake, kamaboko, and green onion. Cover and cook over high heat until liquid again comes to a boil. Uncover and add the spinach. Carefully crack the egg on top of the green onion, cover donabe, and turn off heat. The egg will poach slightly. Uncover and serve immediately with garnishes of nori and optional hot pepper spice.

Note: To eat the egg, you have the choice of consuming it whole or swirling it around in the hot broth, in effect scrambling it.

Variations: Instead of a raw egg, you can add 1 hard-cooked egg that has been peeled and cut in half, thus suggesting the full moon. Other ingredients can be added, such as parboiled carrots, tempura shrimp, and crab legs.

SOBA WITH ZUCCHINI AND MUSHROOMS

Yield: 2 to 4 servings

When buckwheat was first introduced to Japan in the eighth century, it was eaten as a gruel to stretch the amount of rice in the diet. In the seventeenth century, buckwheat flour was combined with wheat flour and water to make a dough for noodles, sobakiri.

Serve this as a side course. Other vegetables can be added or substituted for the zucchini. And try adding shrimp or pork.

2 tablespoons cooking oil
2 cloves garlic, peeled and minced
3 very large *shiitake,* soaked for several hours, then drained and sliced into matchstick-size juliennes
½ pound zucchini, sliced into 2-inch juliennes
4 ounces *soba,* cooked and drained
1 to 2 tablespoons soy sauce

In a large skillet, heat the cooking oil and season with the garlic. Add the mushrooms and zucchini and stir everything together. Cook over medium heat for a few seconds. Add the soba and soy sauce and continue to cook, stirring, until everything is heated through and coated with soy sauce.

CHILLED NOODLES WITH CUCUMBERS AND MUSHROOMS

Yield: 4 to 6 servings

In summer the Japanese enjoy cold dishes, especially those made with noodles. To serve this as a main dish, add slices of cooked cooled omelet or pork.

SUMMER SALAD DRESSING
½ cup rice vinegar
1 teaspoon cooking oil
½ cup soy sauce
¼ cup beef broth (or *dashi*)
2 tablespoons sugar

4 large *shiitake,* soaked for several hours,

drained, and sliced into matchstick-size juliennes

- **¼ cup beef broth (or *dashi*)**
- **2 tablespoons soy sauce**
- **2 tablespoons sugar**
- **½ pound *soba* or *somen*, cooked, drained, rinsed, and chilled**
- **2 large cucumbers**
- **Salt**
- **2 scallions, chopped**

To make the salad dressing: Combine the vinegar, oil, soy sauce, ¼ cup broth, and sugar in a saucepan. Simmer for 5 minutes, cool, then chill.

Place sliced mushrooms in a saucepan with the remaining broth, soy sauce, and sugar. Heat the liquid, stirring for 3 minutes. Remove the mushrooms and set aside. Add this liquid to the chilled cooked dressing. Continue to chill sauce.

Heap noodles in a large serving bowl and refrigerate.

Peel cucumbers. Slice in half lengthwise and remove seeds. Lightly sprinkle with salt and let drain for a few minutes on paper towels. Rinse and pat dry. Cut into 3-inch lengths, then slice into matchstick-size juliennes.

Arrange cucumbers and mushrooms attractively on top of noodles. Pour sauce over vegetables and noodles. Garnish center of platter with chopped scallions.

MENRUI WITH DIPPING SAUCE

Yield: 4 to 6 servings

Cold noodles are often chilled further with ice cubes before serving. This sauce for dipping cold noodles is flavored with mirin, soy sauce, dashi, and bonito flakes. The strong-tasting garnishes are not added until the last minute so that they do not lose their texture in the sauce.

MIRIN–SOY SAUCE–DASHI DIPPING SAUCE

- **¼ cup *mirin***
- **¼ cup soy sauce**
- **1 cup *dashi***
- **2 tablespoons dried bonito flakes**
- **Salt**
- **4 to 6 ounces *somen*, cooked and drained**

GARNISHES

- **3 tablespoons finely grated *daikon***
- **1 tablespoon grated ginger**
- **4 scallions, green top part only, thinly sliced**

Place mirin in a saucepan over medium heat (if desired, you can ignite the mirin to burn off the alcohol) and add the soy sauce, dashi, bonito flakes, and a pinch salt. Bring to a boil, then strain through a sieve. Cool to room temperature.

Place cold noodles in a glass bowl. Each person gets an individual bowl filled with sauce and an individual plate with garnishes. Noodles are eaten communally with chopsticks; each person takes a small portion of noodles, dips them into the sauce, and eats.

ZARUSOBA

Yield: 6 servings

The Japanese use a zaru, a round bamboo basket or bamboo-lined box, for this popular summer dish featuring iced buckwheat noodles. The noodles are piled into the basket. Then each person takes a small portion of the noodles, dipping them into a sauce made of soy sauce and dashi and garnishing with scallions and nori.

- **1 pound *soba*, cooked, drained, rinsed, and drained again**
- **2 sheets *nori*, toasted and crumbled**
- **3 scallions, including at least 3 inches of the green stems, sliced into thin rounds**
- **2 tablespoons *wasabi*, mixed with just**

enough cold water to make a thick paste, then set aside for 15 minutes

1½ cups *mirin,* soy sauce, *dashi* dipping sauce (see preceding recipe)

Place cooked noodles in a bamboo basket or divide into six serving bowls. Top with crumbled nori. Serve with individual plates of scallions and wasabi and individual bowls of dipping sauce.

Variation: Kishimen noodles are traditionally served in a similar manner for a dish called kishi zaru.

KUDZU NOODLES WITH PEAS

Yield: 4 to 8 servings

Kudzu noodles are fun to make. If in a pinch for time or ingredients, however, you can substitute cooked, chilled shirataki or harusame. Other vegetables or sliced raw fish, such as octopus, can be added to this dish. Grated daikon or grated red maple radish make excellent spicy toppings. Serve as a chilled side dish.

1 recipe fresh *kudzu* noodles (or canned or dried *shirataki* or *harusame,* cooked and chilled)

½ cup fresh peas, blanched, or frozen peas, defrosted

SOY SAUCE–VINEGAR DRESSING

3 tablespoons vinegar

3 tablespoons soy sauce

½ teaspoon lemon juice

1 teaspoon sugar

Black sesame seeds or crumbled *nori,* for garnish (optional)

Drain kudzu noodles from bowl of iced water; carefully pat dry with paper towels. Place noodles in a serving bowl and toss with peas. Combine dressing ingredients in a small bowl and stir to dissolve the sugar. Pour over kudzu noodles. Toss carefully. If desired, garnish with black sesame seeds or crumbled nori.

For additional rice and noodle recipes, see:

Soups and Stews
Osechi Ozoni
Pork Balls with Kinome Soup
Special Udon Nabe
Sukiyaki Japanese Style
Sukiyaki American Style
Shabu-Shabu
Salads and Vegetables
Mrs. Ozaki's Osechi Salad
Tofu and Miso
Beef and Rice Stuffed Tofu Pouches

DESSERTS, CONFECTIONS, AND SWEET SNACKS

After a many-course Japanese dinner, a simple dessert of strawberries or a slice of melon is refreshing. In fact, the most commonly served dessert for a Japanese meal is seasonal fresh fruit. At times, however, a more complicated sweet dish may be desired. These differ greatly from what American tastes may consider dessert. Cooked chestnuts in sweetened syrup, sweet potatoes, red beans, and lima beans are standard home-style sweets. Perhaps our down-home rice and bread puddings can best be likened to those Japanese recipes. Another recipe belonging in this category is a form of gelatin, made of agar-agar (kanten).

Tea ceremony moist sweets and confections are far more elaborate than the home-style desserts. Their outer appearances are very beautiful. Many are wrapped in edible leaves, decorated with symbolic shapes, or colored to especially please the eye. The newcomer to these sweets will be taken by surprise with the first bite—instead of chocolate or sweet creams, he or she will find a paste of beans, either chunky (tsubushi-an) or smooth (koshi-an) in texture.

The bean paste, or bean jam, used extensively for desserts and confections is referred to as *an*. Most often azuki beans are used for an; they are boiled in water with sugar. In Japan, an is very often purchased from a confectionery shop, though on special occasions it will be made at home. In the United States, you can purchase these prepared beans at Japanese confectionery shops and at oriental markets in cans.

Japanese bakeries and confectioneries in major American cities display beautiful goods, many resembling French pastries. When you bite into a dumpling, a cake, a doughnut, or a candy, however, do not be surprised to find a filling of sweetened beans.

SWEETENED RED BEANS

Yield: About 2 cups

Japanese families often keep a supply of sweetened azuki beans on hand in the refrigerator so they can quickly make up a dessert for a surprise visitor. For a simple dessert, you can serve a small scoop in an attractive dish. Sweet beans are often combined with gelatin cubes, canned or fresh fruit, shaved ice with sweet syrup (like a snow cone), ice cream, or toasted mochi (rice cakes). The topping might be a bit of honey, brown sugar syrup, or molasses. If you encase small, plain rice balls made of mochigome (sweet rice) with azuki paste, you will have the traditional sweet, ohagi (rice dumpling). For an unusual breakfast, try spreading these beans on buttered toast or pancakes.

1 12-ounce bag *azuki* beans, washed, then soaked 12 hours in water to cover
1 scant cup sugar
1 tablespoon salt
¼ cup honey

Place pot of beans and water over high flame and bring liquid to a boil. Cook, removing scum with a slotted spoon. Stir occasionally. As the water reduces, be careful to stir more often; eventually you will need to stir constantly. After about 40 minutes, when the water is almost completely absorbed, add ⅓ cup sugar and the salt. Stir constantly. In 10 minutes, add another ⅓ cup sugar. (If you add the sugar all at one time, the beans will become too liquid.) After another 10 minutes, add remaining sugar and the honey. The total cooking time is approximately 1 hour.

Allow beans to cool before eating. They are usually served the following day. Turn beans into a casserole and refrigerate. Cooked beans will keep for several weeks.

Note: Some people prefer a firmer bean. In this case, you may wish to shorten cooking time by about 10 minutes. For a softer paste, carefully mash the beans with a wooden spoon as you stir and cook.

CANDIED CHESTNUTS (KURI NO KANRO)

Yield: 4 to 8 servings

Chestnuts, a popular ingredient in Japanese cookery, are available in many forms. You'll find them raw, cooked and canned in a sweet syrup, and roasted and sold in paper bags. Freshly cooked in a syrup, they're a delicious sweet ending to a meal. You can use a spoonful or two as a topping for ice cream or cake.

¾ to 1 pound fresh chestnuts (about 20 to 24)

SWEET SYRUP
1 cup sugar
¼ cup water
2 tablespoons honey

With a very sharp knife, carefully cut a small X into the flat side of each chestnut, taking care not to pierce or cut up the meat. Place chestnuts in a medium pot, cover with water, and bring to a boil. Continue to boil for 10 minutes. Drain and rinse with cold water so you can handle. Carefully peel the chestnuts. Rub off the inner brown papery skin. (This is the oily, bitter part of the nut.) Whole chestnuts are more attractive, so try not to break them up. This takes a lot of practice.

Place peeled chestnuts in a pot of water to cover. Simmer for 30 to 40 minutes, until tender. Drain.

In a small saucepan, slowly cook the sugar, water, and honey together to make a syrup. If sugar is cooked too rapidly, crystals will form. When sugar is thoroughly dissolved and the mixture is a light gold syrup, add chestnuts to syrup. Simmer for about 15 to 20 minutes, stirring occasionally. Allow chestnuts to cool in the syrup. Serve. Refrigerate leftovers.

MANJU (DUMPLING WITH SWEET BEAN FILLING)

Yield: 12 larger, double-layered circles or 24 small balls

Until recently, few Japanese kitchens had ovens, which explains why there are not many home-style baked goods in the Japanese cuisine. When an elaborate pastry is desired, it is purchased from a neighborhood bakery. If a Japanese homemaker makes a dough-based dessert, it will generally be a steamed dumpling. Manju, a sweetened dough with bean filling, is such a dessert. Even though manju is considered a sweet or tea snack, I find that the taste is quite subtle for the American palate and that therefore they are best served with meals, much as you might serve hot biscuits.

DOUGH

- **1 cup all-purpose flour**
- **½ cup sugar**
- **½ teaspoon baking powder**
- **½ teaspoon baking soda**
- **½ teaspoon salt**
- **3 to 4 tablespoons water**

FILLING

- **2 to 4 tablespoons *azuki* paste (*an*), pureed sweetened chestnuts, or sweetened white bean paste**

Additional ¼ cup flour

To make the dough: In a mixing bowl, combine the 1 cup flour, sugar, baking powder, baking soda, and salt. Slowly add the water, stirring well until you have a firm ball of dough. You may not use all the water.

Prepare the filling ingredients. This is a perfect recipe for using leftover sweetened beans. (See recipe in this chapter.)

On a flour-dusted surface, roll out dough to about ⅛ inch to ¼ inch thickness. Cut dough into 2-inch to 3-inch circles and carefully stretch or flatten.

There are two styles for filling. I prefer to spread a generous ½ teaspoon on half of the dough circles, then to top with an unfilled circle and press the edges with the tines of a fork to seal. According to the traditional method, place a small ball of bean filling in the center of each circle and shape the dough around the ball, pinching to seal, with seam side underneath.

Home-style manju is steamed rather than baked. Place manju in a single layer on a kitchen tea towel, and place towel on a rack in a steamer. Steam dumplings over simmering water. Small balls require about 15 minutes; large double-layered circles, about 20 minutes.

Cool slightly to handle. Manju can be eaten immediately.

Variation: Dough can be tinted with food coloring or powdered green tea.

MANDARIN ORANGE MERINGUE GELATIN

Yield: 8 to 10 servings

Once you understand the basics of making Japanese gelatin with the seaweed agar-agar (kanten), you can experiment with a variety of ingredients and natural food colorings. In this recipe, I have made a meringuelike gelatin and incorporated mandarin oranges—a favorite of the Buddhist deities that are believed to bring good fortune in the new year. Fresh strawberries are frequently used with this sweet; the red and white together symbolize felicity. The white meringue also reminds us of winter snow in the mountains, while the strawberries make us think of spring in the field.

- **1 stick uncolored agar-agar (about 10 grams)**
- **2 cups water**
- **1½ cups sugar**
- **2 egg whites, at room temperature**
- **Grated rind and juice of ½ lemon**
- **1 11-ounce can drained mandarin oranges (or tangerines or strawberries)**

Tear agar-agar into tiny pieces. Wash, drain, then soak in the 2 cups water for 1 hour. Cook in a saucepan over medium heat for about 8 to 10 minutes. Start stirring *after* liquid comes to a simmer. Add the sugar. Reduce mixture by about half.

Beat egg whites until stiff. Gradually beat the sugar-gelatin into the egg whites. Then beat in the lemon rind and juice. At this point the mixture will resemble a meringue. Fold mandarin oranges into gelatin mixture.

Prepare an 8-inch or 9-inch square mold by wetting with water. (I use a Japanese square mold with a lift-out tray.) Spread mixture into wet mold. Refrigerate for several hours. Cut into squares to serve.

YOKAN

Yield: About 7 dozen pieces

A jellylike candy, called yokan, is a popular homemade sweet, made with agar-agar (kanten), sugar, and beans. In this recipe, I have used red kanten and green lima beans. The final color is a rich ruby red, and the taste is similar to guavas. You can also use white kanten and another bean, or a combination of beans, such as sweetened azuki (an), white white, green, or black beans. Yokan is also made with chestnuts, pureed persimmons, or other fruit pastes. Yokan takes several hours, so prepare on a day when you have plenty of time to stay in the kitchen.

- **2 cups cooked lima beans***
- **1 stick *kanten* (*agar-agar*)**
- **1 cup water**
- **3 cups sugar**
- **¼ teaspoon salt**
- **Powdered sugar for dusting candies (optional)**

*You can use dried lima beans, soak overnight, and cook in boiling water until tender. Or you can use frozen lima beans and cook according to package instructions. I find the frozen beans very suitable for this recipe. Use a 10-ounce package.

With a food processor, blender, or sieve, puree cooled cooked beans to a paste; set aside.

Wash kanten and tear into little pieces. Place in a saucepan with the 1 cup water and let stand for 30 to 60 minutes. If you use red kanten, the water will become red as the pieces begin to dissolve. Place saucepan over low heat and cook until kanten has thoroughly dissolved.

Pour dissolved kanten through a fine-meshed strainer into a large, heavy pot. Discard any bits. Return to low heat and slowly stir in the sugar. As sugar dissolves, add more, stirring constantly. Cook over low heat another 5 to 10 minutes after sugar is dissolved, scraping down the sides to prevent sugar from crystallizing. Constantly stir until the mixture resembles a thick jelly. A candy thermometer should register approximately 240° F., which is jellying temperature.

Add pureed beans to pot; stir well. Continue to cook, stirring constantly for another 30 to 60 minutes. Add salt during the final 5 minutes.

Prepare a two-part Japanese mold, springform pan, loaf pan, or casserole by wetting with cold water. Carefully pour hot jelly mixture into prepared mold.

Immediately spread evenly, as the mixture begins to set once it touches the mold. Refrigerate to cool.

Candy is best served the following day. To serve, cut into 1-inch squares and dust with powdered sugar. Wrap individual pieces in small squares of wax paper. Yokan will keep for several weeks, even months.

Note: Should your candy harden into lumps before it has been evenly spread, return it to the pot and add about ½ cup hot water. Cook over low heat, stirring constantly. Candy will begin to dissolve. If necessary, add more hot water. Continue stirring constantly until fully dissolved, then proceed with recipe.

EGG SWEETS

Yield: 4 to 8 servings

Surprised to find hard-cooked eggs as a sweet? This steamed confection is a favorite among children.

10 hard-cooked eggs, cooled
5 tablespoons sugar
Pinch salt

Carefully split eggs in half so you can separate the yolks and the whites into two separate piles. Grate eggs through a sieve or a fine-toothed grater. Add 2 tablespoons of sugar and a pinch of salt to the whites; mix. Add remaining 3 tablespoons sugar and pinch of salt to the yolks; mix.

Prepare a loaf pan (9 by 5 inches) or Japanese mold by oiling lightly. Press whites firmly into the bottom of the mold. Top with yolks, pushing them down firmly as well. Cover mold with lid or foil.

Using a steamer or a Dutch oven set up like a steamer, place mold on top of steamer rack above approximately 2 inches of boiling water. Cover pot and reduce heat to a low rolling simmer. Steam egg sweets for about 10 minutes. Remove mold and uncover. Allow to cool at room temperature for a few minutes. Then refrigerate.

At serving time, cut egg sweets into 1-inch squares.

SENBEI

Yield: About 18 crackers

There are several steps to making these traditional rice crackers. And at each juncture, they're delicious. When the sesame seed–studded dough is cut and deep fried, they puff up like doughnuts and are yummy as is. Or you can bake them in the oven for a tasty, crackerlike wafer. Properly completed, they're brushed with a simple glaze and allowed to dry out for several hours, resulting in a third treat. No matter which method—or all three—you choose, you'll enjoy senbei with tea any time of day.

1¼ cups all-purpose flour
1¼ cups *mochiko* (sweet rice flour)
2 tablespoons sugar
2 tablespoons toasted sesame seeds
1½ teaspoons baking powder
½ teaspoon baking soda
1 teaspoon salt
¾ to 1 cup water
Additional flour
Oil for deep frying and/or lightly greased cookie sheets

SWEET GLAZE

3 tablespoons soy sauce
3 tablespoons sugar

Using an electric mixer or food processor, combine the first 7 dry ingredients. Slowly add the water until the dough becomes a firm ball. Wrap dough in plastic wrap and refrigerate for about 3 hours, or until dough has somewhat firmed up for rolling.

Roll out dough to about ½ inch thickness on a surface lightly dusted with flour. Dust cutter with flour. (I use a round cookie cutter, but use whatever size and shape you prefer.) Cut out circles of dough, rerolling as necessary until all dough is cut.

To deep fry dough: Heat oil to 375° F. and deep

fry a few circles at a time, removing when golden to drain. Dough will puff up beautifully as it fries. You can enjoy the fried puffs immediately.

To bake: Place uncooked dough circles on lightly greased cookie sheets. Bake in a preheated 350° F. oven for 10 to 15 minutes, or until they turn light brown. Remove and cool. Baked dough circles do not puff up as much as the deep fried; they also have a firmer texture. You can enjoy these immediately as well.

To glaze: In a small saucepan, combine the soy sauce and sugar. Heat over low temperature, stirring constantly, until sugar has dissolved and the sauce has somewhat thickened. With a pastry brush, spread glaze over senbei. Place senbei on racks over cookie sheets.

Preheat oven to 300° F. for 5 minutes and then turn off heat.

Place cookie sheets in oven and allow senbei to dry out for 6 to 8 hours or overnight. Glaze will soak into the crackers and dry a little. Store in an airtight container.

For additional dessert, confection, and sweet snack recipes, see:

Salads and Vegetables
Candied Japanese Sweet Potatoes

BEVERAGES

The most notable Japanese beverages are sake, mirin, and tea, although fruit wines, liqueurs, sodas, and Japanese beer are also drunk.

Throughout the recipe chapters of this book, I have made extensive use of sake and mirin. The newcomer to Japanese cookery may at first be surprised to find these two alcoholic beverages listed so extensively as primary seasoning and tenderizing agents.

SAKE

The history of sake (pronounced "sah-kay") is entwined with much ritual, both religious and social. The Japanese production dates back about two thousand years, when the Chinese people introduced the technique of making sake from rice. Sake was originally prepared as a thick fermented gruel to be eaten rather than as a fine drink. Farmers offered it to the gods in appreciation of the rice harvest.

The finest brews of sake are made with the best ingredients. The water must be pure and the rice must be well ripened and of proper weight and size. The alcoholic content of sake ranges from about 12 to 18 percent. The best grades of sake generally contain the highest percentage of alcohol.

Sake is properly served warmed to about 100° F., close to our body's inner temperature. Consumption of warm alcohol is unusual to American tastes, although it is done with some other drinks, such as hot mulled wine, rum toddy, and cognac. Heating sake does not influence its alcoholic content. In modern-day Japan and the United States, sake is also enjoyed chilled. You will even find it as an ingredient of several fancy cocktails.

To warm sake, pour about ½ cup into a tokkuri (a small porcelain decanter) and place tokkuri in a pot of hot water. Over very low flame, heat the sake for about 3 to 4 minutes.

In Japan, sake is the most popular of alcoholic beverages. It is considered an essential part of all ceremonies. Weddings are solemnized with sake, and sake is sipped throughout the meal at both informal and formal dinners.

At a formal dinner, a pot of warm water is present for each guest to rinse and warm his or her small sake cup (sakazuki). The host or hostess first pours a little sake to check its color, fragrance, and taste. Next, he or she fills the guests' cups. Proper sake etiquette should be followed. You should never fill your own sake cup—allow your host or hostess to do so. Hold your cup with your right hand. Sake should never be poured into a cup resting on the table; lift your cup for filling. To signal that you wish no more sake, turn your empty cup upside down.

Once you have opened a bottle of sake, drink it as soon as possible. You can hold opened sake for up to three months in the refrigerator.

MIRIN

The sweetened, syrupy sake, mirin, is primarily used for cooking and not for drinking. It is made from shochu (Japanese vodka), glutinous rice, and koji (fermented rice enzyme). During fermentation, the glutinous rice is transformed into sugar, so that the beverage has a high sugar content (45 percent). Therefore, its shelf life, after it is opened, is far greater than that for sake. Mirin has been called the secret taste of Japanese cooking.

Traditionally, a cold, spiced, extremely sweet mirin-based drink, toso, is served on New Year's Day. Toso is sometimes made with a sake base so that it is not as sweet. The serving and drinking of toso is thought to scare away evil.

THE TEA CEREMONY

The Japanese revere their tea greatly. An entire way of life has developed around their appreciation of tea. This is known as the tea ceremony.

The tea ceremony trains participants to attain mental enlightenment and physical control. In contrast to the hectic pace at which many of us live, the tea ceremony reflects an ideal tranquillity and peace of mind.

The spiritual and aesthetic concept behind the tea ceremony derives from ancient Buddhist teachings. Honored guests are entertained in a traditional manner in which specific rules of etiquette are followed. Guests express their appreciation and admiration of the tea, food, decor, and utensils—also according to certain rules of etiquette.

All of those involved in the tea ceremony strive to follow the teachings of *chado,* "the way of tea," and to apply its commandments to their daily lives: "We shall continuously reflect upon ourselves to attain this end. As in accepting a bowl of tea, we shall always be grateful for the universal love that we receive from each other. We shall strive to communicate to others the virtues of chado—that we are living in this world by mutual consideration through and for others." (Translated into English, Kotoba, Urasenke, Konnichian.)

The gathering for the tea ceremony is called *chaj,* and there are many kinds of chaj, depending upon the time of day. The more formal chaj, with its very strict display of ritual, takes several hours. During this time, a light meal composed of many courses is served along with koi-cha, thick tea. A typical menu would include the basic five tastes—sweet, sour, salty, bitter, and spicy—in the chosen recipes. In contrast, the less formal and now more popular ceremony is more relaxed, involving friendly conversation. At this chaj, cakes and thin tea, usu-cha, are served. There are two varieties of sweets—namagashi (moist sweets), which are served after the meal with the thick tea, and higashi (dry sweets), which are served with the thin tea. Dry sweets resemble candies.

A powdered green tea, matcha, made from young leaves of aged plants, is the base for these ceremonies. Following tradition, the host or hostess cleans the utensils and places a small amount of matcha along with hot water into the large tea bowls. Using a bamboo whisk, he or she gently beats the mixture to a froth. The matcha now has a creamy green appearance and resembles pea soup. It is considerably thicker and more bitter than everyday Japanese tea. The honored guest takes long sips of the tea, making slurping sounds to show approval and completion. Sweet, rice-based confections are served with the bitter tea. (Sugar, lemon, milk, and cream are never served with Japanese tea.)

To properly perform the tea ceremony, a minimum of two years of training is suggested. In Japan and in the United States, study of the ceremony has regained much of its ancient popularity.

In addition to the matcha used at the tea ceremony, there are another five classes of Japanese tea. (1) Gyokuro: the most expensive and best grade of leaves. The taste is mild. To properly brew, heat water to 140° to 160° F. and add tea; steep 1 to 2 minutes. (2) Sencha: medium-priced tea, often served to guests. To properly brew, heat water to 166° to 178° F. and add tea; steep 2 minutes. Once leaves are drained, you can use them a second time. This tea is most frequently served at the sushi bar. (3) Bancha: everyday tea. To brew properly, heat water to 185° to 212° F. and add tea; steep 2 to 3 minutes. Drained leaves can be reused. (4) Hojicha: roasted bancha leaves. The tea has a smoky taste. Brew like bancha. (5) Genmaicha bancha: bancha that has been mixed with roasted and popped rice kernels. Brew like bancha. If you find this tea thin, you may wish to steep it longer.

Another favorite summertime thirst quencher is mugicha, a wheat tea. It is served chilled, much like iced tea. To make mugicha, add ½ to 1 cup of the roasted barley to 1½ to 2 quarts rapidly boiling water. Reduce heat to a simmer and continue to cook for 3 to 5 minutes. Strain, discarding the barley. Refrigerate and serve chilled with ice cubes.

Other tealike beverages include kobu-cha, powdered kombu and water broth; habucha, stinkweed-seed tea; and sakura-yu, salted cherry blossom tea.

With all grades of Japanese tea, you can be assured the highest quality beverage by following a few basic steps. The water must be heated to the proper temperature. Next, rinse utensils in hot water to warm, then fill with the hot water and add tea. (Never place tea in cold water and boil.) Next, allow the tea to steep properly for the suggested time. Purchase only small amounts of tea and store in a cool, dark place, or better yet, in the freezer. Remember to bring frozen leaves to room temperature before brewing.

To the Japanese, the drinking of tea plays an important role both as an indispensable daily beverage and as a seal to formalize social and business affairs.

WHERE TO GO FOR MORE INFORMATION

If you are trying to locate specific Japanese cooking supplies, utensils, or ingredients, my first suggestions are:

- Check what is available at major local markets and food stores.
- Check your telephone directory for oriental markets, health-food markets, and gourmet cookware stores in your area.
- Contact your local newspaper's food department or local radio station's food show host.
- Check with your local department stores' hardware and gourmet cookware sections.
- Check mail-order companies' catalogues of cookware specialties.
- Check the advertisements in national food magazines.

You might also write to the following stores, services, and companies; they accept mail orders. Remember to ask if they have minimum orders, if they require payment in advance or prefer COD, and if they have printed catalogs and/or price lists.

The Soyfoods Center, PO Box 234, Lafayette, CA 94549; (415) 283-2991. Attention: Bill Shurtleff.

Kam Kuo Food Corp., 7–9 Mott Street, New York, NY 10013.

Shing Chong & Company, 800 Grant Avenue, San Francisco, CA 94108.

Star Market, 3349 N. Clark Street, Chicago, IL 60657.

International Supermarket, 117 N. 10th Street, Philadelphia, PA 19107.

Anzen Hardware & Supply, 220 E. 1st Street, Los Angeles, CA 90012.

Rafu Bussan, Inc., 326 E. 2nd Street, Los Angeles, CA 90012.

Kongo Company, 319 E. 1st Street, Los Angeles, CA 90012 (source for tea supplies).

Chico-San, Inc., 1144 W. 1st Street, Chico, CA 95926.

Oriental Foods and Handcrafts, 3708 N. Broadway, Chicago, IL 60613.

Anzen Japanese Foods and Imports, 736 NE Union Avenue, Portland, Oregon 97232.

Conte di Savoia, 555 W. Roosevelt Road, Chicago, IL 60607.

Mrs. De Wildt, RD 3, Bangor, PA 18013.

Buderim Ginger Growers' Co-Op Association, PO Box 114, Buderim, Queensland 4556, Australia.

Le Jardin du Gourmet, West Danville, UT 05873.

Uwajimaya, PO Box 3003, Seattle, WA 98114.

Bando Trading Company, 2126 Murray Avenue, Pittsburgh, PA 15217.

Aphrodisia Products, Inc., 28 Carmine Street, New York, NY 10024.

Specialty Spice Shop, 2757 152nd Avenue, NE, Redmond, WA 98052.

Northwestern Coffee Mills, 217 N. Broadway, Milwaukee, WI 53202.

Nichols Garden Nursery, 1190 N. Pacific Highway, Albany, OR 97321.

Exotica Seed Company, 1742 Laurel Canyon Boulevard, Hollywood, CA 90046.

Kitazawa Seed Company, 356 W. Taylor Street, San Jose, CA 95110.

The Chinese Grocer, 209 Post Street at Grant Avenue, San Francisco, CA 94108.

Katagiri Company, 224 E. 59th Street, New York, NY 10022.

Tanaka and Company, 326 Amsterdam Avenue, New York, NY 10023.

Yoshinoya, 36 Prospect Street, Cambridge, MA 02139.

Mikado, 4709 Wisconsin Avenue NW, Washington, DC 20016.

Asian Trading Company, 2581 Piedmont NE, Atlanta, GA 30324.

Maruyama, Inc., 100 N. 18th Street, St. Louis, MO 63103.

K. Sakai Company, 1656 Post Street, San Francisco, CA 94115.

Kinoko Company, 8139 Capwell Drive, Oakland, CA 94621.

Nozawa Trading, 870 S. Western Avenue, Los Angeles, CA 90005.

Flavors of Asia, Asianattic, Inc., 8 Briarwood Terrace, Albany, NY 12203 (bimonthly newsletter).

Soyfoods, Richard Leviton, editor and publisher, Soyfoods, Inc., Sunrise Farm, 100 Heath Road, Colrain, MA 01340 (quarterly publication).

For further information regarding your Japanese cooking needs or for other inquiries about Japanese culture, try contacting the following sources:

Matao Uwate, Japanese Cooking School, 110 N. San Pedro Street, Los Angeles, CA 90012; (213) 628-4688.

JFC International, Inc., Diane Plocher, Consumer Service Representative, 445 Kauffmann Court, South San Francisco, CA 94080, or PO Box 3220, San Francisco, CA 94119; (415) 871-1660.

Japan National Tourist Organization, 624 S. Grand Avenue, Suite 2640, Los Angeles, CA 90017; (213) 623-1952.

Kyoto Kimono Academy, Uyeda Building, Room 500–B, 312 E. 1st Street, Los Angeles, CA 90012; (213) 617-0044.

Urasenke Tea Ceremony Society, Inc., 153 E. 69th Street, New York, NY 10021; (212) 988-6161; Attention Mr. Yamada.

Embassy of Japan, 2520 Massachusetts Avenue NW, Washington, DC 20008; (202) 234-2266. Consulate of Japan offices are also located in Atlanta, Kansas City, San Francisco, Seattle, Chicago, New Orleans, New York City, Los Angeles, Houston, Portland (Oregon), Boston, Honolulu, and Anchorage. Check your local telephone directory for address and/or telephone.

BIBLIOGRAPHY

AT HOME WITH JAPANESE COOKING. Elizabeth Andoh. New York: Knopf, 1980.

THE BOOK OF KUDZU: A CULINARY AND HEALING GUIDE. William Shurtleff and Akiko Aoyagi. Brookline, Mass.: Autumn Press, 1977.

THE BOOK OF MISO. William Shurtleff and Akiko Aoyagi. New York: Ballantine Books, 1976.

THE BOOK OF TOFU. William Shurtleff and Akiko Aoyagi. New York: Ballantine Books, 1975.

CHADO: THE JAPANESE WAY OF TEA. Soshitsu Sen. Weatherhill, N.Y.: Urasenki School of Tea, 1979.

CHANOYU: A BEGINNER'S HANDBOOK. Soshitsu Sen. Kyoto: Urasenke Konnichian Library.

THE COMPLETE BOOK OF JAPANESE COOKING. Elisabeth Lambert Ortiz and Mitsuko Endo. New York: M. Evans, 1976.

THE COMPLETE BOOK OF ORIENTAL COOKING. Myra Waldo. New York: Bantam Books, 1960.

COOK JAPANESE. Masaru Doi. Tokyo: Kodansha International, 1980.

THE COOKING OF JAPAN. Rafael Steinberg and the editors of Time-Life, Inc. Foods of the World. New York: Time-Life, Inc., 1969.

DINNER'S READY! AN INVITATION TO BETTER NUTRITION FROM NINE HEALTHIER CULTURES. Sally DeVore and Thelma White. Pasadena, Calif.: Ward Ritchie Press, 1977.

EAST-WEST FLAVORS I. Los Angeles: JACL, 1965–1966.

EAST-WEST FLAVORS II. Los Angeles: JACL, 1977.

EATING CHEAP IN JAPAN. Kimiko Nagasawa and Camy Condon. Tokyo: Shufunotomo, 1972.

HOME STYLE JAPANESE COOKING IN PICTURES. Sadaka Kohno. Tokyo: Shufunotomo, 1977.

JAPAN ALMANAC, 1975. Tokyo: Mainichi Newspapers, 1975.

JAPANESE COOK BOOK FOR SANSEIS. Matao Uwate. Los Angeles: Matao Uwate (110 N. San Pedro Street, Los Angeles, CA 90012), 1976.

JAPANESE COOKING: A SIMPLE ART. Shizuo Tsuji. Tokyo: Kodansha International (distributed by Harper & Row), 1980.

JAPANESE COOKING NOW. Joan Itoh. New York: Zokeisha Publications (Warner Books), 1980.

JAPANESE COUNTRY COOKBOOK. Russ Ridzinski. San Francisco: Nitty Gritty Productions, 1969.

THE JAPANESE GUIDE TO FISH COOKERY. Camy Condon and Sumiko Ashizawa. Tokyo: Shufunotomo, 1978.

THE KIKKOMAN COOKBOOK. Tokyo: Kikkoman Shoya, 1973.

THE RICE CYCLE: THE GRAIN THAT CREATED A CULTURE. Tokyo: Japan External Trade Organization (JETRO), 1974.

SHUN: JAPANESE COOKING, JANUARY-DECEMBER. Matao Uwate. Los Angeles: Matao Uwate (110 N. San Pedro Street, Los Angeles, CA 90012), 1975.

SUSHI. Mia Detrick. San Francisco: Chronicle Books.

SUSHI. Matao Uwate. Los Angeles: Matao Uwate (110 N. San Pedro Street, Los Angeles, CA 91102).

TRADER VIC'S PACIFIC ISLAND COOKBOOK. Trader Vic. New York: Doubleday, 1968.

INDEX

Note: Page numbers in italics indicate illustrations

INDEX